PENGUIN BO

THE WILD SILENCE

Since traveling the South West Coastal Path, Raynor Winn has become a regular long-distance walker and writes about nature, homelessness, and wild camping. Her first book, *The Salt Path*, was a *Sunday Times* bestseller, an NPR Concierge Best Book of 2019, and shortlisted for the 2018 Costa Award. She lives in Cornwall with her husband, Moth.

★

Praise for *The Wild Silence*

"Extraordinary: wise, unflinching, exquisite. Profound."
—*The Observer* (London)

"A thrill to read. The nature writing is beautiful . . . heartening and comforting. You feel the world is a better place."
—*The Times* (London)

"A beautiful, luminous and magical piece of writing."
—Rachel Joyce, author of *The Unlikely Pilgrimage of Harold Fry*

"An uplifting, illuminating read." —*Daily Mirror* (London)

"Heartrending. A love letter to the natural world in all its wondrous glory." —*The Herald* (Scotland)

Praise for *The Salt Path*

"Polished, poignant . . . an inspiring story of true love."
—*Entertainment Weekly*

"*The Salt Path* is an unputdownable tale and a temple to equanimity. . . . It will change you." —*The Wall Street Journal*

"Winn's prose is powerful. She excels at description, and her apt metaphors are rooted in nature. . . . An inspiring read, reminding us that there is salvation in nature, movement and the out-of-doors." —*Star Tribune*

"This amazing tale of resilience . . . made me grateful for my loving family and how they make the journey—even when stressful—a whole lot easier." —*First for Women* magazine

"Winn's chronicle is filled with beauty, humor and surprises. Glorious landscape a given, the loveliest scenery is the pair themselves, their affection and easy camaraderie treasures to behold. Facing grief, harsh elements, starvation and judgment about being homeless, they relish growing feelings of achievement and purpose. When, miraculously, Moth starts to feel better, their future grows more unclear. *The Salt Path* is a great travelogue of surroundings, passersby and local merchants, but its heart is in Winn and Moth finding meaning in the chaos." —*Shelf Awareness*

The Wild Silence

RAYNOR WINN

PENGUIN BOOKS

PENGUIN BOOKS
An imprint of Penguin Random House LLC
penguinrandomhouse.com

First published in Great Britain by Michael Joseph,
an imprint of Penguin Random House UK, 2020
Published in Penguin Books 2021

LIBRARY OF CONGRESS CATALOGING-IN-PUBLICATION DATA
Names: Winn, Raynor, author.
Title: The wild silence / Raynor Winn.
Description: [New York] : Penguin Books, 2021.
Identifiers: LCCN 2020045809 (print) | LCCN 2020045810 (ebook) |
ISBN 9780143136422 (paperback) | ISBN 9780525507956 (ebook)
Subjects: LCSH: Winn, Raynor. | Hikers—Great Britain—Biography. | Winn,
Raynor—Travel—Iceland. | Winn, Moth—Health. | Terminally ill—Great Britain—
Biography. | Husband and wife—Great Britain. | Adjustment (Psychology) |
Cornwall (England : County)—Biography. | Iceland—Description and travel.
Classification: LCC GV199.9 .W56 2021 (print) | LCC GV199.9 (ebook) |
DDC 796.51092/2 [B] —dc23
LC record available at https://lccn.loc.gov/2020045809
LC ebook record available at https://lccn.loc.gov/2020045810

Printed in the United States of America

Set in Bembo Book MT Std

This book is a work of nonfiction based on the life of the author. In some limited cases,
the names of people or detail of places or events have been changed to protect the privacy
of others. The author has stated to the publishers that, except in such respects, the contents
of this book are true. Any medical information in this book is based on the author's personal
experience and should not be relied on as a substitute for professional advice. The author
and publishers disclaim, as far as the law allows, any liability arising directly or indirectly
from the use, or misuse, of any information contained in this book.

For The Team

Contents

PART ONE

Always the Land

The shell must break before the bird can fly.

The Promise of May, Alfred, Lord Tennyson

I can hear the voice, but I don't know what it's saying.
    Somewhere deep in my brain,
        a noise between the rush of blood and electrical charges,
        a sound, or is it

        a feeling?

            It's dark and low, a voice like a hum of words
            rising from a hundred throats,
                or the beat of a drum in tune to feet on hard earth,

    or one bird call

    long and low at dusk
        as the light dips below a ridgeline
        and the land

            becomes blue.

1. Gone to Earth

I should have been in bed, sleeping like the rest of the country, not on an ice-cold rock on a cliff top before the dawn of New Year's Day. But as my eyes opened in the darkness of a winter night, I'd felt the same agitation that had been keeping me awake for months, heard the same sounds whispering in my head, and I'd had to go . . .

. . . through the enclosed, narrow streets of Polruan, where curtains were drawn and quietness had settled. All the revelers, fireworks and noise of the night before had disappeared. A dark stillness had returned, broken only by pools of streetlight and the sense of the river moving, wide and deep near its mouth, but heaving inland with the force of the tide, the surface shattering into a thousand reflected lights. Only one boat was moored in the fast-running current, its bows straining on the anchor chain, its stern drifting in a rhythmic fishtail motion. I walked beyond the last of the houses and out on to the open field. I didn't need a torch; I'd come to know this route so well that even in the gloom my feet found their way to a foot-wide strip of worn earth that winds its way through gorse and rock, up steep-hewn steps where the land falls away to the sea, breaking against the deep blackness of the cliff below. Then beneath the arched, wind-shaped hawthorn, bent and contorted as it shadows the shape of the land. Up rough broken ground, my feet barely visible, through the gate to where the land flattens and the wind rises. I couldn't see it but I knew it was there. I could feel the pull of the coast in both directions and as I stretched my arms wide and blended into the unseen, craggy, well-known shapes my exhaled breath became the wind, as did I.

In a field just back from the coast path I found my way to a small rocky outcrop surrounded by an arc of gorse bushes, where the sheep had worn away the grass as they'd pushed themselves in to shelter from the weather. A place to stop and sit. The agitation in my body began to fade and I let go, slipping beneath the wave of exhaustion. The darkness was dense and impenetrable but the air hissed through the gorse above my head, carrying the acidic scent of the needled leaves, as the weight of the sea on the cliff below boomed through the earth in a steady rhythmic vibration. I curled in a ball, the hood of my coat pulled over my hat, gloved hands under my armpits, and my thoughts finally moved outside my head, dissipating in the wild black air. No voice in my head, only silence. I couldn't think anymore, only feel, and I gave in to sleep, a deep, brief, total oblivion.

A slight wash of light broke the darkness, bringing me back into my aching, cramped body, but I didn't move; I stayed curled tight, my body wrapped, hanging on to a small scrap of warmth. A dark form slipped through the grayness overhead, his firm tail and long broad wings tipping only slightly into the wind as he dipped over the cliff edge, disappearing from view. My eyes held the clearing skyline, waiting for his return, not blinking in case I missed him. My head ached from the effort and my attention slipped to the horizon as the slightest slither of golden light began to break, brief and brilliant, before a curtain of squalling rain far out at sea obscured the wonder. Then he came silently back from below, rising into the sky without effort and hanging above the scrub of the headland. His dark back and black-tipped wings almost blended with the low sky; only the flash of white above his tail gave him away as a harrier hoping for breakfast.

Uncurling with a dull pain in my hips, I crawled out from beneath the gorse to see a badger leaving the coast path and climbing up through the field toward some undergrowth at the far fence. His short, stubby legs moved quickly through the patchy tufted grass. Caught out by the light, up too late, stirred from his winter slowness, he'd been driven into the cold night by hunger, but now he needed to be back in his sett, deep underground, safe, warm and hidden from view. He paused at the wide entrance to his tunnel, looking around, checking the air. Then he was gone, slipping into his safe invisible world. He'd gone to earth.

In the faint graying lift of light I climbed on to the last rock and sat with my feet hanging over the edge. At the edge of the land and the start of the sea. In a space between worlds, at a time between years, in a life between lives. I'm lost, but here, at least for a moment, I'm found.

Back through the village and still nothing was stirring. In Fowey, on the opposite side of the river, a few lights were on. People were groggily making coffee, turning up the heating and going back to bed. I followed the path-wide streets to the huge looming bulk of the chapel, through the iron gate and along a concrete-paved corridor between the building and the cliff face. Through the door to the narrow apartment at the back. The cold had crept into my bones and my body ached all over. But I thought I'd found a sense of understanding that I'd been searching for since the day we arrived at the chapel, since the day we'd walked through that door for the first time. The day we'd put our rucksacks down on the bare floor at the end of a 630-mile walk, unlaced our muddy boots and tried to rediscover how to live under a roof. Finally I thought I knew why I couldn't settle, why I was restless, sleepless. I made tea and took it up the stairs to Moth, my husband, lover, friend of over thirty years.

He was lying spreadeagled on the mattress in the bedroom; even the growing light of the day finding its way through a stained-glass window hadn't woken him. Nothing seemed to wake him; he could sleep for twelve hours and still need more. But I shook him and started his day as usual, with tea and two Rich Tea biscuits.

"Moth, wake up, there's something I've got to do."

"What? What are you doing—why are you dressed?"

"I couldn't sleep."

"Again?"

"I know, I'm so tired, but there's something I have to do."

Pushing the foam mattress to the corner of the room next to the cardboard wardrobe where our clothes hung left a large space on the lino-covered floor. We took a green package out of the rucksack that stood in the opposite corner, unzipped the case and shook out the familiar bundle of nylon. Unfurling the tent, I was hit with the smell of damp and sand, wind, rain and ozone-fresh, gull-filled air. I was outside, in the wild, on every shade of red, black and brown soil, in damp mossy woods and deep hidden valleys.

"You do what you need to do but I think I might still use the mattress. I'm actually getting used to the comfort again."

"Okay, but I need to try this. I can't carry on without sleep."

I clicked the duct-tape-bound poles back together with a rising sense of anticipation as they slotted into position and the green dome rose into shape. Crawling into the damp-smelling space it created, I was overcome with a rush of joy. Moth went to make more tea while I dragged in the old battered inflatable mats and sleeping bags and took a pillow off the bed. I was back. This was it. My face sank into the pillow, the world slipped away and sleep washed over me on an incoming tide of relief. I'd gone to earth.

2. Invisible

When the Christmas holiday ends and students miserably return to the classroom, very few are in their mid-fifties and starting to forget as fast as they learn. We stood in the kitchen-living area of the chapel going through Moth's daily checklist before he headed to university for the day. Phone, wallet, glasses, check; van keys, check; notepad with the list of what you're doing today, check.

"See you tonight then."

"Yep, see you later." And he was gone, but I could still hear his footsteps walking unevenly down the side of the chapel into the dull light of a winter morning. Closing the door I was back inside the long narrow corridor-like space of the apartment. I sat at the table with a cup of tea and thought about the day ahead. Waiting for the bread to pop from the toaster, my eyes scanned the bookshelf, searching for something to delay the moment when I had to open the laptop to spend more hours in the soul-destroying hunt for an employer who was on the lookout for an unqualified fifty-something with no employment record. The small bookshelf held just a random selection of books that had come out of a packing box. A few scattered volumes picked up in the last hours before we left our house. Whenever I looked at those books they took me straight back to that last moment before we walked out for the final time. Evicted from the dream that had been our family home, where we ran our holiday rental for visitors to come and stay, where we kept sheep and grew vegetables, the home where our children grew up, our world for twenty years. Before a financial dispute with a lifelong friend ended in a court case that resulted in us being served with an eviction notice. Those few books collected before we closed the door and left our old lives behind, never to return, held the sound of bailiffs as they hammered at the door, the fear of not knowing if we would ever find shelter again, and an overwhelming sadness. But if I'd known this would be the only box of books we'd bring with us into our new life I might have packed a better selection. I ran my hand across them in search of something, anything to take me out beyond the walls, beyond the chapel. *A Field Guide to Fungi*, maybe, though probably not in January; *Outsider II*, definitely not; *Five Hundred Mile Walkies*, that book, the one that had led to the most unexpected adventure. No, there was only one that would do the trick. *The South West Coast Path: From Minehead to South Haven Point*, Paddy Dillon's beautiful guide-book to the 630-mile path. The book that had guided us all the way to Polruan. The friend in our pocket as we decided not to give in to the chaos of homelessness, but to put our rucksacks on our backs and walk the whole length of the path Paddy describes, living wild, homeless and penniless on its cliffs and beaches.

The plastic cover on the little brown book was still intact, the pages bound together with a black elastic hair band. As I took it off the stiff pages bulged in ripples that had echoes of a hard sand beach on an outgoing tide. Between the pages, some stuck together in rain-damaged clumps, were postcards, feathers, grasses, scraps of paper and flowers. Memories of a path that falls from cliff top to sea level and back, until the roller coaster of wilderness has followed the whole coastline of the southwest of England and the walker has climbed the equivalent of Everest nearly four times.

I buttered the toast and waited for the phone to ring. Moth's call to say that he had arrived at the university, and wasn't sitting in a café in Truro or walking on the beach at Watergate Bay because he'd begun to drive to university, then forgotten where he was going and convinced himself that he had some other destination to go to. I thumbed the pages of the small book, almost reluctant to look inside. It held sunlit, windswept memories of months spent on cliff tops in all weathers. But there was something else in there: darker memories of the pain and sadness of the awful week that had driven us to make that walk. We were different people then, desperate, anxious, frightened people, trying to cram twenty years of life into packing boxes with only days left before we had to leave our house, thinking that losing our home was the worst thing that could possibly happen to us. But a routine hospital appointment during that week had changed those thoughts. As the lights of our life were going out, a doctor sat on the corner of his table and switched off the final lamp.

I closed the book. Did I really want to go back to that week, to feel the horror again? Too late: it was already with me. No escaping the memory of Moth's body clenched tight as he was diagnosed with a neurodegenerative disease that had neither treatment or cure. No escaping the sense of fear that returned whenever I remembered being told that the pain in Moth's shoulder, a numbness in his left side and dark fog of mental paralysis slowly taking his thoughts wasn't just old age, but actually corticobasal degeneration, CBD, a creeping unstoppable disease with only a short time left to run its course to the end. And as the doctor painted a picture of Moth's body forgetting how to swallow and pneumonia making him choke on his own saliva, we realized how wrong we'd been: far worse things were waiting for us than becoming homeless.

I put the kettle back on. He should be there by now—why hadn't he called? I turned the pages, carefully peeling apart the clumps of dried paper, Paddy's descriptions of the path leaping out in punctuations of memory. "Drifts a little inland and uphill": I laughed at the thought of us standing at the start of the walk and reading that line as we looked at a steep path following a zigzag up a near-vertical cliff. But as the pages finally began to separate, Moth was there in the margins and I could see his face as he looked up at me in the torchlight of a dark evening, when the last of the light had faded over the horizon and the green dome of the tent enclosed us in the two sheets of our damp, nylon home. Still the same wild, unstoppable man I'd loved for all of my adult life, sitting on his sleeping bag as I lay in mine, heavy-eyed but watching him write. He was there, smiling as he wrote in tiny spidery words in the margins of the guidebook, capturing the days we had just spent on cliff tops and beaches, camping on headlands and rocky ledges. "Camped on Leskey's Ledge, more in the sea than beside it." "I'm so hungry I ate Ray's biscuit, don't think she noticed." "Opened the tent to find we're only a meter from the cliff edge." "Blackberries." "The sea is like syrup, I have become the sea." "Held Ray's hand at the edge of all things." "Today I walked with a tortoise."

Touching the faded penciled words, I was with him in the wind and the rain, watching his feet as they followed the path ahead of me, blown forward into a new world. A world of university and the chapel, where the Coast Path ran past the front gate and I waited for him to return. He hadn't called—where was he?

As the pages slowly separated, page 140 appeared: Portheras Cove. "Dolphins and high tide." "I ran with the tent above my head." "Is this real?" That magical moment when we realized that he was defying the doctors who'd said CBD had no treatment or cure and his health couldn't improve. The night when we ran up the beach in the moonlight. Running away from the incoming tide, holding the fully erected tent above our heads, and learned how to hope again. After the walk, before he started university, we'd told the doctor about how Moth's health had improved, how he had done something that every authority on the illness said was impossible. The doctor hadn't been excited.

"Start the degree if you want to, but be prepared to give it up." Implying Moth might not make it to the end.

We didn't believe him, didn't want to believe. And yet as the time passed and the pressures of his degree meant Moth was becoming more sedentary, the health and ease of movement he'd found on the cliff tops was leaving him. In the quiet coldness of the winter the stiffness had returned, his aching body slowing again. Each day now began with a struggle to stand upright and as he took each shaky early morning step a creeping sense of inevitability had set in. A reluctant acceptance of what the doctor had said; he probably wouldn't be able to finish the degree. He certainly wouldn't finish the course if he kept disappearing; maybe I should start taking him to uni and picking him up later? No, it was a struggle for both of us to survive on his student loan; we certainly couldn't afford the petrol needed to make the journey twice a day. What I needed was a tracking device. I closed the book, overwhelmed with the sadness of the thought that the day would come when Moth couldn't remember what we did. The day when CBD had crept so far that the clear, magical, wild experience we'd shared was lost to him forever and I'd be left alone with the memory. The day when the guidebook would be the only record that our walk had ever happened.

Where the hell was he?

I switched the lights on. Midmorning; the sun had already moved beyond the point where it shone into the apartment and it was getting darker. I finished the tea and sat at the table gazing out of the tall chapel window that looked out on to the wall of the neighbor's garden. At six feet high it half-filled the view, but above that was the upper terrace of garden shrubs and a magnolia tree. A large brown rat dropped out of the ivy and walked across the top of the wall; then he stopped, looking in at me, his round eyes staring until he turned around and went back the way he came. I opened the door to see where he'd gone. I could hear him, but I couldn't see him, just the wall of ivy that clad the cliff face a meter and a half away from the door. From the dark damp corridor of greenness between the chapel wall and the cliff, my eyes followed his trail of rustling leaves upward through the ivy. Up there, between the buddleia bushes and the roof of the chapel, was a thin blue strip of sky, a world where the sun shone and the wind blew and I knew I had to be there; a dark sense of enclosure had borne down on me and I had to get out.

Grabbing my coat and phone, I hurried out into the street, intending to follow it up to the open cliffs, as I had every day since we'd moved to the chapel. The narrow street, hardly wide enough for a car to pass through, seemed full of people. People walking, talking, loud gesticulating people. I walked a short way along the road, but was suddenly gripped by an overwhelming sense of panic and pressed myself against the garden wall of a terrace of houses until the people had passed. What was happening? I couldn't understand the pulsing sensation in my head, and the reddening face. Not a hot flash, they were in the past, but what was happening? Was I ill? More people walked by, noisy, busy people.

"Hi, lovely day."

It was all I could do to mutter a muted "hi" in response. I didn't know what to do or which way to turn, but found myself running back to the chapel, slamming the iron gate behind me and disappearing down the concrete alleyway. I lay on the floor of the apartment trying to calm my breathing, my thoughts racing. Gradually my head stopped pounding and I realized that in the year since we'd arrived at the chapel I'd barely said a word to anyone other than Moth or our two children when they phoned or occasionally visited. When out alone I didn't speak if I could avoid it; if I was with Moth I let him do the talking.

Had I tried to talk to anyone since we'd moved there? There'd been opportunities in the shop when I could have had a conversation while the lady behind the counter filled my bag and asked me, "Are you living here now? I've seen you a few times. Where have you moved from—out of Cornwall, obviously?" She had done so numerous times, but I'd avoided a conversation on each occasion, just muttering "thank you," grabbing the bag and leaving. There had been moments when people in the street had stopped to look at the façade of the tall, imposing chapel and asked about its history, and I'd said I wasn't sure but I'd get Moth because he knew all about it. Then I'd scuttled to the back of the chapel and stayed there. I was in a state of hyper-alert over-awareness whenever I left the apartment. When we walked the path, our rucksacks stuffed with our possessions, I'd had no problems, so why now in the village did I feel this need to be invisible? Any hard-won grain of self-belief I'd found while we were walking had vanished, lost in the sea mist as it crept up the river. I sat up, angry with myself. So much time spent avoiding any interaction with people was ridiculous. I'd let this thing get out of control.

I found the laptop and put on the meditation channel I'd recently discovered. The cross-legged guru spoke to me in smooth tones.

"Breathe in and follow the breath out, and focus on the breath. Let go of all thoughts and follow the breath."

I followed the breath. I was good at this. I could empty my head and follow my breath as if I was born to it. But even as I breathed, the sound crept in and wouldn't leave. A voice from some hidden, subdued, suppressed part of me that wouldn't be quiet. That deep resonating sound which felt like a question.

The phone rang. Yes, at last.

"Where are you? Don't tell me you're in St. Ives?" Last time he'd forgotten where he was going, he'd called me from a café on the north coast, an hour away from uni. Maybe this time he'd headed west.

"Not today. I met one of the other students in the car park and she finally found the courage to ask me what I was doing in Cornwall and why I was on the course." Moth was finding sharing the course with a roomful of twenty-somethings quite difficult; they seemed to live in an entirely different world from him.

"Can't believe no one's asked you before. What did you say?"

"I stuck to the line we used on the path—that we've sold the house and I'm studying as part of a career move into teaching."

"Not really a lie, just a half-truth, but you've said it now so she'll tell everyone else. Can you keep it up?"

"Saves me having to explain how we lost the house and became homeless—it's just easier—but now they probably think I'm an ultra-wealthy mid-lifer having some sort of existential crisis."

"Only a minor misconception then."

I sagged into the chair with the relief of knowing he was where he should be. If only I could cope with this change in our lives the way he did. He just carried on being his full-on, outgoing, gregarious, story-telling self, despite occasionally not knowing where he was. The ragged, distorted threads of our lives were slowly beginning to re-form, but there was something eating into my peace of mind. Not just Moth's health but something else, in the dark confusion of my own head in the early hours of the morning, when I opened the door and looked for the sky and saw nothing but a thin strip of gray between the chapel and the rock face, when I walked into the street and it was full of people and there was nowhere to be alone. On so many days like that, I followed the path to the cliffs to stand with my face in the wind and feel the force of the weather: something that felt real. And always the voice in my head growing louder, like an onshore wind bringing a storm from the sea. Or was it the voice of my mum saying "I told you so"? It was hard to say.

★

Making my bed in the tent in the early days of the new year, I thought I'd solved my sleep problem: I'd simply been missing the familiarity of the tent; things would be absolutely fine now. I'd get more sleep; then I'd be stronger, more in control and able to focus my thoughts on living our new life in the village and making sure Moth didn't get lost. I huddled in the green dome in the corner of the bedroom, away from people and the world, unaware that only a few days later I'd find myself in the middle of the country, as far from the sea and the tent as I could possibly be.

3. Hireth

Death paced the hospital ward, but didn't stop at her bed. He cast a glance as she sat upright, her hair combed, her new blue cardigan clean and neatly buttoned. Not yet, not today, not on a Sunday. Today the deep, lung-shrinking wheeze of pneumonia had subsided and I sat by her bed as we thumbed through a glossy magazine. Moth was only a few days into the new term when I'd had the phone call. The hospital call that you always know will come one day, but never this day. Mum was in the hospital with pneumonia, they thought she was slipping into sepsis and I needed to be there. Three days later and she'd shrugged it off and there was talk of her going home.

"Maybe tomorrow you could bring some nail varnish and make me look glamorous like the girls in the magazine pictures? It'd give us something to do. I'm getting bored now."

After the stale air of the hospital, the dark cold of a late January night was a relief. I closed the van door, started the engine and headed back to Mum's tiny cottage. Along the lanes of central England, lanes so familiar I could have driven without headlights, to the warmth of her kitchen and the familiarity of her things. Her home, but not mine. My home, the place that formed me, molded me into what I would become, was in the valley below, hidden in the black stillness of unlit countryside. I could feel its presence like a body in the room. Tomorrow I wouldn't go to the hospital until later, maybe the afternoon. Before that I would walk across the land and follow my older, smaller footprints through the fields I knew so well.

★

Stepping out into the winter morning and a comforting pocket of warmth in the open porch at the back of the cottage, I reached up and put the key on the ledge, careful not to dislodge the dry and dusty swallow's nest. Such a well-chosen spot, where the morning sun takes the coldness of night at the earliest moment. They'd be back in the spring, squeezing new mud into the cracks of their old home, diving out in surprise every time the door opened. I followed the garden down through dewed grass and bare rose stems to the path that dropped into the mist in the valley. My vision was reduced, but I could hear the Canada geese on the lake. I didn't need to see; I already knew what the view would be. The spring migrants were arriving, stirring the complacency of the geese that chose to stay and overwinter there. They wouldn't be building nests yet, just squabbling over space and food.

Beyond the lake, their calls followed me faintly through the fog, and then it was all around: my roots, my childhood, the source of everything I was, a land so familiar I could map it in my mind like my own skin. I wouldn't go to the farmyard yet, I'd go through the fields first and look down at the farm, stall the moment, suck it all in.

I passed the sawmill where generations of villagers had cut the timber for houses and fencing. The carcasses of huge oaks, elm and beech had lain here, to my child's eye mountainous and never-ending. All gone now. The timber sawn, the saws gone, double-glazed windows where there had been broken dust-covered panes, roses by the door. The mist began to clear in the early yellow light as I walked out of the quietness of a copse of beech trees above the row of cottages and on to the Mountain. From the high point I could look down to the cottages where the estate workers had lived. The Scottish carpenter and his family in the larger cottage with the big garden, overflowing with vegetables to feed their five children; the plumber in the middle with the wife that no one ever saw; and the gardener to the big house in the last cottage. As I climbed the hill away from them the first car was leaving, a commuter heading to work in the town from a smart modernized house in the countryside. The grassy slope wasn't a mountain, just a field on a steep hill, but we called it that. From there, I knew I could see it as I turned away from the tree-lined hilltop and looked back into the valley. And there it was, glowing faintly pink in the morning sun. To anyone else it might have appeared as just a farmhouse in the distance, but I could see the details. The sash windows of the formal façade, the crumbling clay bricks and slate roof, and behind, out of sight, the main body of the house jutting out and forming a T to the front. I could almost hear its presence.

I headed on through High Ways field, the largest field on the farm, always kept for arable crops. I'd spent summers there, following a potato spinner as it passed up and down the ridged rows, throwing white soft-skinned new potatoes on to the damp earth. Walking bent over, collecting the potatoes into a bucket, emptying the bucket into a bag, the bags on to trailers, off the trailers into the sheds, from the sheds to a lorry, from the lorry to the shops and the chip shops. And winters, in the cold, damp and frost, cutting tops off turnips with a billhook and throwing them into a small wooden trailer to take back to the farm and tip into a shredder to feed to the bulls in the pens. When the other children from my school were playing with toys, or in the playground, I was here. Mud on my hands, in the sun and the wind, alone with the thoughts in my head. On the rare occasions when I did spend time with the others, it was as if I viewed them from a distance. Later, as a young teenager, I'd thought I wanted to be the same as my school friends, to focus on makeup and clothes. But, hard as I tried, I couldn't shake the sense of having one foot on the disco floor, one foot in the mud.

Down from the arable fields, through the woods of tall

deciduous trees, carpeted with bluebells in the spring and lined with campion and cow parsley in the summer. I'd spent days at the edge of these woods. Ten years old and I should have been playing with friends, but instead I sat alone where the woods became field and watched the rabbits moving across the grass. Hundreds and hundreds of wild brown rabbits grazing in the grass fields and moving across the winter corn like locusts. I'd loved the power of standing by the fence, almost obscured by the turning post, until I could see a haze of brown across the hillside, and then dashing out of hiding to clap my hands and watch the blanket of rabbits look up from eating before rushing toward their warren, like brown water sucked down a drain. As I grew older, I stopped clapping and instead spent hours just watching, observing the hierarchy of their brown world. The older ones venturing into the wider field, the young ones staying close to the mouth of the burrows, and the watchers. The rabbits that didn't hunch over to eat, but stayed upright, looking, listening and then sounding the alarm. Stamping their strong hind legs against the ground, creating a thudding noise that connected all the others with its signal, causing them to stop eating and, as one, run to the holes on the hillside and vanish.

When I reached the gamekeeper's cottage at the edge of the wood, I scanned across the field, but could see only green. I stood and instinctively clapped my hands, waiting for the brown movement. There was none; the field was still in the cold, damp winter air. The gamekeeper kept foxhounds for the hunt here, in kennels with outside compounds made of high iron railings. They bayed in loud voices that echoed around the valley whenever anyone passed. Strong, muscular, powerful dogs, but the gamekeeper could walk among them as they licked his hands like pets waiting for a treat, not the ruthless killers they were. I'd seen them rip a fox apart and I didn't need to be told to stay away; nothing could have made me go near them.

The gamekeeper's cottage stood at the furthest corner of the Park, a field where the sheep were held during the lambing season. The field dipped down behind his house, forming a corner between the kennel and the wood, and this is where the sheep would come. Sheltered by the woods, but exposed to the foxes living just beyond the treeline and right next to the hunting dogs whom they should have run from in fear. And yet, day after day, ewes chose that spot when their lambs were close to being born. Taking the risk that the foxes would be held at bay by the presence of their predators, they chose this place because when they were at their most vulnerable shelter was everything. A contradiction at the edge of the wood. But the railings are gone now, the kennels are a bungalow and a brand-new four-wheel drive stands outside the gamekeeper's cottage. Something else has changed too. As I walk over the ground that's so familiar I could have left it yesterday, something's different. The villagers have gone, replaced by commuters and retirees, taking the working heart out of the estate. But they've been gone for years; it's something more than that, something more fundamental that I can't quite put my finger on. I shrug it off with the thought that maybe it's me, and my response to the land; maybe I'm viewing it with different eyes.

To the Park. When the old farmhouse was the main house on the estate this would have been its formal entrance, with a gravel drive lined by oak trees. But in the eighteenth century a new hall had been built, leaving the old one to become just a large faded farmhouse. Only two of the oaks still stand, bark split with age, branches distorted, but still pushing to the sky, still searching for that one last ray of sunlight. The roots lift in swollen mounds around the base of the trunks; one is so pronounced it forms a lumpy seat around the base. I sat down to take in the best view. I could hear the echo of my own footfall, circling the tree for hours on late-summer days, hopping from root to root as if they were stepping stones. Not bored or listless, something else—something like mesmerized.

And there it was. In the dip below, at the base of the bowl, the bottom of the valley: the place from where all the paths of my life run upward and away. The sun was higher in the sky now and the bricks had lost the pinkness, turning to their true orange-red. Whenever I took this walk and sat in this spot I was surprised. As I looked down at the house I still expected to see the immense weeping willow tree that had stood in front of the façade, obscuring its face, keeping its secrets. With my eyes closed I can hear the clattering hush of its branches, swooping in tendrils to the ground. I'm running toward the curtain of green, my small hands reaching out and grasping bunches of whip-thin growth and swinging in the air through the height of the tree, or just hanging hidden in the leaves, watching. And my mum's voice: "Get down from there! How many times do you have to be told?" But I don't get down; I swing through the green to the firmness of a branch and watch through the delicate whispering elongated leaves as they search for me, pushing the tendrils aside.

"This needs cutting back. Cut it so it's out of her reach."

So every spring the tree was pruned until the whips hung in a short-cropped bob. But the willow's growth is like no other tree and by midsummer the leaves were sweeping the ground again and life inside the green dome was mine.

The mobile phone ringing in my pocket brought me back to the moment. As I opened my eyes Mum's voice trailed away and the tree was gone, the house face exposed. A perfectly proportioned face of five windows and a Georgian entrance with polished steps. Nothing to hide now, no secrets kept behind the leafy veil.

"Your mum's had a stroke. I think you need to come to the hospital straightaway."

"But how? She's coming out on Wednesday—you said she was better?"

"Just come now; we'll talk about it when you're here."

Back in the stifling, cloying heat of the hospital wards, the nurse led me to an office where a doctor was waiting.

"Your mum's had a stroke, a total anterior stroke. It's severe and still progressing."

"Still progressing? But she's in the hospital. Just give her the drugs to stop it."

The doctor shook his head, with an expression between sympathy and exasperation.

"What about all the adverts? You know, 'act FAST' and save the person. She's in the hospital—how much faster can it get? And total anterior—what on earth does that mean?"

"It's a large cortical stroke. We don't know how large until we have the scans, but we can already tell it's severe and extensive."

"Extensive?"

She lay motionless on the bed as it was wheeled back into its place. The occupants of the other beds all watched in silent vigil and I could see the confusion in their faces. This was the respiratory ward; they were used to oxygen masks and nurses, but not this. The nurse drew the blue curtains around us and we were alone. I picked up her hand, lifeless and uncontrolled. The doctor returned with the results and spoke in a hushed voice.

"She appears to have no feeling in her body; she's totally affected. As I said, it's a total anterior stroke; it has the effect of a hammer blow to the head. She's retaining some organ function and her lungs are working; we don't know how it's affected her brain, but she's probably not there. There's nothing that can be done. It won't be long; she'll be gone soon."

I stroked the hair back from her closed eyes. She'd always

been so concerned about her hair. Always neatly cut, and permed and set in rollers every week. Even in the potato fields she'd worn a headscarf over hair fixed with hairspray. So many of our arguments during my teens had been about the state of my hair.

"Mum, can you hear me? I'm here." I held her limp hand, stroking her fingers, still broad and strong. "I'm here." Her eyes slowly opened; her mouth was moving, but no sound came out, yet I could see her in the blue-gray eyes. Fear, confusion, a panicking wild animal. "Mum, you're on the ward, you've had a stroke, but it's okay, I'm here." Then I saw it, a look of horror and recognition, and I felt a spasm of throat-clenching nausea. She was there, present, alive and trapped. "Just close your eyes, Mum, try to sleep, it'll help." Help who? It wouldn't help her.

As she slept I cut her fingernails, filing them carefully into shape, then painting them with her favorite pearl-pink nail varnish. When I finished I laid her hands back across the bed, their pink tips looking strangely out of place on her wide hands. The lights dimmed for the night, and I sat in the blue cocoon, watching numbers rise and fall on the monitor.

4. Running

"Don't go in the woods. The gamekeeper sets traps for the foxes that'll have your foot off like that." Mum claps her hands, locking her fingers together, imitating the gin trap closing and biting off my foot. "You know this—how many times do I have to tell you? But get a vase anyway."

I carefully place the armful of bluebells on the table and go to the pantry for a vase. I'm still in there when I hear Dad come in.

"What the hell, has she been in the woods again? Get those stinking things out of here." Through the crack in the pantry door I can see him sweep the bluebells off the table and throw them into the garden. "You, get out of the pantry. You do not, ever, go in the woods. Get your boots on. If you've got nothing better to do than that you can come and do some work with me."

Two days had passed and Mum was still breathing; the wild, conscious light in her eyes was fading, but her body didn't let go. She'd been moved to the stroke ward, where the nurses better understood her needs. It seemed her greatest need now was food, but she couldn't swallow—her throat no longer heard the messages from her brain. That morning they would insert a feeding tube up her nose and down her throat so liquid food could reach her stomach. The night before, the small, dark-haired nurse had explained how it worked. "Best not to come in until after the procedure, love. Looks worse than it is; give yourself the morning off."

So I went to Black Woods. Drawn there without thinking, without planning, instinctively, compulsively. I'd known the dangers in the woods when I was a child, I'd heard all the warnings, but I went anyway. I had to go. And now, nearly fifty years later, the same pull found me sitting on a rotting branch among the trees. In the spring the woodland would be carpeted with bluebells, thousands, millions of dancing blue heads in every direction. Although there were central strips of dark pine plantation, the bluebells gave away its history as being an ancient deciduous wood. That sense of age was still there, dark, enclosed, protected, otherworldly, and at the center of that, in the heart of the woods, was the gamekeeper's territory. That was where the pheasant pens had stood.

A large cleared area had been surrounded by a high fox-proof fence and within that was a lower fenced section where the wooden pens were. Here the pheasants were reared from tiny chicks to adults. Crouched in the undergrowth, hiding, I'd spent hours watching him caring for the tiny day-old balls of fluff with their distinctive striped backs. As they grew he moved them through the series of pens until they were scrawny, scruffy juveniles old enough to leave the pens. Then they were released, outside the pens but still safe within the high fence. These were tame teenagers, free to roam, but always home for dinner. In the evening, just before dark, the gamekeeper would come with a hessian sack hung over his shoulder, scattering grain on the leaf litter. And whistling. A low repeated monotone whistle, but the birds knew the sound and came running from every direction, hundreds of trusting birds running to their carer, the man who had been their source of protection and food throughout their short lives. I would creep away then, getting back to the farmhouse before dark.

Back in the woods now I'd picked up a long stick without thinking and scratched through the leaves ahead of me, rhythmically, side to side, mine-sweeping for gin traps as I had as a child. But they were long gone. Sweeping the leaves aside exposed a hole in the ground, a tunnel leading deep into the earth. Much bigger than a rabbit, smaller than a badger: the mouth of a fox den. But there were no foxes there: the entrance was covered in dry leaves; no footprints marked the mud at the entrance. They'd gone, moved on.

I didn't need to crawl under the wire fence of the pheasant enclosure; it was broken and curled and I could walk in where the heavy wire gate was swinging off its hinge. Inside the cage, ferns and brambles had reclaimed the woodland floor, but I could still hear the whistle. There would come a day for every group of young pheasants, a day when their flight feathers had grown and the gamekeeper opened the gate. That day he would whistle to them from beyond the pen and they would run out behind him to the wide wood, pecking their corn, oblivious to the gate being shut behind them, totally unaware of what lay ahead. An adult life where they were free. Free to live as wild birds, or to return each night to the corn and the whistle, which they did, every night, trusting the gamekeeper implicitly. Until the day he came without corn, but with noise and dogs to drive them forward until they burst into flapping, squawking flight at the edge of the wood. On a flight path that took them straight over the waiting guns.

Something seemed to have changed. The pens had gone, and the pheasants, the foxes and the gamekeeper. It was beyond that, something more, something I couldn't name. I knew the bluebells were still there, waiting in the cold earth to re-emerge when the days lengthened. Just as they had that day when I'd picked hundreds of them, hoping to fill the dark serious house with their scent, and comfort my mum, crying at the kitchen sink after Dad had thrown a curled torn envelope on the table and stormed out. But as with that day, no amount of bluebells could make this day bright.

★

The tubes distended her nostrils, projecting alien tendrils from a face reddened and starting to bruise. I combed her hair, trying to swallow my horror. Her eyes were closed, but as they opened tears were falling and they looked away from me. I sat and held her hand with a touch she couldn't feel.

"All right, dear, all in place now, aren't we? We'll try again with your lunch in a minute." The nurse turned to me, beckoning me outside the curtain. "We don't think this is going to work—her stomach's rejecting the food, probably because it's affected by the stroke too. We're trying again now, so just go and get a cuppa and the doctor will have a chat with you later."

A thought was starting to form, but I crushed it and turned away from its whisper.

Desperate for air and light, I found myself outside the hospital, walking briskly from the grounds down the path toward the park, past the allotments and up a hill I hadn't climbed in years. And then I was there. I sat on the stile where a footpath crossed through a hedge of hawthorn and hazel and the town stretched out across a wide river plain below. The first time I climbed that stile I'd been a teenager, decades ago. I'd walked along the muddy path at the edge of town in the dark, but as I stepped over the stile the town was no longer gray and dreary but magically lit with a million lights. He'd caught my hand then, the boy in the trench coat, his hair blowing in the cold wind.

"Wait, wait here, don't go down the hill yet. Look at this— this is what I wanted to show you. It's transformed at night, the reality disappears and it becomes this other world."

I was going nowhere. It was the most intense moment in my young life as Moth opened his long blue coat to let me shelter inside and we looked out over the glow of the town and the rushing lights on the dual carriageway.

"You know I've never felt this before, but I think I love you."

I rolled his words in my head, over and over until they grew into a bright ball of warmth. I'd never heard those words spoken before. Not in real life, not in my house, not in my life. They were words from books and films, words that conjured color and passion and fullness and I let them wash over me, bathing me in a cloak of beauty, safety and possibility.

I pulled that cloak around me now on a dull, cold January afternoon and let the comfort of it soothe the panic. The stile was rotting, barely taking my weight, and the town hung in dank dampness, the roar of the traffic below increasing. But I could feel the warmth of the cloak that had wrapped me every day since that night and I held it close as I walked back on to the ward and sat in the doctor's room.

"I'm afraid the feeding tubes aren't working. Her stomach is rejecting the food. Now, we're not sure if that's because the whole stomach has stopped functioning, or just the upper part."

"What are you saying?" He was so casual, so matter of fact: was he saying what I thought?

"We think the nose tubes should be removed as it's clearly causing her distress."

"And what then?"

"We can surgically insert a tube into her stomach, but there are problems with that. Still, we'll be doing the best we can."

I couldn't grasp what he was saying—problems?

"I can't take any more of this niceness. Just tell me what's happening. Tell me the truth."

"The problem is if we insert the tube her body might continue to reject the food. And if it doesn't then there's still the problem of infection. Eventually, at some point, infection will be the cause of death."

I couldn't speak, but became transfixed by the shape of his mouth as the words continued to fall out. Textbook words that he was totally unmoved by, but I'd asked for them.

"What will happen if you don't do the surgery?"

"The stroke will kill her. She can't survive for long, it's too severe."

"So you're saying she can't survive, it's just a matter of now, or later."

"Yes."

"But infection will eventually kill her if you use the tube. When, how long?"

"Nine months maximum, that's if her stomach doesn't reject the liquid and if her digestive system is still working."

"And if you don't use the tube?"

"We'll stop the antibiotics and the fluid drip, the pneumonia will return and due to the inability to swallow she'll aspirate."

"Aspirate?"

"Choke on her own saliva. She'll probably die in two to three days."

Those words again. It had taken months after Moth's diagnosis for the nightmares about the meaning of those words to stop. I tried to close my mind to the sound of them. But the words reared back into my consciousness with their roaring whisper.

"Why would you do that? Why would you stop the antibiotics and the fluid—that seems insane?"

"Because without the stomach tube she'll starve to death, so we'll be moving into a phase of non-intervention unless there's some other organ failure before then."

"Well, what do you think should be done?"

"We think we should insert the tube, tomorrow or the next day, because that's the next step. But it's your decision."

My decision? I stood to leave and had to grab the chair; my legs were fluid. *He's telling me to decide how and when my mum should die.*

Back at her bedside and she was sleeping. I tried to catch my thoughts but they skidded by too fast, half a century of memories. How could I decide anything that wasn't colored by our past? I needed space and sky and the roar of wind in trees and crows tilting as they were blown off course and rain on my face; I needed real and I was running, running.

Through the wet meadow that always flooded in the winter. Past the dyke that I used to climb into, wading through water as high as my Wellies, with earth walls above my head, poking sticks down the water-vole holes. Across the tiny brick bridge over the river where the mallard ducks collected. Through the gateway where Mum would put the tea flasks on hot summer afternoons when the field was full of the busyness of haymaking. Beyond the clay pit with the smooth wet sides that I slid down in wild, childish, mud-crusted abandon. Up the hill with the ridge in the middle that gave a perfect lift to a fast-flying sledge on snow. Beyond caring that this was someone else's land now, that it had never been ours anyway. Running, running.

To the woods. The dark, still quietness of the pines. No life there, no dancing bright leaves on summer days, no call of birdsong in spring. Silence. I lay on the dried soft ground and crunched handfuls of crisp dead pine needles until the pounding in my head subsided. Real: this was real. This earth, this land, these trees. Real, safe.

Hidden in the darkness of the straight, vertical trunks I was invisible, my existence blurred. These trees had always been here for me, bushy and low when I was young, tall and swaying now; I'd come here through every twist and turn of my young life to be in a wild place, an animal behind a screen of bark looking out on the human world. A lifetime, from childhood to middle age, all of it compressed into one moment, one choice. Looking through the trunks, I saw the village spread out through the valley. From the farm below, to Mum's cottage and the churchyard beyond: her lifeline laid out from start to finish. And in between the trees and fields, my life was interwoven. With my eyes closed, I let myself feel the wind in the treetops, and the sharpness of the needles, and the faint scent of pine filling my aching head. So much loss. I needed the soft earth to suck me in and fold over me, to hide me from any more loss.

My thoughts began to calm, to settle into the quiet hush of early afternoon. There was no choice; I already knew the answer. And yet even the thought of it felt like the ultimate betrayal. This ninety-year-old, strong, independent woman had proudly told the story of how she was the first woman in her village to wear trousers, of how the other villagers had reviled her for it. She had been a teenager in a pre-war world that was soon to be invaded by a group of drinking, smoking, trouser-wearing land girls. They were women set free from the confines of their restrictive lives and seizing the freedom of the new world that was opening up to them in the vacuum left when the men went to war. Reading between the lines, it seemed Mum had been both horrified by their counterpoint to her strict Victorian upbringing, and excited by the possibility. One woman especially seemed to have had a lasting effect on her life: the artistic, book-reading Glin. They had become close friends and she'd visited us throughout her life, appearing annually, unannounced, in a camper van with piles of books for me and chocolates for Mum. She always brought the possibility of the different, with her short-cropped hair and men's jackets. She would stay for a day or two, during which Dad would stay in the fields all day, only coming to the house for food and sleep. Then she would be gone; I'd wake in the morning and the camper van would have left, and I'd begin to read her books.

Over the years the pile of books from Glin grew, and so did my ability to annoy my mum. The greatest punishment in her arsenal was to send me to my room, where I had to sit and read on sunny afternoons when I wanted to be outside, or sometimes for whole days at a time. When I was very small it was an irritation, but soon it became like no punishment at all, and there were times when I'd do something wrong as early as possible in the day so that I could finish a book. Climbing trees and wading through streams, safe in the knowledge that Jack London's *Call of the Wild* was waiting on top of the pile that had yet to be read. Or I could always go back to *Ring of Bright Water*, or *Watership Down*, or any of the other books that took me to places where the wild animals lived. I began to dream of writing my own book, and instead of reading started writing stories and imagined holding my own book with a picture of a penguin on the spine. Until I found the letter; then the dreams were put on the shelves with the books and a harsher reality stepped in.

In the cottage, I folded her clean nightie and towel, putting them in her bag. Bed socks: her feet were like ice; I should take socks. But they weren't in her drawers. All her other clothes were there; I looked again and, as I lifted up the neatly folded cotton hankies, there it was, the curled, ripped envelope. Looking exactly as it had when I was a child. She wouldn't tell me what was in the letter, so I'd searched for it. For years. I'd given up looking, thinking it must have been thrown away, but when I was twelve I'd found it by chance in a sewing basket. It was the moment of finding a hidden tomb on an archaeological dig. That moment when you know you'll see through a doorway to another world, one that's always been there but hidden from view. And now, all these years later, she still had the letter. I didn't need to read it, I knew what it said, but I took it out of the envelope one more time. Those familiar words that were no more than black lines on white paper, and yet I'd spent half my life thinking what the contents of that letter meant and how it had colored our family life. Years of piecing together my own version of the story, using it as the answer to so many questions. The fields, the woods, the land on which I grew up weren't ours. It was a tenanted farm. Dad had asked what the procedure would be for the tenancy to be inherited and he had received his reply. The tenancy would not pass on; when the estate owner died, the estate, with all the farms and houses that it held, would be sold and the tenancy would end. To be renewed by the new owner, or not. I wouldn't stay on the farm forever; I would have to leave, to work away from the farm and create another life. That was when I put the notebooks and pens away; there'd be no more stories about the wild things.

I spotted the socks, all of them in a plastic bag under the bed. Why would she do that? I took the socks and went back to the hospital.

A change of shift had brought another doctor, another face.

"We can get her into surgery for the tube tomorrow morning. Obviously, in her condition, there are risks with the anesthetic."

"No."

"Sorry?"

"No, she wouldn't want it. She'd hate to be lying there depending on others for everything. She'd hate this. I know she is hating this."

"But we need to do it. It's the next step."

"No, you don't need to at all. Just let her be. It's what she would want." Did I know that? Was I sure? Could I possibly make that decision without any cloud to my judgment? If I stuck to it would I always question myself, always doubt the choice? Of course, there was no question of that.

"I'm not sure if we can allow that."

"The other doctor said it was my choice. It isn't about me, it's about Mum, and I'm sure it would be her choice." Did I really know that? How could I possibly know? Even as I said it, I could hear the gamekeeper's whistle, that long monotone whistle from the woods.

The doctor referred the issue to the consultant, who insisted on a meeting with a Macmillan nurse, so that I "fully understand my decision." So I sat in another corridor and waited for the nurse, but she didn't come. I didn't really need the meeting; I already understood so much more than the doctor could imagine. In the years since Moth's diagnosis thoughts of death and the process of dying rarely left my head for more than a day. Years filled with time spent in the hospital corridors learning how to wait and how to be afraid. Time spent on open cliff tops trying to grasp the finality of death, and to accept it as part of life. And yet I could still only see death from the point of view of an observer, not as someone holding on to the last thread of their existence, so how could I make the ultimate decision for her? How could I? I needed her to tell me, to show me something from her trapped world.

I stopped waiting for the nurse, went back to Mum's room, held her hand and stroked the lifeless, papery grayness as I fell over the words. Stumbling through the impossibility of explaining how she would end her long life, and how a choice had to be made. How could she possibly tell me anything? I should have protected her from the truth and let her think she would get well, if she was still able to think at all. I gave up and let go, sobbing without control, tears flowing from a well of loss that just kept growing deeper. As I wiped my face, smearing away salt and snot, she opened her eyes, those watery blue-gray eyes. They hesitated for a while at the end of the bed, focused on something out of sight and then turned to me, holding my gaze as her mouth moved, a slight, barely perceptible movement. And a whisper, so faint I had to put my ear to her mouth.

"Ome."

"What, Mum, what is that, what are you saying?"

"Ome."

"What are you saying, Mum, are you saying 'home'?"

Her eyes fixed on my face and then they closed and she slipped back into sleep. Home, what did she mean by home?

The Macmillan nurse came and sat by the bed.

"I was waiting for you in the corridor."

"I know, I'm sorry, I was delayed."

I told her about "ome" and what I thought it meant: that Mum wanted to go home to die, as Dad had when the cancer he'd tried to ignore finally overtook him. So she talked to her and carefully explained the situation, without tears or drama. But there was no response.

"We can't allow her to go home; her care needs are such that she needs to stay here. Are you sure you heard her say something? It seems very unlikely."

"I did. I know I did."

The consultant came, ticked boxes, signed forms, the antibiotics were removed and she was wheeled from the ward into a side room. A room of quiet, ultimate stillness, completely alone. She was in the dying room.

"How long?"

"Three, four days at the most."

I moved into the room with her.

5. Trust

I needed Moth to be there, to share the horror of the decision, to just be present in the space next to me. But the word "aspirate" was too close, too real; I couldn't let him witness it. However Mum died it would be her death. Not his. But if he was there in that dying room I couldn't keep the two separate in my own mind, and I needed to hide him from it, hide him from the possible horrors to come. Hide him from death. And Mum wouldn't have wanted him there; in fact she'd have hated him being present.

Moth had blown into my life on a Wednesday afternoon, his hair hanging in Celtic plaits, his old RAF trench coat flapping behind him. I was eighteen, barely an adult, when he'd ignited my life with a wild electricity that hadn't faded. His raw, visceral, impassioned spirit joined every fight to protect the environment and he'd lived his days following a dream: that he would be able to make people understand we had one precious land which had to be protected. He'd spent weeks up trees and on encampments blocking the building of new motorways, and weekends outside the railings of Sellafield nuclear power station fighting to stop the outdoor dumping of radioactive waste. But the protests were ignored, the concrete came anyway and the waste continued to be dumped in the pond. I was overwhelmed by the light he seemed to emit; it shone through every dark, dusty, undiscovered corner of my world. Naïvely, I'd believed that my family would feel the same. They didn't.

Moth was strangely, almost magnetically drawn to the countryside, to the wilderness. He'd grown up in the town, but even as a child his eyes were turned toward the trees and the hills. His thoughts were always of when he could next pass from the gray to the green. In the months after we met, whenever we could, we went to the Peak District and walked across every hill, moor and valley that we could access for a day trip. I'd spent my life in the countryside, so that wasn't why I went—for me those walks were about being with him. But for Moth it was something else; he was drawn to nature like an addiction and without that regular shot of green he found the rest of his world unbearable.

Walking was one thing, but Moth was always looking for something else, for a more intense immersion in the outdoors. On a morning when we should have been in college, we were at his house, T. Rex playing on the wooden record player. As Marc Bolan rode a white swan, Moth stood by his bedroom window, looking hazily blue in the sunlight as it reflected from the mirror. I'd only known him for a few months, but he'd created a whirlpool in my life, a kind of madness where all I thought about was him. He'd pulled on his jeans and was holding his T-shirt in his hand, but hesitated by the window, looking up the street and then waving.

"Who are you waving at? You're not dressed."

"Just the old lady over the road. Doesn't matter—I've waved to her all my life. I never close the curtains." He seemed restless, as if he was waiting for something to happen. "Let's go rock climbing. Come on, I'll get the rope." He climbed with his friends, but I'd never been. He tucked the T-shirt into his jeans and did up the belt. I briefly skimmed over the scenario in my head. Just time to get to the rocks, then get home without my parents even knowing that I'd skipped the day off college. Of course I was going.

We parked my tiny battered Fiat car at the foot of the Roaches,

a band of gritstone rock rising out of the Staffordshire moorland. We'd walked there many times, crossing the crenelated
escarpment from Rockhall Cottage to Lud's Church and then
returning along the road, Moth pointing out climbing routes
he'd attempted with his friends. Getting out of the car, he put
his faded blue canvas rucksack on his back, with a pair of EB
rock-climbing boots dangling from it and an orange rope
thrown over his shoulder, and we began the walk up to the
rocks. He was explaining how the texture of the sole of the
boots had a sticky effect on the rock, allowing for a better grip.
I looked down at my cheap plastic trainers and wondered how
they would stick.

"Don't worry, I'll lead, so you'll be following up, and if you
slip I'll have the rope secured so you don't fall."

I put on his spare harness, closing the buckles to their tightest
setting. It was still loose—what if I fell out of it?

"It's just an easy route, so you'll be fine." He explained how
the rope ran through a metal belaying device that clipped to my
harness. "Let it run through your hands while I'm climbing,
then secure it off like this when I stop. Then if I slip I won't crash
off; it stops the rope from running and breaks my fall." He pulled
the rope to one side to imitate me securing him.

"What if I can't hold it?"

"You will. I trust you."

And he was gone, heading up the rock wall with certainty
and confidence, while I stood on a rock slab at the foot of the
climb. I shuffled my mustard-colored trainers, looking up at
what appeared to be a flat wall of rock rising straight up into a
blue sky. Each time he stopped I secured the rope. I'd got this; it
was going to be fine. The ground was dry and dusty and as the
day heated up and the rocks became warm, the smell of the pine
trees below began to fill the air. Moth reached an awkward spot
and leaned out away from the rock, holding on with one hand so

that he could get a better look at the route above, his feet stickily gripping the small indentations in the rock as he said they would. The shape of his lean body arched away from the gritstone caught the light, creating an almost surreal silhouette against the blue sky. I had to take a photo, to capture the moment. As I bent down and picked up the camera, letting go of the rope to take the photo, he leaned back an inch too far and without my hand on the rope to stop him, started to fall. Dropping the camera, I snatched at the rope, slowing his fall, but not soon enough to stop him hitting the rocky ground at the base with some force.

"What the . . . ? Why didn't you stop me?"

"I picked up the camera."

"You're kidding me. It better be a bloody good picture."

"I don't know if I even pressed the shutter. Are you hurt? Shall we go back?"

"Yeah, it feels weird when I breathe, but you're climbing this before we go." He stood up stiffly and quickly climbed to the top without hesitation, belayed and waited for me to follow. I couldn't. What if he let me slip just to prove a point? "Come on. Trust me—you'll be fine."

I started to climb. Easier than I thought: my fingers found the grips; the footholds felt secure. But as I reached the very spot where Moth had leaned out my trainers slipped and I was off the rock. A momentary lurch and then a snatch on the harness and I'd stopped falling and was hanging in the air.

I could see his face over the rocks at the top of the climb, his hair blowing in the wind beneath the red bandanna tied around his head.

"You're okay, I've got you."

I hung in the warm air, the moorlands spreading out around me, but all I could focus on was his face framed against the blue sky. I stopped panicking as the wind blew gently against the rope. I knew I wouldn't fall; he had the rope. I wasn't going anywhere but up.

By the time I'd driven back to town Moth was struggling to breathe. I helped him out of the car and watched him walk into A & E. Then I drove home.

Mum was in the garden when I got there. "Did you have a good day?"

I looked at her weeding the flower beds and wanted to say yes, absolutely yes. I'm in love with a man whom I can trust with my life, and today I learned that even if I get things wrong, I can still trust myself to try again and I think I might be good at photography, even though it's taken Moth possibly cracking a rib to find that out. I desperately wanted to share it all with her. But I didn't.

"It was okay."

I'd tried so hard to make my parents understand Moth, but the more I talked the more their fury grew. They'd rejected him with a venom and ferocity that wiped out every vision I had of what my family was. "You'll regret this, my girl, you'll regret this 'til the day you die." I couldn't grasp it, couldn't understand why they didn't see what I saw. "He's no use to you, he's useless, pointless." I was in agony as I began to try to live between two worlds. Hiding one from the other: my unrestrained happiness as Moth and I grew closer, and maintaining my parents' belief that I was the daughter they wanted me to be. A tearing, hiding, lying impossibility, yet I couldn't choose one above the other. I couldn't face the disapproval and rejection that being honest with my parents had brought. I wanted it all. I wanted to keep all the people I loved in a tight close bubble; I didn't want to be without any of them.

Moth didn't want to just see the natural world, he wanted to envelop himself in it, to feel the elements in their wildest form, as empty of man as he could find. Neither of us earned enough money to travel abroad, but in this country that desire drew him north. So when he began to plan a trip to the Highlands of Scotland I knew I had to find a way to go with him. I couldn't tell my parents, but looking back over the decades that have passed since then, the idea of not simply saying to them, "I'm going on a camping trip with my boyfriend and if you don't like it, well, tough," seems faintly ridiculous. Yet I couldn't: their views and their hold was so tight, the recrimination so difficult to endure that I simply wasn't brave enough to face it. But I was going with him anyway.

Of course I was going with his whole family, of course I had my own room, of course Moth's parents would be with us all the time. At Moth's house I emptied my clothes from my suitcase into a rucksack he'd borrowed from a friend. I hoisted the huge, red, hard-framed, rusty lump on my back, the very first time I'd felt the sag of weight on my shoulders and the security of the waist-strap around my hips. Moth tightened the shoulder straps and my eight-stone, twenty-year-old frame was held in a straitjacket. I had no idea how I would be able to move with this thing strapped to me, but all I felt was wild excitement. Moth plaited his hair, put his ragged waistcoat over his collarless shirt and tweed cropped trousers, laced his walking boots and we were ready, we were going, we were actually doing this. His dad gave us a lift to the railway station to catch the night train to Inverness.

"What do I do if your parents phone the house?" Moth's dad straightened his flat cap and looked quizzically out of the car window.

"They won't, you're supposed to be in the north of Scotland on holiday." What if they did? What if they checked it out? I pushed the thought to the back of my mind as we got on the packed night train. There were no seats left so we sat on our rucksacks in the corridor as the country slipped south and we got closer to the big adventure.

It's difficult to sleep on the floor of a train; the jolts, bangs and smells are hard to shut out. Yet in fitful snatches of darkness I dreamed of an oddly shaped mountain set against a purple sky, and rain like a solid curtain. As dawn broke we were north of the border, in a strange and foreign land that I'd never seen before. And a young German called Johann was sitting on a rucksack next to me.

"You're heading for Ullapool? Fantastic place, but you should go north of there and see the mountain Stac Pollaidh. Amazing place, you'll never forget it."

Moth had his OS map out looking for the mountain Johann was suggesting.

"I'd thought of going here." I could see Moth's finger hovering over the area of land he'd been talking about for weeks, a patch of undulating contour lines that stretched away from roads or habitation into an indistinguishable area of green. "To Ben Mor Coigach, then along the ridge to Sgurr an Fhidhleir—the Fiddler." Even the name had a dark, slightly threatening edge. The details had gone over my head. It was the first time I'd gone away for more than a day without my parents, and I was with him. Even in the dusty coldness of the train carriage I could still picture the way his body moved under the sweaty, slept-in shirt. I could imagine the way his shoulders curved and feel my face against the skin of his back as he cooked mushrooms in a frying pan after afternoons of skipping college, then work, afternoons of losing ourselves in our own world of obsession.

"It all sounds good to me. Let's do Stac Pollaidh as well." I was going to be alone with him for a whole week, just us, together. I didn't care where he took me. I'd have gone anywhere.

The bus from Inverness was hot and stuffy, but as the doors opened in Ullapool the clear air hit us like chilled champagne. Empty and cold, but white with a glorious, fizzing brightness.

We walked around the small town on the western coast of Ross and Cromarty, eating chips, watching the fishing boats in the harbor and looking for a B & B. The following morning we bought some food supplies for the next few days and checked the weather report on the harbor master's door: clear skies for the next two days, light winds and maybe a little drizzle the day after. We lifted our rucksacks and began the long walk from the town to Stac Pollaidh.

"This is going to take all day and I just want to get there. Shall we hitch?"

"Okay, why not." I put my thumb out in hopeful expectancy.

We climbed out of a camper van driven by a Swedish family, with three children, a dog and a clattering cowbell suspended from the roof, and stood at the foot of the mountain. The heat was already rising as we began the walk up through heather and jumbled rock. The heat became intense, turning the warm morning into a baking-hot afternoon of clambering over sharp steep sandstone. I'd had no idea how hard it would be to climb a mountain with a full rucksack on my back. I seemed to be dragging a boulder of weight with me, turning every step into a gym-style weightlifting exercise. It was as if there had been a shift in gravity and some unknown force was now bearing down on me, requiring a huge concentrated effort to overcome. I gritted my teeth and followed Moth's heels as he bounded up the hill with a monstrous rucksack stuffed with a tent and big clanking billy cans. I couldn't give in, couldn't be that whinge-ing, whimpering girlfriend and ruin his longed-for trip. Finally, gasping and sweating in the hot air, I dropped the pack down on the ridge and tentatively touched my shoulders, red raw from the straps. The very first time I'd stood on the top of a mountain in Scotland, and it took my breath away. The wild remoteness of Assynt stretched beneath us and away to the sea and the Summer

Isles. A vision like nothing I'd ever seen before, a green and blue shimmering heat-haze of glory.

"You did really well. Didn't know if you'd make it up there."

I was pulsating with pride, glowing in his praise as I peeled my green T-shirt out of my puckered skin. But as my eyes moved away from the view to the west, there it was, in the south: the dark heart of Ben Mor Coigach.

"There it is. I can't wait to head up the valley toward it; I've been thinking about this for weeks."

I looked at him, blond hair blowing in the wind of a mountaintop, excitement filling his face with light. Where he belonged. But down there in the south was a trail of miles over peat bog and rock to a dark imposing jutting blade of mountain, hidden deep in the black wilderness. A tiny tinge of fear crept across the sun.

We caught a lift with a group of Spanish twenty-somethings to a campsite in Achiltibuie, miles away to the west. A night on a campsite before the planned two nights of wild camping on the trek to and from the ben. We pitched the tent and I rushed to the toilet block in hope of a cool shower to soak my raw, bleeding shoulders. There were no showers, but the Spanish girls were stripped and washing at the sinks. I was shocked. I'd lived my life under Mum's Victorian values, where baring anything more than my arms in public was seen as just *not nice*. I desperately needed to wash, so took my T-shirt off and dabbed water on my shoulders, feeling oddly exposed in a wooden shed at the edge of the world.

"What sort of boyfriend is he? Making you drag a weight like that about." The Spanish girls were crowding round looking at my dismal shoulders.

"I wanted to come."

"Ha, really." They took the sponge off me and slowly and carefully bathed the raw skin, picking out the threads of green shirt.

"It's not my rucksack—I borrowed it. It doesn't really fit me."

"Never borrow kit for the hills, it always causes pain." They smoothed the skin down with antiseptic cream. "Keep your shirt off; you need to let it see the air."

With the damp T-shirt in my hand I walked back to the tent, through a strange new world of liberation. It was the first time I'd camped since a school trip to the Peak District, but to be zipped inside a tiny enclosed green space with Moth was no hardship. The next morning the Spanish van dropped us back on the side of the road. They disappeared, waving until they were out of sight, and silence fell. A dark green-gray silence. The stillness of the peat bogs in the heat of summer, after the nesting birds have fledged and gone, when the heat sits on the heather in an airless blanket.

The air didn't move; rather we pushed through it as we began the long slow incline toward the foot of the mountain. The light had an intense reflective clarity, highlighting the rocky outcrops in strange 3D exaggeration, brightening the greens and blacks of the hillside, as if we were viewing a screen with the color wrongly adjusted. I stopped repeatedly to readjust the spare T-shirts I'd folded over my shoulders to protect the damaged skin, and the morning wore into afternoon. The peat was dust dry, cracked and shaped into small ridges and valleys around every rock and heather outcrop. We filled our water bottles in a small trickle of stream in late afternoon and then, over a final crest of heather, it appeared. The dark, wild tsunami of rock and heather rising ahead of us, filling the sky in every direction: Ben Mor Coigach and the vast near vertical walls of the blade of rock, Sgurr an Fhidhleir. I couldn't breathe. This was the mountain in my dream on the train.

"Moth, I dreamed of this place; it was awful, the rain . . ."

"But it's not raining and the forecast's good. Let's get up to the lochan and put the tent up, come on."

Lochan Tuath sat flat calm and black at the foot of the Fiddler, the oppressive slab of rock now towering into the sky. I turned my back to it and focused on peeling the T-shirt off and washing my shoulders in the ice-cold water of the small lake. We sat at the edge, grateful for a growing breeze that carried the midges away. I was in paradise; we were completely alone in this vast wilderness, no one to see, no one to judge, no need to hide or pretend. The light almost faded, leaving just enough moon to pick out the Fiddler, flanked by steep sides of tough grasses that seemed to slide toward the peat bogs below. A surreal noise drifted on the wind from the side of the mountain. At first it sounded like a faint wind through a broad wind chime, a hollow deep sound that came and went on the breeze. Then louder, a choir of voices in another language, somewhere far in the distance.

"What is that?"

"It's the voice of the mountain. It's calling."

We were about to get in the tent, silhouetted in the moonlight on a raised dry patch of ground beneath the black wall of rock behind. We were almost in, we could so easily have missed them. A herd of red deer passing by, heading away downhill with a purpose, calling to each other with a deep, wild song all of their own. We watched them disappear over the brow into the valley below, then crawled into Moth's tiny green tent, barely more than a one-man, with a single wooden pole to support the door end and hardly enough room for your head at the other. I was living a magical, unsurpassable moment of life. Tomorrow we would climb the ben and the Fiddler, suck in the spectacular wonder of the landscape, then back to the tent for another night before heading away. I drifted into sleep, lulled by the ripple of the flysheet in a gentle night wind.

I woke in complete blackness, unsure where I was, and fumbled around for my watch. Two a.m. I put my head back against Moth's chest, warm, rising and falling rhythmically, and caught the sound of a distant rumble. Not his breathing, something outside, distant but growing louder by the second. Moth was awake now.

"What the hell is that?"

Louder now, the noise had grown to the volume of a train, a pounding roar that grew and expanded and encompassed. Then it came. A pushing, pulsing wind that sucked the air from the tent, forcing the side in until we were wrapped in stretched cold green nylon that seemed to be scooping us from the hillside.

"What the fuck?" Moth was out of his sleeping bag, trying to hold up the wooden pole, but without enough room to sit upright he couldn't grip it. "Get your clothes on, get your clothes on . . ." He threw himself flat out in the tent, pressing his huge size twelve feet against the pole, his legs taking the full force of the wind. I panicked my way into clothes and boots, shoving what I could get my hands on into the rucksacks, trying to get clothes on to Moth while he braced the pole and held the wet suffocating tent from his face.

The pole snapped, split in two between his feet, and the tent became a swirling nylon bag, barely held down by our weight. Moth tried to lace his boots in the blackness of the vortex.

"Feel for the plastic bag at the bottom of my pack."

"What? Why? Everything's wet anyway."

"It's a survival bag. We'll get out of the tent and get into that."

"What? I'm not going out there . . ."

The zip of the tent doorway ripped apart and the wind was in: there was no choice. Peeling ourselves from the wetness we fell out into the dark night, and as the weight of the second rucksack left the nylon the tent cycloned into the air, ripping out the steel pegs, taking insulating mats and torches, spare clothes and bags of wet food in a wild missile that disappeared into the night. Moth desperately tried to unfold the bright orange survival bag without letting it go.

"Get in, but throw the rucksack in first or I'm going to lose it."

I slid into the bag, only opening my eyes in short snatches as the spears of rain cut blindingly into my eyelids. We were in, in a bundle of rucksacks and wet sleeping bags and running water, lying on an exposed mountainside miles from a road, even further from habitation. In a plastic bag.

We lay on our stomachs, holding a tiny gap of bag open as lightning ripped the sky apart and for split seconds the Fiddler appeared in huge, terrifying glory. A roaring, growling anger of wind pushed furiously at our orange capsule, but we were low in the heather and hard as it tried we didn't move. The rain battered the plastic sheeting, spearing the back of our heads as water ran past our hands and into the bag through the tightly gripped opening. We couldn't close it completely, couldn't take our eyes away from the wild chaos, so kept a crack open, peering out, transfixed. Moments of blinding lightning lit sheets of water as they were lifted from the ground by the wind and thrown upward to meet the deluge from above in rolling balls of water that reflected the terrifying black monster of a mountain a thousand times, until we became the mountain. Wrapped in the howling black anger, we were engulfed by the unstoppable power of the storm and the sense of nature as one horrifying, beautiful whole. We gazed out between our hands, speechless. As fear began to subside we were overwhelmed by the swirling maelstrom of elements, until we felt as if we were part of it. Lost and dispersed in the unending cycle of water, earth and air.

A faint light began to creep through the water-filled world and we returned to being two people lying in a plastic bag half full of water, hands clasped together in defiance of the rapidly growing possibility of hypothermia. And yet still there was no sense of panic. Something had happened in the darkness. I felt the heat slipping from his hand, a hand I now knew as if it were my own. In the wild grip of nature we had formed a bond that didn't need words, a bond as palpably real and completely untouchable as the song of the deer in the quiet stillness before the storm.

"We've got to go. We could die if we lie here any longer."

We struggled stiffly out into a wind so strong we could barely stand and had to kneel to roll the water out of the plastic bag and crush it into a rucksack. The world had changed. Not just between us, but around us too. Dry parched peat bogs had become a sea of water. Rivers, streams, waterfalls and heavy falling rain. The calm flat lake that had been clouded with gnats and midges the night before now had waves three feet high and our tiny mound had become an island.

"We have to try to find a way down. Take our time and look out for rocks—we'll be stuffed if we fall and injure ourselves."

I followed him blindly, trusting without question that he would find a way through, barely able to see through the rain. Picking our way around boulders hidden in water, wading through torrents where there hadn't been a drop the day before, lashed by rain, in a wind that gusted strongly enough to blow us over, I put my foot to the ground and it didn't stop. My right foot disappeared and in a split second my left knee buckled and I was up to my thigh in a sinkhole, stopped only by my rucksack wedging me at ground level.

Moth hauled me out by the rucksack straps and we lay in the water, exhausted.

"We'll be lucky if we get out of this." This had been my dream on the train. In the growing light the mountain took on the strange shape of the form in my nightmare and a fatalistic acceptance began to lull me to sleep.

"No, get up. We're going to be fine—we're nearly there."

I staggered back to my feet and followed him down from the mountain, finally dipping below the cloud line as the road appeared ahead. But between us and that was the final hillside, no longer a dry dusty path over mountain grass and heather, but now a broad, unavoidable waterfall of rushing foam.

"We can't climb down through that—we won't be able to keep our feet."

"No, you're right." Moth took his rucksack off and with a strange smirking look back at me, clutched it to his chest and sat on the ground. "But we can slide."

He was gone; in a gush of spray he was through the forty meters of water and standing at the bottom. I knew I had to follow, even though it was against every instinct to throw myself down a hillside, but I was shivering and beginning to feel a malevolent sleep tugging me into submission. I skimmed through the icy water and we crawled the final few feet up to the road. We were stamping on the tarmac trying to keep our circulation moving, rivers of water running from our clothes, when the postbus pulled to a stop beside us.

"Need a lift?"

The café in Ullapool had just opened. In disbelief that we had survived we squelched in and sat on the plastic benches of an alcove and waited for a breakfast to appear. The warm stillness of the café seemed completely unreal; we stared at each other across the Formica table, unable to formulate words for what had happened as water ran from our packs in streams across the floor and a haze of steam rose between us. The waitress came and put the breakfasts down.

"Where on earth have you two been? I'll get a mop." The food sat in front of me and my focus narrowed to the sausage and beans and the thought of how they would feel in my mouth. I was desperately hungry, but the need for sleep overtook hunger and my face slid on to the plate, warm egg spreading up my cheek as I closed my eyes and gave in to exhaustion.

*

We returned to our separate homes, finding it intolerably hard to be apart. Something had changed. No longer just young people bound up in a passionate obsession, we had formed a bond that had a power neither of us really understood. We'd become one in the madness of that night in the plastic bag. Not just with each other, but with the uncontrollable elements that had nearly been our downfall. A wild unity had crept into our veins and our future was defined by it.

6. Burning

I'd begged Mum to explain exactly what it was that they hated so much about Moth, but it was like trying to catch a frog in a bucketful of tadpoles. Each answer almost formed the real reason, but none did so fully: "His hair's too long," "His jeans are ripped," "He's going to turn into a dirty smelly old man," "He's lazy," "He doesn't drive"—ridiculous answers. But eventually something came close: "He's not like us, he's a townie." There it was, but not quite, a tadpole with legs but still hanging on to its tail.

I was angry, I felt betrayed, but however valid their argument seemed to them I stayed with him anyway. The moment he'd entered my life he'd filled it to the brim; there couldn't be anyone else. It finally came to a head when we bought a cottage on the outskirts of the village, a tiny house with a long garden: my happiness was uncontainable.

"Moving in without getting married, that's disgusting; you're an embarrassment."

We worked on the house, drying out the damp, repairing the broken windows and putting in running water and a bathroom, but we didn't move in. I couldn't take the final step of defiance. I needed them to love what I loved; I needed them to understand. But there was no stopping it now: the volcano was always going to erupt. It came on a polite Sunday afternoon over a plate of salmon sandwiches and Victoria sponge cake.

"I'm ashamed of you. You had so many opportunities to marry a farmer. What use is he to you anyway? He has no land. You'll never be happy without land."

There it was, croaking, wet, slimy, blinking into the light.

A fully formed frog that could never hop back into the bucket of vague suggestion. I was too bound up in the moment to hear what they were really saying, and they didn't have the words to express themselves. All I heard was, he wasn't a farmer, so he wasn't good enough.

We didn't move into the cottage; instead we got on a train to the Isle of Skye. The registry office on the island was closed for renovations, but had temporarily set up in a spare room at the back of the builders' merchant in Portree, the capital of the island. For some oddly superstitious reason we spent the night before our wedding in separate bed and breakfasts, meeting in the morning in the car park among the builders' vans. We were a spectacle, an unexpected source of amusement for the people hanging out of the builders' merchant's window, laughing and clapping on a Monday morning. We shone out against the gray tarmac, Moth glowing in a bright cream suit he'd had made by a local tailor, and me in a white dress I'd bought in a Laura Ashley sale. Clothes smuggled north in our rucksacks, hidden from each other on the train. In the dark dusty room we held hands and said yes, absolutely we do, without fear, or doubt, or hesitation, behind a curtain made from hessian sacking that separated us from the shop, while a builder was buying "half a pound of lost-head nails."

The next day we stood on the summit ridge of Bruach na Frìthe in the Black Cuillin. The first day of thousands of days. Clouds rose from the valley behind. Appearing from nowhere to pour over the ridge top in a river of running moisture, clinging to the rocky precipitous side of the hill and sweeping away to dissipate in the warmth below. Our lives stretched ahead, a running river of days as the sun shone overhead in a clear blue sky.

Then we returned to our tiny house, with no plaster on the walls or bed to sleep on, but overflowing with hope and enthusiasm.

*

We still had to tell my parents what we'd done. We'd sat on the mounded oak roots in the park as my stomach churned and I tried to breathe, in the moments before we walked down to the house and unfolded the marriage certificate on the kitchen table. I'd lain on the grass there as a child during the lambing season. I'd been sent to bring a ewe and her lamb back to the farmyard. As I lifted the just-born lamb, making little lamb bleating noises to encourage the new mum to follow, I realized she was about to give birth to another, so put the lamb down and stopped to wait. Lying on the grass, the cool earth damp beneath me and white clouds drifting overhead, the ewe lying next to me as the second lamb slipped into life, I knew something stronger, more powerful than anything I'd known in my short life. It was all one: the earth, the grass, the ewe, me, the clouds. Just one huge whole, one cycle of completeness. I wasn't on the earth but of the earth. It was a profound, deep molecular understanding that shaped the rest of my childhood and kept me separate from other children, and attracted me to Moth; it would allow me to survive homeless on a cliff top with awe and inspiration; and on that day it saw me walking to my family home, about to cut the cord between myself and my parents so savagely that it could never really mend. But their words still rang in my ears: *You'll never be happy without the land.*

I'd moved into the dying room with Mum, sleeping on the upright chair by her bed. Nurses came and went, tending to her needs; doctors came, looked at her and then left, saying, "Not long now"; the air in the room shut down in still, suffocating finality. In the dimly lit corridors of the hospital, each night a man came shuffling from the men's ward in his striped pajamas, entered the women's stroke ward and went to the bedside of the same frail old lady. Each night he held her hand and talked to her: "Mum, wake up. Mum, take me home. I need to go home."

Each night as he shook her awake and she shouted that she was being attacked, the nurses would come and quietly escort him away. She wasn't his mum, but somewhere in the darkness at the end of his life he was looking for the way back to the beginning.

Four days passed, then ten, and still the doctors came, ticked their boxes and said, "Not long now." Mum's eyes opened occasionally, looking at me for long moments, then at the bright light of the window, but mainly they stayed focused at the end of the bed, before closing again. Her breathing became heavier and the pneumonia crept back, drying her mouth and blocking her throat. Days became a series of long-drawn-out seconds, crawling into minutes. I listened constantly for a variation in breathing, any sign that the agony of watching her go would end soon, but nothing changed and the days dragged on.

I began to understand that nurses aren't allowed to tell you about anything except practicalities and mid-level doctors are programmed to pass you on to the consultants, so to catch one of those as he flew past was the only way to get an answer. Waiting for an unending time in the corridor, afraid that if I looked away he would pass like a wisp of smoke, I watched as desperately ill people were wheeled into the ward and then as one was transferred to an identical room opposite Mum's, the family following, heads bowed and weeping. I was back in the corridor two days later when they shut the door on a quiet, still body, shaking hands with the nurses and leaving for the last time. The faces on the ward changed, people went home, their lives shaken and altered by strokes, but went home all the same, and finally on the third day I caught one. He looked briefly at Mum, ticked a box and was about to vanish when I stopped him.

"You said three to four days, so why is she still here? If I'd known, if you'd explained . . ."

"Most old ladies on this ward are frail, but your mum, she's strong, she has a willpower to keep going. But soon, now the pneumonia's here."

The walls of a dark pit of self-recrimination began to rise around me. If she had the will to keep going now, against all the odds, maybe, just maybe, if I'd allowed them to insert the feeding tube it might have bought her time to recover. Had I chosen to allow her to die when she could have recovered? I went back to her room, pulled a blanket of horror over myself and listened to her harsh breaths.

"You're doing yourself no favors here, duck. She's going nowhere today. Get out of this place for a bit—you'll feel better."

That word "duck," that colloquial word, it bore the sound of childhood and home and belonging. I looked at the nurse as she held my arm and guided me to the door. I hadn't met her before, but something in that one simple word made me trust her enough to put my coat on and leave.

With no thought or sense of reason, I returned to the woods. It seemed so obvious; it was the only place to be. I had to be there, safe, held. Exhausted but alert with a numb, hollow fear, I lay on the dry bed of pine needles and watched the sun move across the sky between the dark branches.

I left the wood, past the black stump of the old elm tree. It had been a tall, mature tree, growing alone on the hillside, burrowed under by rabbits and giving shelter to cattle as they stood beneath its branches, swishing away flies with their tails on hot summer days. It seemed to have the strength to live forever, and yet one night at the end of summer, when I was only seven, just before the start of school, Dad had woken me to get dressed and go outside.

"Where's Mum?"

"Still in bed."

This felt momentous. It had never happened before: he'd woken me to take me out into the adult world of night.

"You have to see this. I've never seen it before; you'll never see it again."

I held Dad's weather-cracked hand and followed him into the field behind the house.

"Dad, why? Why have you set the tree on fire?"

"I haven't."

The elm that had stood alone in the field for possibly two hundred years was alight. Vast, leaping flames engulfing the branches, bursting into the black sky with bright orange heat. So much power released from one tranquil, green, shady habitat.

"But why is it burning?"

"I don't know. It's as if it lit itself, as if it chose to burn."

During all the years I shared with that practical man, who prided himself on "calling a spade a spade," this was the closest that he ever came to wonder. As the bright light lit his face, that's what I saw: awe and wonder at the spectacle, a reaction so profound that I was witnessing it being burned into his psyche. As the tree crashed to the ground and we cowered from the ferocity of flying sparks and burning branches, I could feel something in his hard-worked hands soften. The tree continued to blaze on the ground, but nothing else around it caught fire; it burned alone. The tree released its own intense life heat, and all around it the night stayed still and calm; the cows grazed and the stars didn't go out. As the flames subsided we walked back to the house; he was silent, but I could still see his face lit by a natural magic.

I walked away from the stump, a mass of intense emotions that I could barely name. My past, my present, my family and in there, among it all, Moth, casting a shadow across every day with the knowledge that this wasn't the only choice I would have to make. That the choice I'd made for my mum I would have to face for him too. Or would he choose his own time? Choose his own moment to let go of his bright green light and say, This is the most perfect day I'll ever see, and for that to be enough. I pushed the thought back into the shadows. Not now, not now.

In the churchyard the truth of life was laid out in neat rows. The farmers from the village, my grandad, the people from the cottages, the old estate owner and his family, my aunt and uncle. Everyone who had peopled the village of my childhood were there, collected together with my dad. I knelt by his grave, ripping the long grass from around the headstone with my hands and putting fresh flowers in the holder. I couldn't feel peace there, just a sense of them all gone, sucked into the vortex of life that drew them all into the cold ground of a windy hillside. The weight of death was crushing me in visions of Moth standing at the church gate, waiting his turn.

"Dad, please. I can't take this, she can't go on like this, please come and get her, please."

Feeling the pull of the hospital, I called back at the cottage and had my first shower for days, did some washing and looked for a book to read through the long hospital nights. She still had a box of books taken from the shelves in my old bedroom. I'd taken a few over the years, but somehow that box hadn't been collected. Fingering the yellowed pages and folded corners of books I'd loved in my childhood and teenage years, I spotted one I didn't know so well. The ruined house on the cover was familiar but the contents were elusive, blurred by time. I put Mum's clean things in a bag and the battered old copy of *Copsford* by Walter J. C. Murray on top.

7. Breathing

Her breathing was heavier, catching on unseen obstacles, causing her mouth to dry and block with unswallowable saliva. It had to be removed with swabs to let the air past. At two in the morning, there was no time for sleep. Just time to listen to the breaths, saving them, storing them for when there would be no more. I opened the curtain, letting the car-park lighting turn the room into a burned-yellow crypt.

I put my feet up on the bed and tried to let sleep come, but there was no hope of that, so I propped *Copsford* on my legs, letting it catch the light from the window. Why couldn't I remember this book? But as I opened it and thumbed the worn, discolored pages, a faint memory began to stir. I did remember it. It was one of the books that had come from Glin, Mum's artistic, book-loving friend. I'd tried to read it, but, too young and disappointed by the lack of animals, I'd discarded it on the bookshelf. Too young to understand what had driven the young Walter J. C. Murray to leave the city and live for a year in the ruined house depicted on the cover. A year without running water, or electricity, in a house where rain leaked through the roof and wind howled through the doors. Maybe now it would make sense. As the night wore on and nurses came and stood by Mum, watching, listening, I read my way out of the room and into a hidden place in rural post-war England. But in the quiet stillness of the room I became increasingly irritated by Walter Murray and his inability to stick to anything. He grew up in Sussex, playing in the fields and lanes of the village where he lived. Too young to be affected by the early years of the First World War, when he was

finally old enough to join the war effort he entered the Merchant
Navy, only to find he hated the nauseating endlessness of the sea,
so left and joined the RAF. But he was never to become a pilot;
the war ended before he learned how to fly. Returning to the village of Horam, he was listless, an irritated youth who felt he'd
missed out on the big show, so he packed his bag and left for the
city and a job in journalism. But he was bored by reporting on
trivial incidents and again began to grow dissatisfied.

I became quickly bored with Walter and put the book down to
go out into the corridor for a cardboard cup of tea from the drinks
machine. The man—his name was Harry—came shuffling toward
the women's wards in new blue checked pajamas, taking up his
seat by the sleeping old lady. "Mum, Mum, let's go home." I waited
for the nurses to usher him out, but they didn't come. He held her
hand, stroking it carefully, almost tenderly, as she started to rouse.
I expected her to shout, but she didn't, she just reached out and pat-
ted his arm. "We'll go home tomorrow. Go back to bed now and
get some rest." Harry stood up without resisting and left the ward
the way he came, a hunched old man, but inside the shell a lost,
frightened little boy who just knew he had to get back to some
vague memory of an earlier time. I went back to the room, shutting the door quietly behind me. Mum's eyes were open, staring
again at the end of the bed. I tried to stand in her gaze, but she
wasn't seeing me; something else held her transfixed.

"Try to sleep, Mum. I've got this book . . ." I began to read to
her and within seconds her eyes were closed and her breathing
heavier and harsh. I knew how she felt; there aren't many things
as sleep-inducing as a teenager who can't just get on with something. But I stuck with it as Walter became disillusioned by his
dull job and his dismal accommodation, even finding he no
longer had inspiration to write: the one thing he'd hoped to do.
He was suffocated by the city and started to dream of returning
home where he could "live close to nature." The pages turned

and I stopped needing him to explain himself; I knew him already, I knew what he was searching for—it was the same force that drove me to walk the cliffs or run to the woods. The same inexplicable, magnetic pull. Hooked now, connected, unable to stop reading, I followed Walter's year of living alone in the countryside, immersed in the wild exuberant nature of the English landscape in the mid-twentieth century.

As night turned into morning and the hospital day began, I started to understand what it was that didn't feel quite the same about the fields and woods of the estate. What it was that had changed in such a silent way that its passing was hardly noticeable. There was a lack of something, but that lack had been almost invisible until I held up the mirror of *Copsford* and what was reflected wasn't the estate of my childhood. I looked up from the book at the leafless branches of the birch tree outside. Of course the hedges weren't full of wild flowers, or the grass buzzing with bees: it was the end of January. But it was something less obvious, something more than the converted sawmill and the commuters living in the farmworkers' cottages. It was a stillness, a wild silence beyond the emptiness of the pine trees. A silence on the wind, the deadness of something having gone. The farm had become a different, neater, more barren place, the wild things had gone, the skies were quieter and the earth was empty and dark. An invisible change, almost imperceptible until it shone out in *Copsford*'s blinding light.

Then everything changed.

"I can't stand to think of you there. Don't you need me with you? Let me come." It was hard for Moth not to be with me; it made no sense to him. "I know she hates me but it's too late for that."

"I know, but please don't come." I could already feel the difficulty of what was happening that day and I couldn't have him there. It was almost too awful to cope with myself, but if he was in the room he would know what it was to die this way and I couldn't let him see it—I could barely hold Mum's death separate to his as it was. For him to be in the same room would have meshed the two inextricably in my head and I was already close to drowning in my own maelstrom of thought. "Please don't."

The harsh, snatched breath had become a deep wheeze. Every intake a growing battle, and with each hour it became worse. I called the nurses in.

"She's choking. Can't you do something?"

"She's on nil-intervention. We'd have to get approval from the consultant. He told you she would aspirate."

"What the hell? How could I know that aspirate meant this? You can't let her suffer."

The wheezing became a hauling suction of air, her body taking over in a primal, instinctive fight for oxygen, her face and throat distorting with the force of each deep, desperate attempt to breathe. Her lungs were producing vast amounts of mucus, but her throat couldn't swallow.

Hours passed in the agony of watching her suffer. Hours of doubting the decision and hating myself for making it. Hours of mind-shattering, nauseating despair as I fought for each breath with her, thinking each one must be the last and she couldn't possibly survive this. Exhausted, harrowed, I held her hand and watched in useless horror. As the afternoon wore on, when I thought neither of us could take any more, the matron appeared.

"We're going to give her hyoscine. It's a drug that will stop the mucus production and ease the choking."

Slowly the miracle relief left the syringe and her throat began to relax, the breathing became quieter, and the stillness returned. I crawled on to my chair, curled in a ball and shuddered with sobbing. I just wanted blackness, where no thought or sound or fear could enter.

"I'll get you a cup of tea, duck. That's the hard bit over now."

Over now, it was nearly over now. But it wasn't. I was sobbing through one death, with the weight of another bearing down on me. I had to call him.

"It's been an awful day, but just tell me about yours."

"Why won't you let me come?"

"Just tell me about your day."

"Another weird one—definitely not the best. I had a really blank moment like I'd just switched off without knowing it, then I was so stiff I could hardly move. The lecturer was shaking me, saying I'd been staring out of the window for ages; then I couldn't get up, nothing seemed to work, so someone drove me back to the chapel. Today I'm doubting if I'll make the end of this degree, let alone teach afterward. I'm just going to go and lie down. Can I call you later?"

I curled back into the chair, pulling the cotton blanket over my head and dragged *Copsford* into my cave with me. Take me away from this, Walter. Take me to green spaces and country lanes filled with herbs and wild flowers. Let me pick agrimony and comfrey with you. Take me away; give me the green safety of my childhood. I began to reread the book in the filtered light from the fluorescent strip. The world, Mum, Moth, all of it shut outside, just alone with Walter, wading through a stream on our way to pick blackberries.

In the twilight of a hospital night I couldn't hide anymore. Moth had begun university in hope. Not the sort of hope a normal student would have, that their degree would give them a long and prosperous future. His hope was that he would survive to the end of the degree and in doing so maybe his brain would stay alert enough to take him on to the next stage of his life. But he didn't have to tell me; I knew he was slipping backward from the high point at the end of the path. That euphoric point when he'd taken his rucksack off and his body had lost the stiffness and restraint of CBD and moved to his command. Or was he actually slipping forward, slipping into the future that had been predicted?

We began our epic walk of the Coast Path with no sense of hope or possibility. Moth had been told he couldn't survive, that the tau protein in his brain had stopped functioning in its normal way and was now clustering together in what the consultant called aggregates. A creeping process of tau phosphorylation, which would slowly close down the parts of his brain that instructed his body what to do. I imagined the tau forming like plaque on teeth, but in a place where the brush wouldn't reach. So it could spread and grow until it suffocated all those beautiful brain cells that told Moth how to move, to feel, to remember, to swallow, to breathe. And yet as we walked along that incredible strip of wilderness, forgetting the existence of the normal world that lay to one side of the path, with our eyes always drawn to the endless horizon of the sea on the other, exhausted and starving, something had changed. He had changed. He'd grown stronger, the fog in his brain had cleared, his movements had become surer, easier to control. Why, why, *why* had that happened? There had to be a reason, but maybe it was time to accept that the doctors were right, that there was nothing that could be done other than face the inevitability of the end.

I couldn't accept it. At the first crack of light through the window I picked the phone up.

"I don't care how tired you are—get up. You have to walk; you have to move. Just get outside and move."

"But I can't. I feel like shit."

"I don't care. Get up." I put the phone down and went into the corridor for another tiny tea from the machine, then picked the phone up again.

"You're still in bed; I know you are. Get up—you have to. Please just get up." There had to be a connection, a physical, chemical, biological reason why he'd improved when we walked. Whatever it was, we had to look for a way to replicate that effect. If we couldn't find a way, we'd have to put on our rucksacks and walk again, indefinitely. He was on the slide to the bottom of CBD, with no twists or turns to slow his descent; we had to find a way. "Moth, put your boots on. I don't care how you feel; you have to keep fighting. Just get up and try. Please try . . ."

We were walking the first time we'd realized that Moth had some kind of problem. Our twenty-fifth wedding anniversary. No big celebration, no noise or commotion, we hadn't even told the kids which anniversary it was. It was a day just for us to be together, but we still felt we should do something to mark the moment.

"Do you fancy walking up Tryfan? We've always wanted to but never given ourselves the time. Let's do it today."

Tryfan is a sharp ridge of a mountain in Snowdonia, tricky to get to from any side, and more of a scramble than a walk to get to the top. But it pointed out from the Glyderau hills, in a definitive, memorable way that somehow seemed to fit the day.

"Okay, today then."

Leaving the van by the YHA building at the foot of the mountain, we began our walk, climbing easily up the rocky steps from the tea hut. The air was clear and early summer warm, skylarks hanging over the heather bogs with their clear, unmistakable song of the sky. The towering arc of the Cwm Idwal cliffs lay ahead with the lake at their base reflecting bright sparks of sunlight. We weren't drawn in to follow the path that runs a pinball route beneath the rock walls, but branched away left, following a line across the rocky flank of the hillside, past the fast-falling stream to its source at Llyn Bochlwyd. We stopped to eat, drinking the tea from the flask and feeling the ache of legs that had been away from the hills for too long. Moth put the flask back into the daysack and handed it to me.

"Can you carry this now? Don't know what I've done to my shoulder, but it's really aching today, I can't seem to lift my arm properly."

"Isn't it any better? Do you think it could have come from that fall through the barn roof in April?"

"Could have, I don't know—it didn't seem to hurt at the time though."

"Give me the pack then."

We continued up, rising sharply. Avoiding the eye-watering, knuckle-whitening Bristly Ridge that has rock-scrambling enthusiasts dribbling with excitement, we opted instead to find our own way to the top and began to scramble through a scree of large rocks and boulders toward the summit.

"I've got to stop."

I thought I'd misheard him—he never said stop; I'm always the one who needs to put the pack down and admire the view. We sat on a rock, the Ogwen Valley stretching away west, a deep groove of dark rock, oozing peat bog and high peaks where only the sheep belong. Multitudes of orange and blue specks were leaving the cars that were beginning to cluster on the roadside.

"We should carry on. It's going to get busy up here soon."

"Don't know if I can. I feel dizzy. I can't look down—I think I'm going to be sick."

"What's wrong? Have you eaten something that hasn't settled? It was only a cheese sandwich . . ."

"No, it's not that, it's something else."

"What? What is it?"

"I don't know. I'll try; maybe it'll pass."

At the top of Tryfan are the Adam and Eve stones. Two column-like boulders that stand vertically on the exposed ridge. To truly say you've done Tryfan you have to have leaped over the one-and-a-half-meter gap between the two boulders, and having done so wins you the "freedom of Tryfan," however that presents itself. Our climbing days had faded away when the children were born, when being around for them meant life was too precious to risk on the fickle hold of a climbing aid. We weren't there to prove anything to anyone, or to have a tale to tell in the pub. That leap represented far more to us: we were there on that day to say yes, yes we'd make that leap of life again together as we had twenty-five years earlier. It was to be our wild, exposed retaking of vows: to each other, to nature, to life. But as Moth retched up his cheese sandwich and sat with his head in his hands at the foot of Adam, it wasn't to be. Looking at the precipitous fall down the other side of the boulder, I wasn't sorry.

"Stupid idea anyway. It's not as if we've anything to prove to each other after all these years." I tried to make light of what was one of the rare occasions in his life that his body had failed to do what he asked. "Maybe you've got vertigo. It's just middle age creeping up on you."

"Don't joke—I think you're right. I don't actually know if I can go back down."

We sat on the exposed mountain ridge as the light faded and the brightly colored specks returned to their cars and drove away. The moon rose above the arching eastern skyline, washing the mountain tops in pale waves of light, obscuring the valley below in darkness, highlighted only by the lights of passing cars.

"I'll be with you forever, Ray, because it's where I want to be. Will you do the same?"

"Of course. Where else would I be? Forever."

"But that might not be too long. We've got to get off Tryfan in the dark, without a head torch."

"Forever it is then, even if that's just half an hour."

8. Painless

"As we don't know if she's in pain we have to choose whether or not to give her painkillers." The consultant stood outside the dying room tapping the clipboard with his pen. "I would err on the side of the likelihood that she is in discomfort, which we have a duty to alleviate, and begin a morphine drip."

It had been two weeks since the consultant had said Mum would live for two to three days and finally the morphine was here. This was it. Dad had reached this point on his bed in the sitting room of the farmhouse, while Mum made scones for visitors in the kitchen. I knew what it meant: another choice to make, another box to tick to ease her along the path to death. I chose for her; I chose to bring death on a floating cloud of opiate. No more struggling for air, no fighting to cling to a life that was over; these days, hours, moments had to be gentle. An easy goodbye on the warm summer breeze of morphine.

The Macmillan nurse leaned across the bed to explain to Mum about the drug; there was no response, other than for a long moment she stared again at the end of the bed. I glanced in the direction of her vision and for the faintest second I thought I saw him there, flat cap pushed back on his head at a strange angle, that funny lopsided grin. Her eyes closed and as I looked again Dad was gone, a hopeful figment of my imagination wishing he'd come for her as I'd asked him to so she wasn't alone.

Together in that long, quiet night, as the morphine driver filled her veins with stillness and her breathing dropped to a calm and shallow movement of air, my thoughts were full of doubt and fear. The choice I'd made to let her die rather than try for life by inserting the feeding tube was beginning to torment me with a worm of recrimination that couldn't be buried. And fear. A growing, burning sense of panic, forming itself like a white-hot ball in my stomach. On the Coast Path I thought I'd found a way to come to terms with knowing that Moth would die, to accept it as the hardest part of life. Death had become the ever-present shadow in the corner of our lives, but now I was living through the same death that was predicted for him and I realized that, as much as I thought I'd come to terms with that, there could never be a peaceful acceptance for me; I would be forcing him to fight long after he chose to lie down and let it be. My mind was running in panic through a room of fire with no exit doors.

I dozed fitfully through the night, my face on her cool, dry, unmoving hand, until woken by the faint gray light of morning. I sat back in the chair, straightening my stiff joints, putting my feet up on the bed. The blue covers, silvery in the early light, moved almost imperceptibly with her breath. Her waxy face had taken up the same translucent color, outlined by light from the window behind. Then a mist. A mist like steam leaving a hot, wet athlete at the end of a long run. Lifting from her body in a gentle rising haze. I didn't want to drag my eyes away, but glancing around the room I couldn't see it anywhere else. It was just there, in the outline of her quiet stillness: a slow movement of molecules through time and air, energy from her cooling body passing into the morning, into the flat dull atmosphere of the room. I took a deep, deep breath and held it tight.

Over now, all over now.

I walked slowly back across the estate in the late afternoon as the light began to fade, making my way, as I knew I would, to the darkness of the trees. And now at last, with my fingers pushed into the composted pine needles, I knew why. I finally knew what had driven me to suggest that we should walk across cliffs and beaches, through woods and valleys, sleeping wild, living wild. I could feel it now, cold, gritty, dark. I could feel it pushed beneath my fingernails and dusty in my hair. It was the thing I'd fooled myself into thinking I could live without, the one part of me that my family had understood better than I did. I'd always known what the voice in my head was saying. It was the land, the earth, the deep humming background to my very being. I ran to it when all else fell apart. I needed the safety of being one with the land; the core of me needed that sense of complete belonging as fundamentally as the air I breathed. Without it I would never be whole. It was always the land.

I rearranged the wreaths on the grave as a cold wind blew up from the farm in the hollow below. Walking out of the churchyard, crunching the smooth, round pea gravel beneath my feet, I left them there: my family, my history, all the connections to my past. I got into the van and closed the door on the estate and my childhood, cutting the final tie. Heading south, back to Moth, to our new empty life and the strip of concrete that led to the back of the chapel.

PART TWO

Pushes the Sea

Read again my friend, watch how the words bend.

"come, will you join me in my precision?,"
Anno Birkin

I can hear it,
hear it but not hold it,
feel it but not touch it.
It wraps around me like a breath,
soothing,
cooling
and the voice falls
and becomes a tone
and I'm closer to its source.
And in the breath, a smell,
rich, deep, acidic, wind-blown over dense heath,
through tall seed heads of ripe grass.
And the tone rising, rising, until it's clear, clean,
sky-lark sharp on racing cirrus clouds
and I can touch the voice,
feel its words
and they're full and total
and carry the truth
in a stinging cold rain
dried by hot sun.

9. Matter

Quantum physicists would explain the possibility of something coming from nothing by the theory that when matter and anti-matter particles come together in a vacuum they cancel each other out; they're annihilated. But if you change the energy in the vacuum to an electromagnetic field then that annihilation event produces energy, a whole set of new particles which have a mass. I'm no physicist, most of my physics classes at school were spent reading a book under the lab bench or staring out of the window. But having lost just about everything we owned and entered a life that felt like a hollow space in which I was merely existing, then perhaps I was in that vacuum. And yet even in a vacuum it's possible for the energy to change, almost without warning.

Death wasn't new to me—I'd known it before—but now the tyranny of its finality returned as if I'd met a complete stranger. I was once again astride the void between life and death where days lost their meaning, overshadowed by the darkness of infinity. Doubt about choices I'd made and fear of those I still had to make, playing on an endless loop of regret and fear. Day on week on month, alone in a bubble of silence as Moth studied and the world went on around me. The only sound was the resonance of the voice in my head, never quiet, hollowing my thoughts into echo chambers of its insistence.

On the cobbled streets of the tiny city of Truro, Cornwall's county town, a group of homeless people were gathered outside the bank. Sleeping bags on cardboard, clothes worn and dirty,

faces showing the harshness of a life spent outdoors in every
weather. Never hesitant, Moth stopped to speak to them.

"All right there? Anything you need?"

I watched him stand and chat casually with the group as if
he'd always known them. His strangely lopsided stance was
more exaggerated than it had been when we were walking, but
otherwise he was the same person who had dropped his rucksack on the floor of the chapel for the first time, his homeless
life behind him. Confident in himself, sure of who he was, no
reluctance to re-engage with life. When he avoided mention-
ing having been homeless to his peers at uni, it wasn't out of
fear of their reaction, but because he was so engrossed in the
coursework that he couldn't be bothered with the distraction
of having to discuss anything else. Not like me, hiding in the
shadows.

"Just the usual, food and a roof. TV might be good, bored sick
of talking to this lot."

"Could help you with some food later, not a lot I can do about
the rest. Ray?"

I thought about the contents of the fridge, and the small
amount of student loan we had left. Pea risotto again.

"Yeah, no problem, we'll pop and get you something from
the Co-op."

We headed back to the group with a bag of the food we would
have wanted when all we'd eaten for a week was twenty-pence
packs of noodles: bread, fruit, cheese and a couple of pasties. An
offering to share around. I folded the empty bag and had to ask
a question that had been scratching in my head as I sat in the
chapel, out of sight of the world.

"If any of you found a home and you moved in and started
living a normal life again, how do you think you'd be? I mean,
do you think it would be hard? Not paying the bills and finding
a job, not all that practical stuff. But do you think it would be

hard to go inside after living outside for so long? And what about other people—do you think you'd find it easy to slip back into normality, that you'd just be able to interact with people in the same way you did before you were homeless?"

Moth looked over at me, half sympathetic, half annoyed.

"I've been in and out of homelessness for a while." An older man in a trilby hat, with a brown dog that licked my ankles, seemed to have no hesitation in talking about his feelings. "Not in my own place, but I sofa-surf when I get the chance. I like the comfort of inside; I have no problem at all getting out of the rain. But there's a freedom outside and when I sleep in the woods it feels right. Feels like I belong. Other people though—fuck me, that's another matter."

The younger men were laughing at him, mock crying, dabbing their eyes.

"Shut up, the lot of you. You're just afraid to say it—you're the first ones out to the woods and on to the coast, because it's where you feel right. Feel human. But other people . . ."

One of the younger ones stopped laughing and looked up.

"Just taking the rip, mate, we all know it. But people, well, you can't trust 'em, can you? Even if they seem to be helping, you can't trust their motives. Feels like someone always wants to know a bit more so they can find an easier way to do you over, move you on. And here, with all the tourists, well, we're just a fucking eyesore, aren't we? Everybody wants us gone. How would you get rid of that feeling? Be bloody hard, wouldn't it? That's why we all stay hidden. It's not like in the big towns; in the countryside you can't sleep on the street, you've got to keep out of sight."

We walked away, Moth's hand a little tighter around mine. He knew why I felt as I did, he just felt powerless to help me beyond it. Trust. Such a slippery, elusive concept. Like an eel in your hands at the side of the river: release your grip for a second and it's downstream and out of sight. You may never catch it again.

We bought a copy of the *Big Issue* from the seller on the corner and headed back to the van with a bag of frozen peas and a pack of rice in our bag.

Winter passed, spring came then warmed into summer as I hid on the exposed cliff tops. Hiding from other people, hiding from myself, where the sea was always in motion and the cry of the herring gulls on the wind unending. Midsummer: the sunset had moved beyond the west and was heading north as I crouched among the rocks near the cliff, watching the badgers scuffle out of their hole and head off into the undergrowth. The nights were so short now the badgers needed to be out before darkness really came, or the sun would return before they'd had enough time to find food. It was too early in the year for ripe fruit, too late for birds' eggs; they needed all the time the short nights would allow to suck up the hundreds of worms and grubs they needed to eat each day. The sun had finally dipped below the horizon behind me, leaving the sky to the south holding a mirror to the dying light. Pale turquoise blue growing darker by the second, stretched from Bolt Head in the east to Lizard Point in the west, scattered with thin clouds that moments before had been low and white, but now were brightly lit in reflections of pink. Torn ribbons of color fluttering across the evening sky, a maypole dance of light.

I followed the colors as they receded behind the land, back down into the village, to the darkness of the chapel where Moth was writing up an assignment, and to another sleepless night.

"You know what you're doing, don't you?"

"No, no, I don't know at all, that's why I'm trying to explain it to you. What am I doing?"

"Can't you see it? You've gone back to how you were as a child, how you were when we met. You're hiding from the world; you're back behind the sofa. When you were faced with something or someone new, you hid from it. Afraid to face the world. That's what you're doing now." Moth delivered his casual psychoanalysis while packing cheese sandwiches and a notebook in his uni bag. But he was right. I had been a shy, introverted child. Always running to hide when a visitor came to the door, happy and confident alone outdoors, but reluctant and afraid when faced with people. Until I met him. As I grew to know him, just the look on his face as I caught his eye across a crowded space was like a hand reaching into the darkness of my hiding place and guiding me out. One look from him and I could walk across a room full of strangers as if I belonged there. But here alone in the chapel I'd lost that sense of strength. He was right: I'd become that reticent child again.

"I can't get behind the sofa. It's too small."

"Idiot. You're hiding behind me, or round here at the back of the chapel. You've got to get a grip on this before it takes over. How did you overcome it before?"

"I met you."

"But there was more to it than that. Where have you gone? Where's the woman that finished walking the Coast Path, strong, determined, forcing me back into life, making me get up each day and keep going? Look for her—I know she's still there." He put the bag down and hugged me and I didn't want to let him go. Stay here and hold me, I feel safe when you're here. I slid my arms under his and held him tight. There was less of him; he'd reduced, the strong muscles that had enveloped me in the past seemed to be shrinking. I held his arms and they felt much smaller. How had I not noticed this earlier? Too wrapped up in myself and losing Mum to pay attention. Or had winter and layers of clothes disguised it?

"Are you losing weight?"

"Yeah, must be, my jeans are looser. Don't know how, considering the amount of pea risotto you feed me on. Anyway, I've got to go, I'm late already."

I stood at the front of the chapel and watched him walk up the road. He made slow progress with an unsteady, lopsided gait, and his jeans really were baggy. He was vanishing like sea mist in the heat of the sun. Unnoticed, just quietly evaporating into the morning air. I shut the door on the back of the chapel and curled on the sofa. How had I been so blind? So absorbed in my own self-pity that I hadn't seen how quickly he was declining?

I needed to know more about CBD, to understand it for myself, not simply accept the morsels of information given by the doctors. Did it really cause muscle wastage, or did Moth need to eat more? Or maybe his body wasn't digesting his food properly. He'd refused to learn anything about the disease, preferring to accept each day as it came. But I couldn't do that anymore; I had to know everything. I'd spend a little time with Google now, maybe just an hour.

An hour became a morning, as a life-draining, body-twisting disease spread itself out before me in advice sites and chat rooms. The voices of the carers, recounting the lives of their loved ones changed beyond recognition, lives confined to chairs, hoists and straws. The sadness was total. Not once, among all the lines, all the lives, was there a glimmer of light, a word of hope. The day wore on. I switched on the lights and made more tea; late summer but the sun had already finished its short journey across the window of the chapel and disappeared from view. Stories of pain, loss of control, of dementia. I wanted to go back, to take away what I'd seen, to not have looked. But there was no way back. I could see the disease now in all its life-changing horror.

I closed the laptop and opened the door, watching the rain

falling in heavy drops, bouncing off the leaves of the ivy wall. So much rain—you'd think the plant would drown in so much water. But I knew that couldn't happen, the degree Moth was studying in sustainable horticulture had led him to read about the amazing power of plants to control their own responses to the environment, only taking up as much water as they need. Scientific research that showed it would take more than a few days of standing water before the plant's internal regulatory system was overwhelmed and it did drown. Research. There must be scientific research into CBD.

Hours became a day, which led into days. I helped Moth stand in the early mornings, encouraged him through the difficult first movements, made cheese sandwiches and waved him off down the street. Opened the door when he returned, then made mash, then pasta, then baked potatoes, amazing dishes from a bag of frozen peas and an egg. Student food, paid for with a student loan. And I studied. Finding my way into a rare disease, about which so little seems to be known. As the days became a week, then a second, I followed research into CBD through efforts to find ways to diagnose and then to analyze the progress of the disease, through failed trials with drugs, to dead ends and down rabbit holes. Lost in a maze of research, and still it rained.

Paddy Dillon sat on the shelf, his book still tightly bound with its hair band. In there, somewhere in there, we'd found a way to hold the disease at bay, but how? There had to be a scientific reason for the improvements in his health when we walked; if we could understand why that had happened, then possibly, just maybe, we could replicate it in some way that would allow us to live a life under a roof and be well at the same time. I went back to the beginning, to understand the very start of the disease, to build a picture of it from the base up. So little information; so little knowledge. And I was back down the rabbit hole reading about connected diseases, other lives changed by tau proteins that have lost their form and function. And there, tucked away in research undertaken into a better-known, more widespread disease, I found something, a small nugget, but something. Small data sets, in one or two random pieces of work. They proved very little, but I was grasping for tiny, almost untouchable straws, so I seized the possibility the results represented and leaped around the chapel.

I opened the door to suck up some air. The ivy was dripping, but it had stopped raining. Out in the empty street, I could almost hear the theme tune to a spaghetti western and expected to see tumbleweed rolling by. After hours of staring at a screen, my head ragged from reading around in circles, the empty, soundless streets of autumn in a Cornish village were almost calming. On a normal day I wouldn't have read the poster on the telegraph pole, even less considered answering the invitation it offered. I would have seen the headline of WI and thought, No, there's absolutely no chance I'm going to the Women's Institute, and walked straight by. I certainly wouldn't have got as far as reading "flower-arranging session" and definitely wouldn't have thought of going. But this day was far from normal. Buoyed by the success of googling a tiny snippet of hope, I was through the door of the community center before I had a chance to overthink what I was doing.

The square, clinical space, with its magnolia walls and small raised stage, bustled with old ladies scurrying. Piles of flowers, green oasis and shallow dishes covered the tables that spread out individually across the room.

"Hello, you're new."

"Yes, I, erm . . ."

"Come and join us. We're creating an arrangement for a side table—you can take it home afterward. It costs a pound. Sit here."

The efficient old lady was gone, busying herself with cutting oasis to fit a bowl, and I sat at a table in the middle of the room, watching the organized mayhem around me. What on earth had possessed me to do this? And a pound, what was I thinking of?

"Well, I don't know about all this—I can't arrange flowers, but I guess I'll just go along with it anyway! Hi, I haven't seen you before—are you new?" A small woman of a similar age to me, with curly red hair, sat down at my table.

"Well, yes, I was just passing and I thought—"

"That's how it starts! There'll be no escape now; the ladies won't let you go. I come and go from the village, two months here, two months in London, but when I'm here I love it. They just take me over. Every day they have a schedule for me: lunches, dinners, WI, card-playing, you name it. But they're so easy, there's no pressure, they just make me feel so included—I love it. I haven't seen you before—have you just arrived."

"No, I've been here for quite a while now, but I don't know anyone . . ."

"Or have I seen you up on the Coast Path? Anyway I'm Gillian—call me Gill. Are you any good with flowers?"

"No, not really."

Later, walking back to the chapel, self-consciously carrying my scruffy flower arrangement down the street, I tried to work out why I had thought it reasonable to walk into a WI meeting. There was no answer to that, so I went back to googling research.

"Moth, I have to tell you this—this is so important."

"What is that? Looks like you've thrown some weeds in a bowl. Why is that important?"

"Not that, but they're not weeds, they're native British flora."

"What are you talking about?"

"Forget the flowers. I've been researching CBD, looking for

the answer to why you were so well when we were walking, and why you're deteriorating so quickly now."

"I didn't think you'd noticed. I tried to keep it from you."

"How can you hide from me? You've never hidden from me. I'm the one that hides."

"I know, but I know you're struggling with being in the village and your mum and everything."

"Well, forget that now, this is more important." I made tea, sat at the table and explained about an obscure piece of research that had been undertaken with Alzheimer's patients.

"But that's not CBD, so why is it relevant?"

"Because Alzheimer's is a tauopathy—different from CBD, yes, but it's still about the tau protein, so there could just be a similarity." I showed him the research and made him read about patients with Alzheimer's who had undergone endurance training and had miraculously regained some cognitive abilities which doctors had believed were lost forever.

"Don't you see, that's what the path was for us: extreme endurance training. We were walking miles every day, carrying heavy weights on a really restricted diet. It's the same thing."

"Well, maybe . . ."

"Think about it, really think about it."

"But I'm already doing physio exercises every day, and I walk a couple of miles most days. What are you suggesting? I give up my degree, find another trail and keep walking? Just walk indefinitely? I don't know if I can do that."

"I know, I know. But that's not the end of it, there's more."

"Oh . . ."

"I've read pages and pages of science papers that show the importance of being in nature for our physical and mental health."

"Everyone knows that."

"Yes, but it made me think why. Why exactly is it good for

us? It's not just because it's relaxing. There is that, but there's more. Look at this—read this one research paper. It's the only one I can find, but . . ." I turned the screen of the laptop toward him; it showed the summary of an obscure piece of research. "Isn't this what you've just been studying at uni? The chemicals that plants emit from their leaves—I can't remember what you call them?"

"Secondary metabolites. Plants emit them to protect themselves from the environment and pests and stuff."

"Oh, okay, but you can't remember what you had for breakfast."

"Weetabix."

"That's too easy. You always have Weetabix. Anyway, this paper shows humans interact with those chemicals from plants too. There's an actual chemical reaction between our bodies and plant emissions. I mean just read it."

"I was going to eat, but okay."

I put the kettle back on and watched Moth as he focused on the computer screen, a light of realization beginning to cross his face. I poured the water in the cups. Yes. Maybe this wasn't just my wishful thinking.

"It's a small study. My science lecturer at uni would say there'd have to be a lot more research done to say this was conclusive proof, but you can't doubt his findings. He did actually record a chemical change in the patients when they exercised in the natural environment."

"Exactly. Surely this proves it—proves what I've always believed. We need the plants, the land, the natural world; we actually physically *need* it. I'm convinced it's part of the answer to why your health was so much better while we were walking. It has to be."

"Was I well, really? I almost don't remember. There are bits of the walk that I can't picture at all."

"You're joking, surely. I remember it as if it was last month. How can you remember uni stuff but not remember our walk?"

"No, I'm not joking, not at all, and I've no idea why I can remember one thing but not another."

All those nights of wind and stars, the pain, the hunger, the life-changing beauty of it—how could he possibly forget? He was the center point, the pin on which the compass hand of my life spun. Without him present, conscious, aware, my life would have no direction; I would be lost in a darkness I might never find my way out of. His fading memory was opening a bottomless box of loss into which all the memories of our long life together would slowly be drawn. I shut the lid on it quickly. Not today, not any day.

"You have to do more exercise, you need to do so much more than you are, and you must spend more time outside. We need plants; we need green."

"So that's why we have the weeds in a bowl on the table?"

"No, that's another story entirely; I'm almost too embarrassed to tell you about that. Shall we eat instead?"

The moon traced an arc across the bedroom wall, picking out the colors of the stained-glass window as it moved slowly through the night. I could almost feel the deep low tone of a ship moving away from the dock and making its way out to sea, the throb of its engines through the water vibrating the cliffs. It had to be high tide, the dark, invisible depths of the water floating a ship laden with thousands of tons of china clay out through the mouth of the river, releasing it to the wide ocean. The Fowey River is a deepwater harbor, allowing huge cargo ships to pass between the tiny picturesque villages of Fowey and Polruan, going a short way inland to the clay wharf at Bodinnick. As much as 750,000 tons of clay are brought by truck to the port each year from the china clay mines of central Cornwall, and then hauled out in huge iron containers that sink low in the water under the weight of their immense cargo, heading away to ports in Europe and beyond.

The blast of a single horn signaled the ship's safe passage out of the river. But I barely heard it. The voice was loud in my ears, keeping sleep at the door and masking every other sound. Fleeting, untouchable, loud in its silence, a sparrowhawk passing gray on early-morning light, more a parting of air than a visible movement, a sensation of noise without volume. The voice of an answer felt, of an emotion that had no words for its expression.

10. Antimatter

"Hey, here again, this is the only place I ever see you." Gill was right. Since the day we met at the flower-arranging table I had only seen her twice, each time when I was sitting on this bench at the cliff edge.

"I know. It's so open up here, so much space. I come here most days."

"This is your place, your thin place."

"Thin?" I'd heard of this before at an abbey on the Scottish island of Iona, but I didn't admit it; the conversation would be too long and my solitary time on the bench would be broken.

"Yes, it's a concept from Celtic spirituality, the idea of a place where the barrier between now and beyond is thinner, where you're closer to God."

"No, sorry, I don't believe in God, or hereafters. Just the carbon cycle: we live, we die, the molecules go on in some other form."

"Well, call it what you like, but I think this place is pretty thin for you."

We were in our mid-twenties, our life together was still new and the possibilities endless, when we got off the ferry from the mainland of Scotland and set foot on the island of Mull for the first time. The old red rucksack that I'd abandoned in favor of a smaller lightweight one when we prepared to walk the South West Coast Path was almost new, its pockets still waterproof and its buckles still shiny. We'd been married for two years and had spent endless nights after work weighing dried rations into small portions and encasing everything else in plastic bags in preparation for a back-packing trip across the Isle of Mull to Iona in the west. In those two years together we'd backpacked across the Lake District, staying on campsites and climbing mountains as we went. We'd cycled from the Midlands to a wet and boggy mountain in mid-Wales, glad of the bed and breakfasts we'd found ourselves in each evening. Countless walking, cycling and camping trips in between had led us to believe that we should do something else, something a little edgier, something wild. We'd attempted a wild-camping trip once, into the remote, uninhabited expanse of Knoydart in the Western Highlands of Scotland, but unfortunately we'd chosen to go in August. Inevitably we'd beaten a retreat, pursued by a relent-less army of midges and blood-sucking ticks and had relinquished our wild adventure, resorting to staying in hotels where the doors were closed against the biting swarms outside. But this trip would be different: we were totally prepared and it was later in the year, so darker nights but fewer insects.

A few days in and we were beginning to feel more at ease with the idea of wild camping. We put the tent up on the deserted rocky shoreline of Lochbuie, still and dark in the twilight. We were totally alone in the remote wilderness, watching the stars as an insect repellent coil burned inside Moth's felt hat, the smoke percolating through, keeping us midge free and his hat repellent at the same time. In the dying light the oystercatchers came, gathering in noisy groups, but then, silently, as the last light dropped away, running together in lines along the shore, dipping their heads in unison, their orange feet flashing until complete darkness brought a stillness to the water's edge. On the headland the dark, imposing ruin of the tower of Moy Castle, decaying silently under the onslaught of centuries of weather systems, became a silhouette in the moonlight.

Next morning, as the faintest dawn light caught the wind-rippled loch, we woke to the sound of a deep-throated roar, a noise of earth and heather, the call of bogs and rocky outcrops. Outside the tent, just below us on the shoreline, a red stag shook his wide multi-pointed antlers and bellowed out into the early morning, announcing the start of the rut, a guttural uniting of his life with the wild freedom of the mountains.

Days later, among the rocks at the summit of Ben More, the highest point on Mull, the island spread beneath us in an undulation of hills and glistening lochs. On every side a sheet of lush green draped over an ancient volcanic land, falling softly to the sea. And there in an upswell of air, lifting without moving wing or feather, the huge, terrifying, magnificent shape of a golden eagle. Glowing rust in the afternoon sun, his shape filled the landscape as he passed by at eye level, not even acknowledging us as present in his space.

We reached Iona having eaten our way through the bags of food, drunk crystal-clear water from the streams and felt a power in the silence of the hills that had filled us to the brim. Saturated by the empty environment we'd passed through, we had no words to hold the feeling, we didn't need any, the sense of wholeness was enough. We headed toward the abbey as every visitor does, but for us out of curiosity rather than religious belief. A center of Christianity, as it had been since the religion was brought to the island by St. Columba in the sixth century, it's a much-loved place of worship and contemplation. We shouldn't have gone; it wasn't a place for us.

"Are you here to pray?" A resident of the abbey approached us as we entered the cloister.

"No, just looking."

"This isn't just a tourist attraction, it's a center for faith, belief and Christian community."

"I know, but we've just come from Mull, we've had an incredible experience in the wilderness, something almost spiritual. And we were heading here; Iona was our goal. We're back south in a couple of days." Moth, as ever, frankly saying what he felt without hesitation. I held back; I could sense where the conversation was heading.

"There is no spirituality without God. You won't find a thin place out there; it's here in this building, where humans have worshipped God for centuries. This is where you'll find what you seek."

"I don't think I'm actually seeking anything. I'm just open to what comes. What's a thin place? Is it geological?"

I had my hand on Moth's arm; this wasn't a conversation we had to have.

"A thin place is where man can be close to the other world, to God's realm. It's here."

"Maybe for you."

I pulled him away. There was no need to argue with someone else's faith simply because it wasn't ours. There was no right or wrong, just belief or not.

Beyond the abbey the road led us across the island, through the machair of lush grass and dry flower heads to a wide expanse of sand and pebbles: the Bay at the Back of the Ocean. There is no land beyond there, just the rhythmic swell of the Atlantic Ocean. We sat on the shore, the sun catching the waves as they broke out at sea, picking through the stones around us. Among the smooth, multicolored nuggets we turned in our hands were small, perfectly green pieces of millennia-old rock. We'd picked up a leaflet that said these tiny pebbles were known as St. Columba's tears.

"These are the land itself, older than Columba, older than humanity. This is what we are, the land, this is where we come from. The thin place is right here, and it's always here. This place between the stone and my fingers, this is the place where our conscience and the earth are inseparable." Moth held the green stone up to the sunlight.

I watched him lying on the shore, his face intense in thought, clothes worn and stinking from two weeks' wear, a ragged half-grown fluff of beard merging with tangled hair. He was my thin place, though he would never know the depth of it, the place where it all became clear and there was no separation between worlds or time.

As we left Iona we didn't realize that there wouldn't be any more trips like this, or that soon it would be a baby carrier we would lift on to our backs, or that the next time we packed our rucksacks it would be twenty-five years later and under very different circumstances.

I walked back to the chapel where Moth was studying and we would eat another pea risotto. The notion of the thin place hadn't entered my head for decades, but suddenly the time we'd spent on the Coast Path shone brightly in my memory. I could feel it now, the weeks of headlands and skies, the nights of stars and rain, the smell of the weather as it blew in from the sea. I'd sensed something then, a thinness between the wild world and the human, between freedom and containment. We'd walked along the barrier between those worlds and felt something of our natural state of being. Touched a wild connection with the land and held it in the dust on our hands. We weren't the same people who had started that walk; we were changed in ways beyond measure. The echo of that feeling was at the core of the problems I was experiencing living in the village, it was in the cold dark soil under the pine trees on the estate when my mum died, it was in the little girl sitting in the tree watching the wild world go by. I'd touched a thin place and I couldn't go back.

Moth was lying on the bed when I returned to the chapel, a strange thing at midday.

"What's going on? I thought you had to finish that assignment?" I checked myself; I sounded as if I was talking to one of the kids who hadn't finished their homework.

"I'm so dizzy: every time I look at the computer screen it feels as if I'm travel-sick. I just had to lie down."

"You can't do that! You've got to get up and do some exercise—it'll help. I know it will."

"Don't you get it? I can't. I feel as if I'm going to fall over."

No, this isn't happening, get up, don't let this happen, just get up. The doctor had explained that Moth's erratic lateral eye movements were just another symptom of CBD, but we hadn't realized how quickly the symptom would progress or what it would mean. As Moth tried to read the lines on the screen, his eyes juddered, causing a sense of motion sickness.

"No, I'm making you some tea and you have to get up; we're going to walk out of the village, into the sunlight. Just sit up." Cut in two by my own words, I desperately wanted to pull the blanket over him. I would have drawn the curtains, if we'd had any, made him comfortable, let him rest, accepted what was happening. I didn't; I put the kettle on instead. "Sit up, drink this, we're walking this afternoon, sit up."

We stopped on a bench halfway up the hill, Moth sitting heavily down on the lichen-encrusted wooden slats. Gannets circled just off the headland, gliding smoothly through the sky. Circling, circling, then in one powerful controlled movement drawing their wide wings tight to their sides and shaping their long beak and yellow-capped head into one line as clean as a shard of ice, firing themselves into the water. Direct, immediate, a thought, an action, a fish.

"How are you feeling?"

"A bit better."

"Let's keep going then."

"I think I'll have to break up the computer work. No more than half an hour at a time, take a break then go back to it."

"Whatever works—and walk, you have to walk. Remember

how much better you were on Golden Cap. When we started walking the southern section of the path, we thought everything was over and you were running out of days, but after just two weeks you jumped on that trig point and we danced. Don't you remember?"

"I don't really remember Golden Cap."

"Of course you do." Don't forget it, you can't forget it. I could see those wild wind-shaped summers slipping from him like an ice lolly off a stick on a sunny afternoon. If we didn't hold those memories together, would all the life they held slip from view, leaving only a faded picture behind?

"This is a bit like that bench where we met the old men with the blackberries."

"Which old men?"

"You have to remember those men. I remember meeting them as one of the most moving moments of the whole walk. I've held on to what one of them said ever since. Even now I feel that's what our walk was, it summed up everything."

"I can't picture it. Where was it?"

"Just after Zennor, after that day of water when we thought we would drown by just breathing. When the sky was so low we were nearly in the clouds, you couldn't see in front or behind, just damp air. The day after that, when it was still foggy, but felt as if the rain would return at any moment."

"I remember the rain, but even so . . . those men . . . no . . . it's not coming back."

"We sat on a bench, it was early morning and we'd just camped on Zennor Head in the field of cows. Two old chaps walked up from the cove below and one of them had a Tupperware box of blackberries." Please don't forget this. How can you let this slip from your memory? It should be a diamond in your pocket forever. Something to hold on dark days, a fortune in the bank of life. "He offered us a blackberry from the box, and we didn't want to take them because the ones we'd eaten had been too tart and sharp. But that blackberry was like nothing we'd eaten before. It was rich and purple, autumnal ripeness in a bite, the most perfect taste. That's when he said it." I sat back waiting for him to remember.

"Said what? Don't keep me hanging."

My throat was tight with tears of loss and fear of loss to come. He had let go of a moment that hung so brightly on my tree of memory that I could find its glow in any dark place. But for him the light had dimmed and gone.

"He explained how those blackberries were like no other, how they got their amazing flavor."

"How was that?"

I swallowed hard. This couldn't be happening. If this was gone, what else was gone?

"He said, 'You need to wait until the last moment, that moment between perfect and spoiled. And if the mist comes right then, laying the salt air gently on the fruit, you have something that money can't buy and chefs can't create. A perfect, lightly salted blackberry. You can't make them; it has to come with time and nature. They're a gift, when you think summer's over and the good stuff has all gone. They're a gift.'" Our path, our magnificent walk, was slipping away from him. Hold on to it, Moth, hold it tight; it's ours, our bright light in the mess of our lives. Don't let it go; it was ours, our gift of time and nature.

"That's a great story."

"It's not a story." I watched the gannets, swift and sharp, my mind drifting along the path through the days between Zennor Head and Land's End. We'd stood on those blocky granite cliffs beyond Land's End with only a few pounds and a Mars bar in our pockets. Just the two of us, alone at the edge of the Atlantic, only the two wet sheets of the nylon tent to shelter us from whatever the weather systems threw at us. We could have given up then, got on the bus and headed away from the hardships of the path, to sofa-surf with friends and family and wait for a council house to become available. But we didn't. Moth's health had improved in ways we'd been told were impossible and the path had given us something we'd thought we'd never feel again. Hope. We'd held on to that feeling and carried on walking into a future we couldn't see.

"Shall we carry on?"

"Yes, why not, while the sun's still shining."

Hope. I held it warm again in my hand, a smooth, round, sea-worn pebble of possibility.

I left the chapel in the early evening, only intending to walk to the Block House at the end of the street, an old lookout tower positioned on a fin of rock that points out into the mouth of the river. But as I closed the iron gate behind me, Gill walked past.

"Hi! Haven't seen you around for so long. Got to dash but I'm having a bit of a get-together at mine tomorrow. Would you like to come?"

"I, er, I mean, well . . . okay."

Standing outside the door of a virtual stranger with a bottle of wine in my hand made my chest pound erratically. I couldn't seem to breathe normally and my vision was blurring. What was I doing here? I looked down the street at the gap between the houses where the passenger ferry chugged slowly into the quay, returning locals from the chemist and the butcher's in Fowey and taking tourists to and from cream teas. I could be on that ferry; if I turned around right now I could run down the street and be on the boat before anyone knew I'd knocked on the door. Too late: the door was open.

"Hi, come on in, have to say I didn't expect to see you." Had I misunderstood some social code again, and the invitation was just a polite gesture, not a real invite and I didn't actually have to be here? "Let me introduce you." Too late: I was in the house.

A room full of people. Dark heavy curtains against tall north-facing windows, pulled open but still forming shadowed corners. People on sofas and wing-backed chairs. People standing in groups, holding wine glasses, laughing. People at ease in the company. I stayed at the edge as Gill tried to guide me around the room.

"Sarah and Marion, this is Ray, but she lives down the road from you so I'm sure you've met already."

I'd seen one of them before, Marion, a delicate older lady with bright white hair, but not Sarah, the spritely lively woman in her fifties that she was with.

"Oh hello, are you new? I haven't seen you before." Marion stayed in her chair but extended her hand, not to shake mine, but to hold it in her cool gentle grip.

"Er, not really, I've been here for quite a while now." I'd seen the white hair of the old lady in her garden on sunny days, but I'd hurried by, hoping she wouldn't speak.

"And this is Simon." A calm, smiling man in his sixties. There was something about the way he moved, something about the way Gill's face lifted when she introduced him—

"Hi. So Simon's your partner?"

She seemed momentarily shocked and glanced around.

"No, no, no."

"Gill's a great friend. We've been friends for quite a few years, haven't we, Gill?" Simon moved away, smiling. There was something in the denial . . .

Sarah slipped among the group in a smooth movement that displayed the confidence of a person who knows their position in the gathering and immediately started a conversation.

"So who are you, why haven't I seen you before, where have you moved from, what do you do with yourself that keeps you out of sight?"

In one sentence—all the questions that I feared. These people could have been any of the people I'd met on the coastal path, any one of them could have been the person that drew in their dog on a retractable lead when I told them I was homeless, or poked me with their foot and called me a tramp when I'd dropped coins on the ground and knelt to pick them up. Assured, confident middle-aged people, secure in their position in society, the village, their own lives. How could I answer any of their questions without being afraid that what we'd experienced when we were walking would happen again? And I couldn't walk away from these people as we had on the path; I'd bump into them in the village for as long as we lived there.

"I'm . . . We . . ." I couldn't formulate the words. I couldn't say, "I had a home, a place I loved and put my whole life, my whole self into, but I lost it, and you haven't seen me because I've tried to avoid just this moment. The moment when someone asks me to explain myself." There were three people sitting on the green velour sofa pushed almost back to the wall. I'd known a girl who would have squeezed behind there and hidden in the dark, avoiding talking, avoiding questions. As the room seemed to almost lose focus I desperately wanted to join her. Moth had been right, as always: I'd become that child again. "I came here from Wales with my husband. He's studying for a degree at the university."

"And you? You must be really busy, otherwise I would have met you."

Busy hiding. Busy struggling in the bricks, slate and concrete, when all I needed was greenness, and wind, and crows lifting from tall trees, and sparrows squabbling in a hedgerow of shifting sunlight. Meet me on the path and I could tell you who I am, why I am. But not here, not in a roomful of people that I've forced myself into to try to break this strange disconnection. What was I doing? What was I even thinking of doing? The pile of job rejections had grown to the point where there were very few vacancies in the area that I hadn't already applied for and I knew I had almost stopped looking. But as I thought about her question I realized that tentatively, almost as if I was trying to hide it from myself, I *did* know what I was doing. I saw myself in the dark kitchen of the chapel, laptop keys smooth under my fingers, reading research papers, tracing patterns across the keys, tracing lives. The vision caught me in an uplift of air, a warm thermal buoying the outstretched wings of a gull until it turned on the wind and arced away from the cliffs, dipping out toward the open sea. And as I opened my mouth to reply the words came out, unexpected and unannounced.

"I've been doing some research, but now I'm thinking of writing."

"Oh wow. Gill . . ." Her voice was raised now. "Gill, you didn't tell me Ray was a writer."

All the heads in the room turned toward my dark corner by the curtain. Oh fuck. Oh fuck, fuck, fuck.

Away from the village and the party and the people, on a path between high hedgerows of hawthorn, heavy with clusters of ripe red berries, I leaned against the bank of grass and ferns beginning to curl into autumn. Only the sides of the hedge had been trimmed that year, leaving the top growth stretching upward and nearly meeting over the track, forming a green tunnel of branches leading toward the road. I felt small in there, safe and hidden. The same small child who had found her way into the drainage ditch in the middle of the wet meadow, a dark, secret place.

It was early afternoon in the half-term holidays. Mum was asleep in the chair and Dad was talking to a salesman in the farmyard, looking at bottles and cans in the back of his van. I wanted to get in and look too. I hadn't seen all those brightly colored containers before, with their skull-and-crossbone pictures; they were new.

But Dad sent me away and I wandered into the meadow. Below the farmhouse and the barns, past the pigsties where the Large White sows stood on hind legs and hung their front legs over the walls waiting to be fed, like rows of old ladies chatting over the garden fence. To the stream, hung over with willows, and below that, the wet meadow. A field that spent much of the winter under water, when heavy rains made the stream burst its banks and flood the lower land. The sheep were only occasionally let in here; it was too wet for them and caused their feet to rot: a kind of stinking, slimy, sheep version of trench foot. Mainly it was empty and full of tall grasses and wild flowers. Carpets of meadowsweet, knapweed and plantain, the hedgerows billowing with lady's bedstraw. And running down the center, the drainage ditch.

I climbed in, down a rocky patch that formed steps in the almost vertical sides. The bottom of the ditch was wide enough to walk along, but the sides were well above my head. As an adult I came to realize that the ditch was little more than six feet deep, but as a child it was a dark tunnel. On summer days the water in the bottom only just covered my ankles, but in the winter it was brimful and overflowing. Small holes scattered the sides of the banks and I stood and waited until I spotted a brown tubular body plop out of a hole and into the water. The round head and short tail of a water vole was visible in the water for a moment, before it disappeared into the vegetation on the bank. I'd taken a pocketful of barley from the sacks by the grain mill, where the corn was ground into dust to feed the pigs; now I pinched some out and put a small pile in the mouth of each tiny tunnel and waited for the voles to come back. I'd done this many times but, afraid of being rebuked for being in the ditch, I'd never mentioned the voles to anyone. That day, instead of just the usual one vole, five came back. Swimming through the water, climbing up the banks and suspiciously looking around before snatching a mouthful of grain and vanishing into their holes. I was ecstatic. Five voles.

"Mum, Dad, you'll never guess what I've seen. Five water voles, and they're so fat and they've got these little short black tails."

"They were probably rats."

"No, I know they're voles, they're in my book of British wildlife. They look like tiny beavers."

"Where are these rats?"

"In the drainage ditch." I'd said it without thought, but immediately knew it was a mistake.

"What, you've been in that ditch? You know you shouldn't be in there. Go to your room and stay there." As I went upstairs I could still hear Mum. "Get rid of them. I bet that's where all these filthy rats are coming from, out of the water."

I watched Dad from the bedroom window walking across the farmyard with one of the cans from the back of the salesman's van; then I sat on the bed with the British wildlife book, tracing my finger over the picture of a water vole. They weren't rats. But I didn't see the water voles again.

I sat on a rock that jutted out of the hedgerow, among the grass and ferns. Why had those words come out of my mouth? I'd learned from the loss of the water voles that some things are better left unsaid. But I'd carelessly spoken the words of a barely formulated thought. *I'm thinking of writing*: how could I have said those words out loud? Said them to people I hardly knew or was likely to know? Words I'd hardly dared to say to myself, or formulate to Moth. I walked back to the village across the cliffs as a cargo ship left the river mouth, heavy in the water. A lesson learned. I wouldn't mention writing again. I couldn't tarnish the thought by letting it be anything more than a dream, a secret to keep for myself.

11. Electromagnetic

I ran my hands over the brown plastic cover of the old guide-book, idly tracing the ripple of pages with my finger. I couldn't let him lose what was held within those covers; if those memories began to slip then everything else would come tumbling after. His life, everything he'd done, and us, all the memories of our life, would slip from him, lost in the sludge of vagueness. I had to stop it, to find a way to plug the holes in his thoughts. I couldn't stand quietly by and watch the steady, dripping loss of everything that made him who he was.

I opened the book again at the very start of the path. Mine-head. The faded pencil notes in the margin were barely legible after the rain damage. "Day 1—if the rest of the path is like this we don't stand a chance." "Ants, everywhere." Oh, the ants, the flying ants, mounding on the dry path, millions of them in our hair, everywhere. I traced a line on the OS map that ran through the book. The ants were on the flat bit after the really steep start, where the path flattened to moorland. After the ponies. My finger followed the orange line, through the undulations of contour lines and a film of memory began to unroll in my head. The light had been fading when we reached the headland beneath my finger, some cloud starting to blow in: I felt a breath of sea wind touch my face and there in the air I smelled hot dust and dry heather. I was on the path; it was so real that I put my hand up to brush ants from my face. I closed the book and sat back. I had been there: that book could put me back on the path as if I'd just laced my boots and lifted my rucksack on to my back.

If the guidebook could put me on the path, could it do so for

Moth too? Not for much longer: the pencil marks were fading away. Maybe I could find a way to capture them, to keep the notes before they were lost. A way to hold on to the power of what we did so that every time he tried to let go of life, to sit back and let the tide roll in, I could say no. No, no, don't lie down, read this, remember this, remember what we did, how we didn't give in, get up. Keep trying. Please keep trying.

I opened the Word program on the laptop and headed a page: "The South West Coast Path, Day 1," diligently copying out the notes in diary form. Hours later I sat back and read through what I'd typed. The words were there, but not the path. I could hear what the notes said, but without the guidebook I couldn't feel them; they had no strength. This was pointless; it wouldn't help him at all. I closed the laptop, frustrated with the waste of a day. But a thought was growing, the germ of a possibility.

The ivy was beginning to dance in the first spots of autumn rain. The season was changing, the darkness returning. I could have hesitated, held back, talked myself out of it. But winter would be here soon; there were hardly any jobs around now: all the employers were reducing staff for the low season. I'd had no success in the summer, so I was hardly going to find anything now. If I didn't do it now I never would. I put the kettle on. Could I do it? I had no idea—but I could try. I could take the notes and put them into a narrative form, pull in everything we'd seen and felt and heard, breathe some life into the penciled words. I could write myself on to the Coast Path and in doing so put Moth right there next to me, so when he read it he wouldn't just hear the wind, he'd feel it.

I opened the laptop on a clean page. But where to begin? If it was going to mean anything to him, then he would need to know why he'd walked. I would have to start at the beginning. I began to type: "I was under the stairs when I decided to walk."

★

"How was uni?"

"Okay—I made it through the day. Really interesting session on LED lighting this morning. What about you—been for a walk?"

"No, it was too wet. I've been writing."

"Really? What, a letter?"

"No." The wild enthusiasm of the afternoon vanished the moment I had to explain myself. "Do you remember when we first met I talked about how, as a child, I wanted to write, but that I never did? Well, I might give it a go—just see if I can do it. It's something I want to write for you, not for anyone else to read, just something for you."

"Intrigued! Well, tell me more, what is it?"

All the confidence of the day disappeared.

"I can't tell you yet. I need to do it first."

Days came and went, early mornings, wet afternoons, silent days at the back of the chapel as the rain fell. Word on word, page on page. Every painful day as we lost our home, as I lay under the beech trees engulfed in loss when our last remaining sheep died, as we stepped over the threshold of our home for one last time. Feeling again the void of emptiness that came with knowing I would never go back. Then I was away from the cause and released into the consequence, set free on the coastal path and walking.

I took the rucksack from under the bed and unpacked it, holding the familiar worn items, the battered pan and cranky gas stove, the not-waterproof coat that let the rain pour through. Then I repacked it realizing that each item found its way back in almost instinctively.

There was no stopping: words falling on words, words running free on the cliff tops. Rain, wind, gulls piling into turbulent skies on ozone thermals, sun, burning heat and the dry sweet smell of the earth. I was walking again, feeling the bite of the rucksack on my shoulders, the tightness of the hip-strap, the soreness of blistered thumbs where I'd held the shoulder straps away from raw patches of skin. The burning, leathering of bodies exposed to weather without shelter or protection and the soothing sense of rain rolling down hot arms.

I drank tea, ate toast, watched the rat as he became braver and sat on the wall on dry afternoons, looking in at me as I looked out at him. Each of us becoming a little more confident in our world, a little more able to take another step forward.

The leaves fell from the magnolia tree, the horizon of the sun lowered and I stopped seeing it, just a faint light that came and went by midday. It didn't matter, I was sitting at the table but I wasn't in the chapel, I was sweating in searing heat, dehydrated and longing for rain, treating blisters in the early morning and swimming in syrup-calm seas. The kitchen filled with ladybirds as they hatched into flight from dewy grass in the early mornings, and rang with seal calls in the afternoons, while badgers nosed at the doorway. I stood in the dim evening light, faced the wall and spread my arms wide and the rain came stinging on gale-force winds, pounding my face, battering the rucksack. Winds roaring through granite-block cliffs, hurling crows through wild gray skies.

And always Moth was there, keeping me on the path, face to the sun, heading west. His penciled notes taking me from cove to headland, through woods and dark night skies. I followed his heels as the dust rose around his boots and the rain poured from his rucksack. We were there between Paddy's descriptions of the path, reliving every painful step, sharing every victory. Words on words on words, all-consuming memories falling on to the page.

Christmas trees, darkness, six people squeezed into the chapel, cooking a small chicken in a slow cooker, potatoes on the camping gas ring. One day we'd be able to afford a proper cooker, but without it there was still laughter, wine and bodies sleeping on the kitchen floor. Then the children and their partners were gone and Moth and I were back on the cliff catching a sunset in the middle of the afternoon. Dying light painting the sky, the sea, the land in one exuberant brushstroke of color. Fireworks and assignments unfinished. The start of term and silence. Steam rising from a tea mug. The return of rat in the afternoons.

And the words returned. No holding back now. Through every cracker pulled and mince pie eaten, part of me had been waiting to go back to the tent, to the cliff. Rat settled in among the dead fern leaves and I sat at the laptop and let the words in. And the path called me on, through fossils and landslides, white cliffs and red, to a calmer place, a softer place. I stood in the wind, no longer a battering Atlantic gale, now a quieter wind from the south. No longer chivvying and forcing me forward, now a gentle arm, a quiet guide. Moth was on the path next to me, stronger, fitter, lifting his rucksack without help, able to look forward not back. We held hands and walked into Polruan. "We were lightly salted blackberries hanging in the last of the summer sun, and this perfect moment was the only one we needed." I pressed save and closed the laptop.

Through the chapel window the magnolia was forming flower buds and snowdrops had pushed through the cold ground. Rat stretched in the afternoon sun, turned and disappeared into the ivy.

I shook the ink cartridge and put it back in the printer. Maybe there was enough ink. Taking a deep breath, I pressed print. An hour later a manuscript lay on the table in front of me. The bright black lettering of the title on the first page fading to palest pink by the final full stop. I took a piece of string and tied it with a bow, attaching a piece of brown card cut into a gift tag.

To Moth,
HAPPY BIRTHDAY
don't let go of our Path.
Ray xx

"Happy birthday to you, happy birthday to you . . ." I balanced the tray of tea on the bed as Moth sat up, still drowsy under the bed covers. Rowan, our daughter, followed behind with presents and cards. She was here for a few days, taking a break from her life in London, a world away from the hills and streams of her childhood. Somehow, despite the four of us being scattered by the loss of our home, we'd managed to stay close, still connected, still a team.

"Wake up, Dad, and open the cards."

Feeling slightly sick with nerves I rapidly ate the toast we'd made for him and had to go to the kitchen and make some more. By the time I'd returned the presents were open and the cards were standing on the bed. Just one parcel remained on his lap, wrapped in brown paper, waiting.

"I couldn't open it without you. What is this? I said don't bother—we can't afford presents."

"I didn't buy it, I made it."

"Fantastic, homemade presents, they're the best."

Fear, nerves, excitement, all of that and more: I could hardly bear to watch. And then it was out of the paper, out into the daylight. The manuscript tied in string lay in his hands not mine. He moved the gift tag aside and the title leaped starkly off the first page: *Lightly Salted Blackberries*. Not a secret anymore, not mine anymore.

"What is this? Is this what you've been doing?"

"Yeah, I've been writing it for you." I felt shy and nervous, as if it was the first present I'd ever given him.

"All that time and it was for me."

"It's the path, the book of our path. So you can always keep the memory."

"All that time . . . You idiot, come here."

My heart rate slowed. Relief beyond measure. I got back in bed and ate more toast.

"Mum, what is this? You've written a book? Wow, this must be a whole pack of printing paper." Rowan was flicking through the corners of the pages. "And they've all got typing on. Dad, are you going to read this straightaway?"

"No, it's my birthday: we're going to the beach. But I will, I will read it."

"Brilliant. I'll read it too, before I leave." Before I could say no she'd left the room.

"Don't worry, she can read it. She might as well while she's here. But what a thing. What a huge thing to have done."

"I did it for you. It wasn't huge at all."

Rowan's bags were packed, another sad good-bye, knowing it could be months before we saw her again. I hadn't dared ask what she thought of the book. I'd skirted around her as she read intently for two days, wanting her to stop reading and enjoy her time with us, not wanting her to stop reading because that might be a sign she didn't like it. But now it sat on the table, the string retied. Was she going to leave the house and just not say anything about it?

"I don't know what to say."

Oh no, she hated it, too much reality, too many memories of home, and—oh no, I'd forgotten—that scene on the beach.

"It's amazing, it's brilliant. I didn't even know you could write."

"You think it's okay then?"

"It's so much more than okay! You know, you really should do something with it."

"What do you mean? Put it in a binder or something?"

"No, you idiot, get it published."

I'd been alone through much of the previous year. Both my strong and whole self, the person who had finished the path and was able to face the future, and my lost, confused, fearful self who hid from the world behind the chapel. Matter and antimatter brought together in a vacuum. As I wrote the final words and closed the laptop I was back on the path, the wind in my hair and a sense of hope hanging almost touchable in the air. Undoubtedly there'd been a change of energy in my void, and from that energy a book had appeared. It was there, tangible, real, tied in string on the table. Mass had been created in my vacuum. Something from nothing. But if the particles of that mass were to make their presence felt they would have to interact with something; a light needed to shine so they could be seen.

12. Light

"Undoubtedly this DaTscan shows what we feared. If you look at this, here and here, you can see the problems we're facing." The doctor had moved to a new consulting room. No longer overlooking the car park, we now looked into a willow tree, its leaves moving slightly, disturbing the light that fell across the table. We still traveled north to see the same consultant, a journey every six months that led us back to Wales, a tie not quite severed. "See this here, these two tadpole shapes in the center of the brain?" He pointed with a pencil at two dark forms in the middle of the picture on the screen, the putamen and caudate, areas of the brain that control all manner of movement and cognitive functions. "The radioactive material you were injected with should show up as lights in the scan in the areas of the tadpoles that are functioning. Like flying over a city at night, a mass of tiny lights."

I stared at the screen, waiting for the lights to come on. They didn't. All I could see was a faint line of fairy lights strung around the head of one of the tadpoles like fancy dress. Moth moved backward, away from the picture.

"But there are barely any lights."

"That's the problem."

"Surely the scan isn't working properly? That looks as if I'm hardly able to control my movements at all."

"The human brain is an amazing thing and we don't know everything about it. Yours clearly seems to be finding a way around the shutting down of this section. It's taking other pathways."

Sitting again in the hospital car park we were numb. It wasn't the shock we'd experienced with the original diagnosis of CBD, but a sense of disorientation that came from of knowing that however hard we fought CBD it still held a future that couldn't be avoided. We leaned against each other and stared at the pebble-dashed wall of the hospital. Behind us men pulled golf caddies across the green of the golf course, hitting balls with varying degrees of success. With the windows open we could hear the whistle of balls through the air. Balls flying with hope rather than aim.

"I can't do this anymore."

No, no, please don't give up. I held his hand, the same hand that had held mine for the first time as we walked in the park during a college lunch break. The hand that held our children safe and protected, and plastered the walls of our home. The hand that had reached for mine in the darkness of the tent on a windswept headland. The hand that now had a tremor which shook his pen as it tried to write notes for his degree and rolled the peas off his fork on the way from his plate. I held it tight and still. *We have hope.* We found hope on the path and saved it. Kept it safe in an inside pocket for days like this, for a life like this.

"You can't give in, you just can't."

"No, I meant I can't sit in this car park and stare at the wall anymore. Let's go into town and buy that copy of the *Big Issue*. It's out this week, isn't it?"

"Can you be bothered? It'll just be a small piece at the back. They said they'd send me a copy anyway."

"What? Not go and buy the magazine with the very first article you've ever written, your very first piece? Of course we're going to town."

The *Big Issue* seller was just packing his bag away, about to leave his pitch.

"Have you got a copy left? We really need to get one this week."

"Sorry, they've all gone. Why do you need one?"

"My wife's written an article—it's in this week's issue—about a time when we were homeless and went for a walk."

"That's not this week; it was last week. What, you wrote that? I kept a copy cos I keep rereading it. That was a bloody long walk, but good on ya both, what a thing to do. Here, take it." He fished in his bag and produced a curled-up copy with a cover picture of green trees.

Sitting beneath the clock tower in the center of a Welsh town, we flicked through the front and back of the magazine where the smaller articles normally appeared. There was nothing. I couldn't let go of my manuscript, couldn't trust anyone to read it and not diminish it with derision. But Moth, Rowan and our son, Tom, had persuaded me that I did have something to say about homelessness. I'd offered the *Big Issue* an article about the hidden rural homeless without the slightest expectation of a reply. But within days the editor had said, "Send us something and we'll see."

"You look. I can't see it; it must be a really small piece somewhere. I thought it was all too good to be true."

Moth took the magazine from me and started methodically turning pages from the beginning.

"There's no point you doing that. It'll be at the back."

"Just wait."

I watched a busker setting up his pitch—a camping chair and a hat—then taking a small tin whistle out of a tube.

"Oh wow."

"What?"

"Just look. Look, Ray. Your words. You've done it."

Not a small column at the back, but four pages in the center of the magazine, with photographs of us that I'd sent with the piece of writing. A selfie taken on a headland near Godrevy Light-house. Pictures of the tent on Chesil Beach. And words, my words. We had left Wales, heading south to walk an unknown path and now the record of that walk and the homeless people we had met were in print in our hands and we were back in Wales. A strange and unexpected circle. But, looking at the pages, I could only feel disbelief. I couldn't laugh or cry; instead I sat beneath the clock and listened to the busker play Irish folk music. It was a horrid irony. My words were in print, the thing I'd dreamed of as a child had come true, on the day when we watched Moth's lights fading across the computer screen.

"We should go somewhere to celebrate."

"I don't feel like celebrating." I still felt numb, flattened by the coming darkness, and it was hard to acknowledge what was there on the pages.

"What? Just get up and look at what you've done. Something you thought was beyond reach. And this man, this editor, he took your work and believed in it enough to get it into print. He told you he would and he did. This is what I've been telling you: not everyone's bad, not everyone's to be mistrusted. We've had a shit time, but this is the start of something, a new path—I can feel it. So get the fuck up and come on. We're celebrating."

"But where . . ."

"Cnicht, I think. It feels right for today."

A small mountain in Snowdonia, from the south Cnicht looks classically conical, a cartoon mountain, but on the top it becomes a ridge running in a boggy line toward Snowdon. The first time we stood on the summit our children were small, carrying sand-wiches and Pokémon cards in their own tiny daysacks. They'd struggled up the stony scramble to the summit, exhausted, unable to take another step, until we reached the flat ridge summit and they ran away to play in the heather. Now, we parked the van in

Croesor, a small village at the foot of the mountain. It had been decades since our children had run ahead of us down the track beyond the car park, through a wood and out on to the open hillside. We walked that same path now, the air thick with memories and, in the warm windless July afternoon, midges, rising in their millions from the boggy ground in a biting irritation. But as the path headed upward a breeze grew and had carried them away by the time we reached the rocky, scrambling path to the top. In my head I could still hear the children's voices complaining and I finally had to agree, it was quite steep. On the top it was just as I'd remembered, the land falling away south in a patchwork of fields and wooded valleys, out toward the blue expanse of Cardigan Bay. And away to the north, somewhere behind a band of lazy white clouds, the summit of Snowdon. We stretched the magazine across a rock and reread the article as if it had been written by someone else, about someone else. Moth pulled his feet up on to the rock and hugged his knees.

"I'm not really seeing this; all I can see is that picture on the computer screen. Those lights going out."

"Stop pretending it's just me then, that I'm just feeling sorry for myself."

"All that research you read: there has to be an answer in there somewhere. Maybe you're right, and it's out here in the environment, in our natural wild state. As we were on the Coast Path. Perhaps we just need some land, some space where we can be outside all the time but still sleep under a roof."

"Of course we do, but how's that going to happen? Oh, I know, a miracle."

I lay on my back on the flat dried grass among the heather as broken cloud hung in the sky obscuring the blue, leaving only fleeting patches of bright possibility between the white. A warm wind blew through dry hard stems of heather and scrubby gorse. Purple buds were about to break open to spill honey-scented air across the mountainside and its sparse grass torn by sheep and razor winds. I spread my hands wide on the grass and felt the earth warm and present. A breathing entity beneath my palms. And the voice I hadn't heard for a while was back, clear in my ears, sharp in the air through the rocks, soft in the clouded sky. A smooth ribbon of sound like a heartbeat slowing to the murmur of birds returning at dusk.

"We should go—it's getting late. Shall we go down the way we came, or take the horseshoe past the old mine then cut down the path on the other side of the valley?"

"The horseshoe."

We headed across the dry bogs of the ridge and then down toward the ruins of Rhosydd quarry. Little over a century ago, this had been a thriving slate mine, the barracks and mine workings heaving with men and machinery. The roofs of the barracks are long gone, and the walls are crumbling, but the sense of lives lived and lost is strong. And a magnet for cavers who come to brave the tunnels that are still open underground. A powerful, eerie sound emanated from the broken walls, almost like music.

"What is that? Is it the wind in the walls?"

"No . . . I'm not sure, but it sounds like Linkin Park."

Sheltered behind a higher wall a small fire burned, sending sparks up into the fading sky. A group of people gathered round, sitting talking, strains of the metal rock band echoing out from a small speaker and around the empty walls.

"All right, lads, good spot for a party."

"Yeah, it's not bad."

I could see Moth trying to work out how to take the conversation further.

"Is this the Friday night spot? Perfect for a gathering."

"We're here for Chester."

"Right, a birthday?" Moth glanced at me, shrugging his shoulders.

The men looked at each other, then at the ground as some-one changed the track to one I'd heard playing in the kids' bedrooms when they were teenagers. Of course. Moth clearly remembered too.

"Not Chester Bennington?"

"Yeah, he died yesterday. He was a legend. Nothing's going to be the same now." The troubled, tattooed, immense talent of a lead singer from the metal band Linkin Park, who'd been a big part of our kids' lives, so inevitably ours too. "We're here to send him on his way, lift him up in the smoke and his words, the way he should go."

We sat on the rocks with them, a group of young people in black T-shirts and piercings, tattooed as their idol had been, holding vigil in a ruined mine on a Welsh hillside.

The sky turned to night as the group moved around, talking, singing, drinking, their faces lit by the firelight from wood they'd carried up the mountain. Our lives, life, death, the move-ment of molecules from wood to air, it had all become one. Moth's lights were slowly going out, there was no denying that, but the electrical charges in his brain were finding their own route, making new pathways. For now there was still enough power in his cells for them to keep searching and all we could do was to help them on their way. All we are is an electrical charge, no more than a mass of particles, matter, antimatter, mass and energy. No different from a blade of grass or a spark from the flames, just energy moving in a never-ending flux. While Moth's lights were still shining we would celebrate every one of them and keep each burning in his night sky for as long as we could.

We got up to leave, the final track playing from the speaker, the last of the flames flickering in the dark air as the fire died away.

13. Mass

Late August and the village was heaving with visitors, the silent winter streets an almost forgotten memory. But sitting on the bench in the gorse there was hardly a passerby. In the late-afternoon sunshine the only human sounds came from the beach far below at Lantic Bay. People were dotted over the sand and jet-skis cut figures of eight through the bay and between the boats moored in the bright water. I couldn't stay—I needed to get back to the chapel where I'd left Moth sleeping. For days he'd been overwhelmed by a strange dizziness, as if he was slightly drunk on a swaying boat. A sensation that only seemed to be relieved by lying down with his eyes closed.

I left the bench and cut across the fields. The National Trust rent the land in this strip of cliff-top margin and control the way it's grazed. The grass looked like the fields of my childhood: not smooth-grazed and low, but varying in height where the sheep had eaten but not mown the grass. This lighter grazing regimen allows a scattering of wild flowers to remain, and provides the type of cover that the skylarks love. When I'd walked through here in the spring and early summer, the small brown birds would lift high into the air, singing their bright celebration of the sky, attracting mates and my attention away from their nests. But in late summer the fields were quiet, the birds away feeding. Inland from here the land changed and became what spreads throughout much of the southwest: arable fields of wheat and barley. Monocultures where little wildlife can exist in fields sprayed with pesticides and weedkiller, where the wildlife and the plants it thrives on are driven out of the fields and into the hedgerows and woods. Not the habitat for many of our grass-living birds, who are retreating to the margins, their numbers dwindling.

Following the coastal path down from the skylark fields, through the gorse, to the steep dip in the land where winter storms funnel high winds into a jet-powered blast of air, making it hard to stay on your feet. Past the windblown hawthorn whose roots hold tight while its branches are stretched inland by the force of the wind. Ahead a backpacker appeared from the steep steps that led to the village, rising through the cleft in the rock and vegetation and pausing to catch his breath and look out to sea. A small wooden gate stood between us and as we approached it I could see he wasn't the average backpacker, with the latest equipment and a determined expression. He'd stood and gazed out over the Channel before slowly turning and walking on, unhurried. A bright yellow reflective jacket shone out against the dark gorse, and, on top, an old rucksack with an external frame. Strange to see on a man who at the oldest could only have been in his mid-twenties. I reached the gate before him and held it open for him to pass and as he looked up his face was a showcase of piercings: an open expression adorned in silver.

"Hi, you're backpacking. Where are you heading?" The inevitable question that had been asked of us so many times as we walked the path, but now I was the one asking.

"Not sure tonight. I'll just do a couple more headlands then stop, I think. But I'm heading to Plymouth." He seemed almost nervous as he replied.

"Oh, right, a few more days then. Where have you come from?"

"I started in Penzance. I've been walking for two weeks or so now." He seemed to relax a little as he walked through the gate, but wasn't in a hurry to leave. He didn't look like a person who walked often, although two weeks on the coast had given him the tan lines of someone who had been squinting into the sun and wind.

"That's a great section. I bet the Lizard was amazing in this heat. What brought you to the South West Coast Path then? Have you walked much before?"

"No, though I walked to the shop a lot when I was a kid! No, haven't been living the sort of life where you walk much. I've been sleeping rough in Exeter for the last year, you know, on the streets. But then I read this article about a couple who'd been homeless and walked the Coast Path and I thought, I can do that. So I borrowed all the stuff I needed from the charity people and they helped me get a train ticket to Penzance. It's been really hard though; I'd never put a tent up before, and these boots . . ."

"That's incredible. Have you eaten? Come back with me and have some food, or a cup of tea at least."

"No, I can't. I have to keep going. This walk. This, all of this." He gestured his arm across the sea. "It's changed everything. I have to keep going. I've got a routine now; I know my days. Can't remember when I last felt this way, if I ever felt it. I've got to find somewhere to put the tent, then make some soup. This is my day."

I knew this boy: not his life, but the feeling he was expressing.

"Have you any idea what happens when you get to Plymouth?"

"I'm not sure, but I won't be going back to the way I was. That part of my life's over now. Everything's changed. I've changed."

I watched him go through the dip and over the brow. I couldn't tell him it was my article. This was his moment, his life, his discovery; I couldn't interfere with that.

I pictured the young man walking away beyond the brow, tunnels of blackthorn engulfing him in a green transformative cloak. As it had us. Another life saved by the immense power of the elements on this wild strip of land. I spread my arms and let the rising ozone wind fill my clothes. I'd stopped and spoken to him without thought or hesitation. Had I felt at ease with him, felt a connection? Or was it something else? During all those dark months in the chapel I'd written myself back on to the path, back on to this foot-wide piece of dusty track. Back into the sun, the wind and the green, never-ending horizons. Unknowingly, unexpectedly, I'd written myself back to the place where I felt safe, secure and whole: our wild home. I closed my arms on the salted strength and carried it down the familiar path to the village. But the path had changed; it was no longer the windswept haunt of thrift and kestrels, but a new way, lit by a hesitant light from an unexplored source.

It's hard to spot a fork in the road of life, harder still to make a deliberate choice which way to go. But sometimes you can catch a fleeting glimpse of one as it disappears in the rearview mirror. The outcome doesn't change, but many miles down the road, with the map unfolded in front of you, it's possible to point to the fork and say: Yes, that's where we took a different route.

Squatting in the back of a van on the approach to the M6 motorway, holding a reluctant toddler on a potty, in a traffic jam that had already lasted for two hours, wouldn't be one of the moments when you would expect your life to change forever.

"If this is what it's like on the A road, what the hell is happening on the motorway?"

"You've said it, some kind of hell." Moth was driving, hoping to get the four of us to Scotland for a two-week holiday that we'd planned for months. Maybe this would be the trip when we found our dream home, the ruin in the mountains that we'd thought about for ten years. We didn't know where we'd find it, but we were totally convinced it would be in the north. Tom sat in his car seat, a chocolate biscuit smeared across his face, hair, clothes and now me. Rowan, squirming and annoyed on the potty. The camping equipment mounded menacingly in the space behind me.

"I don't think I can take much more of this—it could go on all day. What happens if we just turn off the road now, just turn left, where does it go?"

"West, if we keep going, west into Wales."

"Shall we?"

"Yes, anything to get off this road."

The sun set over Cardigan Bay as we stood on the side of a hill in a chill wind rising from the valley below. The sea was streaked in every tone of dying light, washing Moth's face in a pink and orange hue. Tom was quiet in the backpack, his face a chocolate smudge on Moth's shoulder, his plump lips relaxing in a gentle pucker, toddler hands fat and sticky, hanging limply from his sides, a deep and peaceful sleep. Rowan, not awake but not asleep, wrapped tightly in a blanket hugged on to my hip, her tangled blond hair catching the last tones of day.

"I didn't realize Wales was so beautiful." Moth had always been drawn north, to the high mountains and the open spaces, but something in the sunset held him entranced.

We held hands and looked out to sea, while the traffic on the motorway inched its way forward. Unaware then that the next twenty years of our lives beckoned in a place we would never have discovered if we hadn't taken an unplanned detour.

As I turned the corner to head back to the chapel Sarah stepped out of her doorway. Fighting the instinct to run, I took a deep breath and stopped.

"Well, hi, how are you, haven't seen you for a long time. How's the writing?"

"It's going well." I could do this. I pulled my ozone-filled clothes just a little tighter, unaware that the chill I was feeling came from the fork in the road that I couldn't see, from a direction I didn't realize existed, from a choice I didn't know I was making. "I've just had an article published in the *Big Issue*."

"Oh wow, well done. What's it about?"

I took a deep breath. A breath filled with the doubt of choices made, of losses endured or yet to come. A breath filled with nights on wild headlands and pebbles from the beach.

"It's about losing our home in Wales and becoming homeless. About choosing to walk the South West Coast Path rather than wait for a council house and the many rural homeless people we met along the way, the hidden rural homeless."

"You lost your house, your home, everything?"

"Yes. I couldn't say before because I know it can make people feel quite uncomfortable. I've encountered that reaction so many times I felt I had to keep it to myself. But today I realized there's no point."

"You don't need to hide that here. There are some people who would react that way, but there are lots of others with a history of life falling apart, people who've come back to live with parents, or just to start again."

"Really?"

"Yes. I think it seems to be a bit of a midlife theme. Lots of us find we have to go back to the beginning of our life in order to start again. Back to where we grew up, or where we were happiest. To a time before things went wrong. I see it like pressing the reset button."

I watched her walk away, then leaned over the wall that protected the narrow street from the drop down to the river. The water was full of boats moored for the summer: yachts, motorboats, the little blue boat that took visitors on river cruises, the black wooden hull of a tall ship, its sails tied down, the crew heading to shore. Children jumped off the harbor wall beneath the no swimming sign; old people in shorts tied their dinghy to the pontoon. Life. Life going on. Lives being lived.

It was all so simple and so clear. Sometimes you just need someone else to switch the light on in your dark place. The strong, fearless person who had finished the path had got lost somewhere in the hospital corridors, lost in a choice that had haunted me. Moth was right; I'd gone back to the start. Afraid of people, hiding, the child behind the sofa. But Sarah was right too; this was my moment to start afresh. The months of being that child again hadn't been wasted time. She was afraid and isolated, yet she had a connection to the wilderness that hadn't left her. She'd had something else, too, a dream that had been broken and lost along the way. I'd stood with her in her room as she stroked the books on her shelves, her small fingers running over the pictures of penguins on the spines, and imagining. The children shouted and splashed as they jumped off the wall, swimming away from the ferry as it weaved between the moored boats and came into the quay. I took one more breath of ozone air and went inside.

Google can find just about anything you need, if you ask the right question. After two hours of searching it gave me exactly what I was looking for. A nonfiction literary agent, not so big that they would ignore me, not so small that they would be ineffective. I uploaded my submission package and sat back as Rat stood up and stretched from an afternoon on the wall. I could see the sun beginning to set on the very last day of our walk along the South West Coast Path. I felt Moth's hand in mine, the scent of blackberries in the air and the overwhelming sense that this moment is the only one we have, the only one we need.

I pressed the reset button.

14. Water

Late afternoon, late August, late summer. The air was still and silent, only broken by the hum of insects and an occasional shriek from the few children who still ran across Lantic Bay. Tail-enders, hanging on to the last few days before being taken home for new school uniforms, exercise books and confinement. Fewer people passed the bench near the rocks on the headland, so I lay on it, knees up, listening to the sounds of nothing, soaking up the last of the light and warmth on my skin before heading back into the village. Back stiff from lying for too long on the narrow wooden seat, I sat up and squinted against the bright sway of light on the sea. Two figures walked across the fields behind me, heads close, deep in conversation. I stood to leave as my mobile sounded the receipt of an e-mail. The literary agent. The likelihood of an agent responding so quickly was very slim; undoubtedly this would be an automated rejection.

My fingers found themselves on the brass plaque on the bench as I sat back down. The last jet-ski of the summer headed for harbor, a spray of water and noise in its wake. The plaque said this had been Peter's favorite spot and his loved ones had sited a bench here for every tired walker to sit and remember him. The couple were cutting across the field waving, but I couldn't focus on them. I glanced at the screen again, expecting the message to have changed, but it was still there.

Gill and Simon climbed over the fence.

"I'm back. How are you? I've been talking to Sarah: she told me how you lost your home, that's so sad."

She knew and yet she was still talking to me.

"How long have you been back?"

"Only yesterday."

Only a day and yet she knew already. The narrow streets: obviously the sound carried. But she was still here talking to me. It was almost impossible to process her words; my hand was still gripping my phone tightly, the email still alight in the darkness of my pocket.

"It doesn't matter here. Lots of us have a history, don't we, Simon?" Simon just smiled and nodded. "Do you ever get on to the river? Someone offered me a canoe to use while I'm here. Do you want to borrow it?"

"Er . . . yes, thanks." They walked away and my head was spinning. I took deep, salt-laden breaths and tried to grasp for something real. A two-pound coin in my pocket. All I had until tomorrow, when we would allow ourselves to take our weekly allowance of money from the student loan. That was real, just enough for two large potatoes and a tin of beans from the village shop. Baked potatoes, that was real. Not people talking, sharing, accepting, no reality there. I looked again at the screen. "I've read the first three chapters. Could you send the rest of the manuscript?" An agent showing interest in the manuscript, that couldn't be real either, that had to be an illusion.

The Fowey River begins on Bodmin Moor, trickling out of the peaty ground in a hopeful stream of water rising from deep in the earth. Falling slowly south, the stream becomes a river fed by tributaries until it gathers enough power to head toward the sea. Before it makes it that far it's sidetracked and siphoned into pipes and taps to provide drinking water for much of Cornwall. But enough water keeps flowing to dilute the salty incoming tide where the river widens and in its lower stretches becomes a tidal estuary. As the tide goes out, deep wide mudflats are exposed between steep-sided woodland, a last remnant of the ancient forests that would have existed here before they were cleared for farming. Crossing the river on the car ferry from Bodinnick to Fowey it's hard to picture the depth of the river, dredged by the harbor commission to keep the mud from blocking the shipping channel. But floating on a piece of foam in the wake of a motorboat we seemed to be crossing a watery chasm.

"So when Gill said canoe, I imagined something like the Canadian canoes we hired when the kids were small, do you remember those? In the Lake District? This feels as if I'm just sitting on the water without sinking." The holes in the base of the two-man foam kayak were supposed to maintain its balance and buoyancy, but two minutes in and I was already soaked to my waist. The foam hovered in the wake of the passing boat as water pushed in through the holes and washed over the top. Unsinkable, in a half-submerged sort of way.

"Yes, I remember those canoes. They were green, weren't they?"

"No, red and orange."

We paddled in weaving, uncoordinated strokes, slowly making our way upstream away from the pleasure boats and commotion. Dodging the car ferry, we passed the looming metal hulk of the clay-loading dock, towering above us half in, half out of the water as we paddled by. Beyond the oil and diesel fumes being washed out to sea and the creek full of moored yachts. Past the old man standing on his ancient wooden-hulled boat, sea-whipped hair and beard, old woolen jumper and boots, dog at the helm, a living snapshot of another era. On to where the river quietens, the mudflats rise closer to the surface and boats are restricted to a central channel. Staying close to the riverbank we skimmed above the mud on the incoming tide, away from the occasional passing boat but beyond the reach of low-hanging trees, in our own channel of water, floating almost silently along the rocky, mud-crusted shoreline beneath the darkness of the woodland. Small groups of white birds perched on the rocks, a stark brilliance against the dark background, their black legs and beaks barely visible as a faint drizzle lowered the light in the woods, deepening our sense that the first few visible trunks shielded a secret just out of sight.

"What are they? White herons? Kind of exotic and out of place."

"They're little egrets, yeah, that's what they are, a type of heron. They're beautiful, but I'm not sure they're a good sign."

Near motionless on the rocks, their whiteness formed a perfect, monotone still life. These elegant birds have traditionally been rare migrant visitors, flying north from the Mediterranean and Africa. But toward the end of the twentieth century permanent colonies began to form along the south coast of England. The Wildlife Trust feel their expansion could be due to the changing climate, the birds being driven north and west as temperatures rise, causing their food sources to dwindle. Not everyone agrees. Possibly by the time the little egret moves to the Outer Hebrides the doubters will be convinced, but by then it could be too late to say "I told you so." The drizzle thickened to steady soft rain as we picked up the paddles and found our rhythm again, the birds dwindling to specks of white on the rocky outcrop behind.

The soft rain became vertical rods of connection between land and sky, drops bouncing from the river with the force of a pebble, leaving ripples expanding and reflecting.

"Shall we stay under the trees, or head back?" I didn't want to give in, but the wetness was making me shiver.

"We're wet to our armpits anyway so it doesn't make any difference. We could explore this little creek while we're here, then head back. This might be the only day we can use the canoe and we certainly can't afford to hire one, can we?" He had a point, but why wasn't he cold?

Paddling back out into the rain we turned into a creek. It

was heavily wooded on one side, old oaks, beech and birch cloaking the steep hill. On the opposite bank a scattered line of trees bounded a steep slope of grass and thistles, where cattle climbed like goats to graze. Huge bird's nests clustered among the branches of willow and oak, where a heron sat swaying in the leaves, its head lowered as the rain rolled from its back. Two others stood motionless by a broken jetty hung with lichen.

"This rain's getting worse. Shall we just pull it under the trees until it eases off? And I need a minute—my shoulder's killing me. Maybe I shouldn't be doing this."

"Or maybe you need to do it more."

We dragged the canoe under the dense trees of the opposite bank, crouched among the roots and waited.

"Jeez, I'm cold now." Finally.

We shivered under the canopy of the trees until the rain slowed with the tide. As we stretched our stiff knees to leave, an apple landed at Moth's feet.

"Where did that come from?"

"Strange, can't see any apple trees."

Deep, slimy mudflats were reappearing from beneath the water, barely covered even at high tide. Within moments of the mud becoming visible, a small flock of curlews landed and immediately began to feed, burying their long curved beaks into the mud, hoovering up whatever morsels of protein were hidden under the surface. These tall brown birds used to be common in much of Britain. In our home in Wales, the burbling call of the curlews had been the sound of spring, as they returned from their winter feeding grounds to nest in the wet meadow and feast on elvers as they ran upstream. But in the last few years before we left the curlews didn't come, their calls silenced. Their numbers have declined by 80 percent in Wales and 30 percent in England in the last twenty years. Vast drops in numbers that have put their survival on our shores in jeopardy.

"Look at that, there must be twenty or more. That's brilliant to see."

"This must be a really undisturbed spot. Curlews, herons, little egrets, who'd have thought there could be somewhere so special, so close to all the mayhem in the river mouth? What the fuck . . . ?" Moth ducked as a half-pecked apple landed on the canoe.

"Are there kids in the woods?"

"Can't see any. I think you'd hear them, wouldn't you? Birds maybe."

"What were you saying about undisturbed?"

We followed the retreating tide to a narrow channel between the mudflats and paddled quietly away. No sounds of humans, or boats, just the push of paddle against water and the knocking of half-pecked apples against the side of the canoe as they floated downstream on the tide.

We left our wet clothes at the door of the chapel as the rain stopped and the sun appeared. Wrapped in towels as the kettle boiled, I checked my mobile: a voicemail from a London number.

"Hi, I've read the whole manuscript now and I'd love to have a conversation. When would be a good time to call?"

15. Air

I stood at the door of the chapel and signed for the parcel, a heavy box that I took inside and put on the table. I sat and looked at it, running my hands over the square cardboard, over the address label with its place of origin printed on the top and the logo in the corner. The kettle boiled and I made tea, then I sat with my knees pulled up on the wooden chair. I could open it now, get the contents out, feel each one, hold it, smell it. Or I could just sit and wait until Moth came back and share the moment with him. Through the window the snowdrops had returned to the neighbor's garden and the magnolia buds were full and ready to open. He'd taken his shed down at the weekend and if I sat on the worktop by the window I could now see between the roofs, to a glimpse of trees in the far distance. I ate a Rich Tea biscuit and waited, the box seeming to grow in size as I watched it. I moved to the worktop, resting my feet on the chair. The box and the trees in one view, the tea steaming between.

Months had passed since I'd walked out of the underground station at Covent Garden in London. Taken the short walk to the Strand, so nervous that I'd struggled to put one foot in front of another or think in a straight line. I'd stood outside a stone archway that led to a gleaming building of glass and steel. So many people, so little sky, I could barely breathe. Our path had led us through the pain and despair of loss to wet nights on foggy headlands—and now to me standing suffocating in front of this glass door. The literary agent pushed it open and waited for me to go through toward the huge picture of a penguin above the reception desk.

"Don't worry, it's just going to be an informal chat with the commissioning editor." The small, elegant woman in a smart blouse and heels made me feel huge, frumpy and inadequate. "You scrub up well" wouldn't be something anyone would ever say to me. I put my hand to my hair, expecting to find twigs and blades of grass—no, just the normal frizzy uncontrollable bird's nest that had never really recovered from our months in the wild. I took a deep breath of stale office air, a deep breath of life, of death and all the complex emotions that brought with it. As we sat on the couch and waited for the editor to come downstairs to meet us, I picked quietly at the blue cloth of the bench seating, startled by a memory of Moth pushing a piece of white fluff around the table as the judge had delivered his verdict and served us with the eviction notice. There was nothing to lose, so nothing to fear. Why then was I so nervous? We'd lost just about every material thing we'd owned and still survived. If I blew the meeting, as I expected to, and Penguin decided they didn't want to publish my book, then what would I have lost? Nothing. Life would be the same, death would still be waiting in the wings and nothing would have changed. Books by famous authors lined the bookshelves, authors who had sat on my own bookshelves, in the days when I had bookshelves. A sharp flash of memory of a life before I had to give away boxes of books and leave the shelves behind. Loss sets you free. In the empty void it leaves, anything can happen. Something from nothing.

We followed the young commissioning editor upstairs to the door of a small room. She paused with her hand on the door.

"We thought it would be easier if we all met you today."

Too late to run now, the door opened on to a round table and four people seated around it, with a life-size poster of Jamie Oliver framed on the wall behind them. There should have been a clear sky beyond the window of the office, but I didn't see it. I was standing at the Lizard Point lighthouse as hundreds of swallows massed, ready to push off from the land and take to the air. Instinctively drawn to the sky, heading south to warmth and food. My head spun with the swooping surety of their flight. No doubt or hesitation, they knew what they had to do. Trust without question or belief, trust as basic and complex as just being. We'd stood at that lighthouse, at the most southerly point on the land, as the wind carried our past away and left us stripped of the weight of our history. We'd turned north and I'd followed Moth's heels on the dusty track away from the past and into the future, trusting only each other and an instinct that told us the path would lead us forward.

A small, beautiful woman seemed to control the room with an easy elegance.

"Have you ever been in a publishing house before? Well, to put you at your ease before we get started, I just want to say we love your book and we'd like to publish it. But you'll have to change that title."

A thousand swallows lifted into the warm wind, into autumn sunlight reflected from outstretched wings the color of midnight skies. As the air cooled and the number of insects lessened the birds simply faced south and let go of the land. Disappeared into the white light of distance. Beyond hope or faith. Instinct is our word, not theirs: they simply spread their wings and trust the air.

It had been months since that moment, months of waiting for the box to come. Finally I heard the iron gate creak and seconds later Moth was back.

"Hi, you're here, how's your day been?"

"Not the best. I've had a strange sensation in my head and neck, as if there's a huge weight pressing me down."

Moth was struggling through the final few months of uni.

A huge and beautiful honors project grew on the table he used as a desk on the tiny landing at the top of the stairs. Large folders of work piled around him and he slowly shrank under the weight of them. As time ran out to get it all finished he was walking less and less. Time running out in so many ways.

"Wow, what's that? Oh, is that it?"

"It has to be. I've just sat with it. I didn't want to open it 'til you were here."

"Well, get the scissors! How have you waited? I wouldn't have been able to resist it."

"You open it. I don't know if I can."

"Don't be ridiculous. Get the scissors and we'll do it together."

As the box opened birds lifted into flight through bright skies, a peregrine swooped over the headland, dolphins swam in wild seas and two figures stood alone on a cliff top, the wind in their hair and hoped.

As I slowly opened the first copy of the book with its new title *The Salt Path*, swallows flew through the endpapers and salt water rolled down my face.

"Look." Moth held a book open on the copyright page. "Look, you've done it." I let my hand hover over the picture of a penguin and it was the hand of a small girl dreaming. A life yet to live before that dream could be realized.

"We did it."

"No, you did it; they're your words."

"But it was our path."

Copies of *The Salt Path* found their way on to the shelves of bookshops across the country as Moth finished his final pieces of work and walked out of the university building for the last time. Weeks later his phone began to buzz with messages from other students from his uni course who'd passed their degrees. They were celebrating their results, but Moth's letter didn't arrive.

"Perhaps it's just lost in the post. Maybe you should call your tutor?"

"No, it's because I've failed."

"If you'd failed you'd still have a letter."

"If I failed I can't go on to teach. I don't actually think I can spend time working on a screen anymore anyway. It's my eyes—doing the computer work in ten-minute stretches is impossible. I know we've said from the day I signed up for the degree that I'd teach, but I think this CBD thing has gone too far now."

We were sitting under the shade of old oak trees hung with lichen that thrived in the clear salt air blowing up the estuary. Every week we followed the Hall Walk as it wound through the trees from Polruan, across the wooden footbridge over the river at Pont Pill, where huge fish swam on the high tide, to the car ferry at Bodinnick. We'd walked in rain and wind with mud above our ankles, past a scattering of snowdrops, through a woodland floor blanketed in bluebells, then hundreds of holidaymakers, to today, a quieter day of hot sun through shady branches. Leaves on the woodland floor crunched in my hand, parched dry, last year's leaves lying dead on the ground beneath the shade of the new growth. Leaning against a tree trunk I could only feel relief. The studying had drained him in every way, but he'd fought through every difficulty to get to the end. Maybe now it was over he could spend more days like this, just moving in a green space, just being. I hung on to every thread of hope as his thoughts slipped and his body stumbled. Slowly, slowly he was eroding, like earth washed from the riverbank in heavy rain, leaving only the roots of him grasping for a secure hold on a slippery rocky surface. His tree about to fall.

"I know, you can't put all that pressure on yourself anymore. We'll have to find another way forward. Who knows, we might sell a few copies of the book, enough to get us through the year and give us time to work out what's next."

Moth's phone was ringing again. More people celebrating?

"It's my tutor." He turned the phone on to speaker, pale and still. Years of work waiting for an outcome.

"Moth, just wondering how you are? You didn't come in for your results the other day, so I thought I better check you're okay. Would you like me to post the letter?"

"I didn't know, I thought they came in the post anyway, thought they hadn't come because I've failed."

"No, you were far too good to fail; of course you've passed."

The call ended and he shakily put the phone back in his pocket.

"I've passed. Can't believe I've passed."

"Never doubted it. We should celebrate." As we walked out into the bright light between the trees, the color was returning to his face. "Can't believe it: Mothman, BSc. So, *so* proud of you. Definitely should celebrate."

"Oh yeah, like a real student. Cup of tea in Fowey then?"

"And one of those great little Portuguese tarts."

"Absolutely, rebel student."

There seems to be no sleep as deep as a neurodegenerative sleep, or at least in Moth's strange and elusive version of CBD. He'd made it to the end of his degree, exhausted, stiff, with pain in his arm and leg and a headache that never left. But now that the pressure of the work was over, all he wanted to do was sleep. Twelve hours a night and he was still tired. So why had I thought that a meditation class would help? Put a tired person in a chair and tell them to close their eyes and be quiet and what are they going to do? Sleep, obviously, but snoring—he could have kept that to himself; it's such a giveaway. I coughed loudly and the snoring stopped. I couldn't meditate, the snore had crept into my space and I was back in the room. I'd tried meditating on the question of what else we could possibly do to halt this rapid decline in Moth's health, but nothing came. The science pointed to the need for vigorous exercise and the natural environment. Both impossible when half of his days were spent sleeping and we lived on a concrete path. We needed to walk again, a long, long walk, but he didn't have the strength to carry his rucksack. Or somewhere to live where he could be on the land, connected to the earth, somewhere green. But that was impossible; we still had a poor credit history from having lost our home, and we were living on the tail end of a student loan and an advance on the book. Not exactly words that any landlord wanted to hear. We were so glad to have the roof we had after our months without a home, and beyond grateful to our landlady for giving us shelter, but we were stuck in an inescapable position while Moth slipped further out of reach. Each afternoon I bullied him into walking, hating myself for the words, driving a wedge between us as I tried to force him forward. I loathed it, but for all the pain it cost, two miles wasn't far enough. It cleared his head, eased the stiffness, but he needed more, so much more. Meditation certainly wasn't helping either, just stiffening his neck further as he sat in the chair. What was I doing? I wanted to cry, and not from the ecstasy of reaching a Zen state.

I glanced around the room. Everyone was perfectly still, eyes closed, minds clear of thought. Simon slowly raised his head from his chest. Calm and precise as ever, he unfolded his hands.

"And slowly allow yourselves to come back to the room in your own time. But remember the saying of the great Buddha: opportunity knocks, but karma tracks you down."

A few weeks into meditation classes and I wasn't too sure if any of the group actually meditated. I struggled, Moth dozed, I couldn't imagine Gill keeping her mind still for thirty minutes and Simon obviously spent the time thinking up Buddha jokes. Only Marion seemed to find peace, drifting into a deep sleep before we'd all sat down and usually waking just in time for tea.

We were all back in the room now. Sarah stretched out of her chair with an easy grace that made me think of ripe barley moving in the wind. I watched her put the kettle on, finding it hard to believe she was close to her sixtieth birthday.

"When do you start the publicity tour?" She put the tea on the table and all eyes turned to me; I shuffled uncomfortably in my seat. I didn't talk much, but had finally found a way to share a space with people and have brief conversations without being overwhelmed by panic. Gill and Simon sat down on the bench opposite, their body language beyond doubt. Two single people, no ties, no family to concern themselves about. Why were they hiding?

"Really soon. I'm trying not to think about it." I could tell from the furtive exchange of looks that they doubted my ability to sit on a stage and talk to people about my book as much as I did.

"And what about social media, have they asked you to do that?"

"Yes, Twitter and other stuff. I've never even looked at Twitter, I don't really get what it's all for."

"It's about connection, connections with other people. It helps spread the word about your book."

"But they're total strangers; I don't know anything about them. How can you trust people not to be really negative and just make it less likely for you to sell books?"

"Well, Moth hardly knows us, but he trusts us enough to fall asleep when he's supposed to be meditating. Sometimes you just need to do that."

"It's not always that easy, Sarah." Gill sat upright; her manner had changed. "When your trust has been betrayed in the past, it can be traumatic. It's almost impossible to regain it, or to give it again freely." She moved slightly on the bench, a little closer to the door. "Trauma can change you, whether it's losing your house, getting divorced or just being betrayed by someone. It's all the same: it leaves a scar."

"Maybe so, but sometimes you just have to jump. Forget the past and just jump. Biscuit, anyone?" Sarah held out a plate.

"As I said, it's not always that easy, Sarah. Sometimes the hardest person to trust is yourself." Gill was putting her shoes back on, preparing to leave.

"Oh Gill, it's always that easy. Ray, you just have to gather it all up and take that leap. Get on that stage and believe in your book. It's not about you, it's all about the book."

"I don't think that'll work—the book is about me, about Moth. It's all about us."

"Who cares, just jump anyway."

PART THREE

Beyond the Willows

When we try to pick out anything by itself, we find it hitched to everything else in the universe.

My First Summer in the Sierra, John Muir

Loud,

in a whisper so obvious I've always known,
in words I've always been able to hear.

The answer
was always there.

16. Jump

Fear has gripped me and I can't do it. I look down at my feet in my black plimsolls, heavy on the last hay bale. A taste of metallic panic fills my throat; my chest flutters with quick breaths. Fear. Air from the void rises cool against my sweat-damp body and I feel the vast emptiness of its space. Sounds carry up: children shouting, laughing. Laughing at me.

"Jump, jump, jump."

I drag my feet away from the edge and catch my heel on the baler twine, taut around the dried grass. Fear explodes in a fizzing stab as I close my eyes and fall backward. The sound of their mocking is farther away but I'm still on the hay. Lying on my back on the hard surface of tightly bound bales, sun-hardened grass, lady's bedstraw, thistles and meadow buttercup scratch at my skin. The rush of fear subsides and my breathing slows in the dense, deep, citrus-thickened air. The familiar arc of the barn roof is close, closer than I've seen it before. Eight years old, but I've never been this high, up among the beams that hold the curve, where a spider closes its web in the corrugated zinc. Slowly, methodically. Heat rises from the hay and meets the sun burning on the zinc, muffling the voices below. I'll stay here, alone, safe. Sparrows squabble and hassle, fluttering noisily around the nest. They left it weeks ago, but still return to perch and argue. I know he's behind me, I can feel his presence. I knew he lived here but I've never been this high, so close to his space. The forbidden place I know I should never come to, but I'm here. The small hay bales have been stacked high into this end of the roof space, but tier down in steps on one side to allow the men to climb to the top and catch each bale as it's sent up on an electric elevator. By the end of this hot, dry summer the barn will be full and tinder dry. To the side of the steps is a wall of hay, a sheer drop to the ground twenty meters below. My cousins are there, waiting for me, by the pile of hay bales we've broken up to make a soft landing spot—hay to cushion the fall. They've jumped already, throwing themselves off without hesitation or thought; now they're standing in the bright sunlight. But I am held here, held back. A barrier of fear like a glass wall. Fear of falling, of landing, of being caught out, of recrimination.

I've seen him skimming the hedgerows at dusk, buff, white and silent, but in this dimly lit space he's gray. His eyes seem closed, but I sense he's looking. Still, motionless in the farthest corner of the barn roof, his feathers sleek and folded. He holds his space here through the daylight hours, but as night falls he'll be gone, out through the fields and scrub. His head moves quickly to the side, drawn by the call of a coot on the pond, then returns slowly, eyes wide and round, fixed on me. I know the coots. I've sat at the edge of the stream among the willows and watched them in their nest. Piles of twigs in the reeds keep the sitting hen just above the water until the eggs hatch and the tiny gray balls fall from the nest into the water, their red heads shaking in wet surprise. Stretched on the willow branches through endless summers, I've seen their pink faces slowly fade and blend with their beaks into the broad white stripe of adulthood. Now, hearing them call, I know they're startled, their stiff gray legs splashing from the shallows to the safety of the deeper water. But as my gaze meets his I realize I don't know him at all; he's a stranger to me.

"Where are you? Wimp, wimp."

"She won't do it."

Their voices are muffled and I let them drift and be hidden by the sound of the stream as it gathers speed down a short waterfall and rushes into the culvert. The deep dark brick tunnel takes the stream under the pigsties, gaining pace as it goes until it explodes into a wide channel through the privet thicket. Another forbidden place, but one I know well.

"Just do it, jump, jump, jump."

Breaking away from the barn owl, I stand up and shuffle back to the edge. The warm wind ruffles my T-shirt and I lift my arms to feel its cooling touch. I rode the culvert with my cousins and they didn't find out, so maybe . . .

I hear my dad's boots before I see him, hobnails on the stones of the stackyard, and I see the rest of the summer holiday stretch before me. Not the short sharp moment of discipline that will be his response, but the days, the weeks of Mum's silent reproach. Her disappointment.

"What you doing, you buggers? You. Get down from there. Now."

There's nothing to lose. Jump or don't jump: the outcome will be the same.

My knees bend and my arms stretch forward, pushing the air past me. As my feet break free of the hay I feel the bird is with me. The tip of his wing brushes my arm as he swoops beneath the beams and out into the fields. The air rushes and time stands still. The barn owl glides beyond the willow trees and I am flying with him.

Free of fear. Free flight.

17. Land

"I don't know why you're asking me, my phone's only for texts and calls, how would I know? Ask Tom, he'll get it." Moth was sitting up in bed, drinking a cup of tea I'd taken him when I realized he was still asleep at eleven thirty.

"Hi, Tom, I can't do this Twitter thing. It's driving me mad. Help me . . ."

"It's easy, but only follow someone back if you want to, if they have things to say that you want to read."

"So who?"

"I don't know—anyone! Who have you got there?"

"What about this man? I think he lives up the river and he seems to have read the book."

"Okay, why not, follow him."

I followed him and hours later received a direct message: "I read your book and loved it, are you still in Cornwall? I have an old beef and sheep farm that makes cider. If you're still in Cornwall I'd love to have a chat, can I call you?"

"Mum, what are you thinking of; you don't just give people your phone number."

"I know, I know I shouldn't have, I feel such an idiot. But there was just something . . . I don't know, do you think I should block the number?"

"No, you've done it now. Just wait and see what he wants."

We stood on the brow of a hill, on a patch of land that had been burned rock-hard in a summer hotter than anyone could remember. The land fell away to the river, where boats drifted on the high tide and light reflected in a white ribbon through the trees on its banks. But up on the hillside there was no water, no green. The scorched earth spread along a broad ridge, grass grazed to soil height by cattle and sheep in every field. As the grass had dried up the confined animals had been driven to eat the hedges and scratch away at the soil beneath in an attempt to find shelter from the burning sun. What could have been lush green hedges, thick barriers between fields and highways for wildlife, were now no more than stark woody stems with sparse patches of shriveled leaves, the roots exposed to the drying air. The earth in submission.

"They've started feeding silage—winter fodder crops—in midsummer. But it's not just here. Farmers can just about hold these high livestock levels in a normal damp summer, but when there's just a slight shift in temperature this is what you get. It's like this right across the south this year: overstocking—and the fields can't take it. But I'm heartbroken to see it here." Sam gestured animatedly across the fields with his hand. A man whose hands appeared never to have seen dirt, or caught the fleece of a ewe thick with lanolin, or laid a hedge. The clean soft hands of an office worker. "It's not as if I don't understand the land. My parents are farmers, I grew up on a farm, across the border in Devon, but we don't farm like this. This is just the use of the land for profit with no concern for its future. I work in the City, always have, so profit and loss is my business. But if you sell out your capital base you've got nothing left to build on and environmentally that's what's happening here. I can't just sit by and watch it anymore." He pushed his hand through his hair and adjusted his designer sunglasses.

I caught Moth's eye. A silent expression of "What are we doing here?" What *were* we doing there? It was hard to say, but I'd known Twitter would cause me a problem, and now here we were. Standing on an unfamiliar, tinder-dry hillside as a result of dabbling with phone apps that I didn't understand.

The burned hill curved up and away from the river to the broad ridge and on the opposite side fell into a quiet sloping valley, with a narrow single-track road running through. Sheep grazed every corner of the land. On the side of the road was a farmhouse that stood opposite a ramshackle zinc shed, held up with old telegraph poles and string.

"This is my passion, this is why I bought the place." Sam gestured toward some scrubby trees that followed the contours of the valley. "Not just for the land itself, but for the orchard. It took thirty years of work in the City, thirty years of waiting to be able to buy this place." Almost imperceptibly the City boy began to slip and somewhere behind the façade was a flicker of something real. Something of the earth. Something I understood.

"I think these trees are special, they're so old and gnarled; supposedly there have been apples here for centuries. I think the history of the connection of man and cider-making here, with these trees, is extraordinary. That coupled with this amazing landscape of the hill going over to the river. Through all those years in the City this was always the dream: that one day I would be able to buy my own farm, to come back to the land and return to my roots. Now I have, and it's here. There are days when the City's too gray and I feel the need for the countryside like an itch I can't scratch; on those days sometimes just knowing the farm is here is enough to get me through. But it's not how I imagined it would be. There are so many problems here—and I can't fix them."

"I don't understand: if it's your dream place why don't you live here?" I looked across the farm, at the dried grass shimmering in the heat haze. This man made no sense. I was back on the path, walking homelessly past empty summer cabins stretched along Hayle Beach. Huts locked up for the winter while their owners returned to another life elsewhere. If he needed a connection to the land so much, then why wasn't he here? Nothing would have kept me away.

"Don't get me wrong, I desperately wanted to live here. My family were excited; we were making the preparations. But then, well, it was my wife."

"What do you mean? Did she change her mind?"

"No. She was diagnosed with breast cancer. It changed everything. The treatment takes time, then the recovery even longer, and we couldn't move while she was ill, so I continued to rent out the farm. And time passes, your focus moves elsewhere and your children grow up without you realizing. By the time Rachel was well, it was too late. The children are heading toward GCSEs; I can't move them from their school, not now."

"So will you move here when the children finish school?"

"No, not that soon. I don't really know when, certainly not in the foreseeable future. Rachel and the children are too settled and happy. If I could just make things work here, then that would be enough for now."

Beyond the broken barn, filled six feet high with years of animal dung and surrounded by metal storage containers, broken machinery and piles of every kind of plastic farm detritus, were more vast corrugated zinc barns filled with straw and animal waste. And between them, piled almost as high as the barn roofs, was manure. A huge stinking pile, running into pools of brown liquid that stood around the barns despite the heat evaporating every other drop of water from the farm. Tom had been right: I probably shouldn't have given him my number. Why had he asked us here anyway? We couldn't advise him about local contractors to clean up the mess.

"The problems have become almost overwhelming. I'd got to the point where I was preparing to sell." His feet shuffled in the dust as he pushed his sunglasses closer to his face and looked down to the creek. "But just the thought of letting it go was almost unbearable. If I sell the farm, I let go of the dream of returning to the land and I just can't do that. That's why I loved *The Salt Path* so much. I read it and knew immediately that you were the ones, you would understand."

There was a still quietness to the room, a silence of age and dust. A small room lined with books and Bibles, a rack of foldable chairs and piles of boxes filled with unused advertising for events long past. Two women sat in the room, calmly chatting about someone they both knew, completely unmoved by what was happening in the huge space beyond the door. How could they act as if this was totally normal when I could hardly breathe? I stumbled to the door, knocking over the rack of chairs, my sweaty hand slipping on the brass door knob. I was out, air at last, but where could I go? The toilet opposite: my only escape route. I slammed the door shut and locked the cubicle door. Just breathe.

The stone church in the Devonshire seaside town was vast. If only I'd come in through the back door, then I wouldn't have seen the endless rows of chairs seating over four hundred people and maybe I wouldn't have locked myself in the toilet. I hadn't been to the town for years. The last time I was here I'd been homeless, following the path as it leads up from the shingle beach and out of town. But the night before, as Moth and I had leaned out of the window of a hotel provided by the festival and watched people walk along the path in the dying light, it had felt as if it was only days ago. I could still smell the red earth as it stained the sea, lighting the seafront in a rust-colored glow. We'd been hungry then, tired, cold and desperate to find some-where to camp as the night closed in, so we'd climbed the fence on to the golf course to the only flat spot around. The sixteenth hole. The next morning we had watched the sun rise, reflecting light from the red cliffs through a heavy sea mist, turning the air pink in an otherworldly glow as the greenkeeper and his dogs had stood accusingly on the course, keen to ensure we left before the golfers arrived. That morning felt more real to me now than the warm bed, hot water and free breakfast of this one. It was still close, present, urgent, the vibrations of the landslip we'd heard that night still rumbling. Oh no—what if the greenkeeper was here?

Five minutes to go. A hum of voices rose outside the door.

I unlocked the cubicle and leaned over the sink, splashing water on my face, forgetting that I'd rashly applied rarely worn mascara. I pictured Moth sitting on the front row, waiting calmly for me to come out, and tried to breathe. Maybe the room wouldn't be full? They'd probably put me in the wrong venue and only a few seats would be filled. My breathing slowed, but the mirror still reflected a pale, panic-stricken face, streaked with black. I tried to wash the mascara off but it wouldn't move and I rummaged in my bag for something that would get rid of it. Lip salve. I covered my cheeks with the greasy Vaseline, like a rugby player preparing for the scrum. As I wiped it off my mobile signaled the arrival of a message. Sam. Again. "Have you had a chance to think about it?"

How could I think about it? To even consider what he'd said would require a leap of faith that we couldn't make. It would require trust, which was something we might never be able to feel again. We would need to put the past behind us, walk away from the memory of where trust had led us before and hope this would be different. But we couldn't do that: simply let go of the memory—the scars were too deep, too permanent. We could never forget. Yet Moth was sitting on the front row, tired, forgetful, slipping quietly into the shadows of his life. He needed air, and wind, wild skies and purpose. He needed to spend his days moving in green spaces. He needed the natural world to wrap him in the green cloak of belonging and help him back to the strength he'd found on the path.

Two minutes to go. The hum was growing into a loud echo around the cavernous roof space. That was it, there were just a few people but the noise was echoing.

Back in the vestry the women were on their feet, waiting.

"Where have you been? It's time to go on."

"I just needed to get some air. Are you ready? Shall we do this?"

The valley curved in a falling arc, the shape of an inverted teardrop, sloping downhill toward the creek. On one side of a newly planted section of orchard I could hear a stream, somewhere behind brambles, scrub and curled wire. Hear it but not see it. The sound of movement, the cycle of water. From land to sea and sky and back to the land. Full circle.

"This is supposed to be one of the places that gave Kenneth Grahame the inspiration for *Wind in the Willows*. Look at this old book." Sam took a copy of *Beyond the Wild Wood* from his bag, a book about the author's life. "I bought this from a charity shop years ago because I loved the picture—it's the creek, and there in the background is the highest field on the farm. I couldn't have imagined then that I would eventually own this place. Like I said, it's a dream."

It did have a picture of a very similar place on the cover. Behind his back I caught Moth raising his eyebrows. Who was this man, and why were we there with him?

"But things haven't gone as I hoped since I bought the farm. No one's understood my vision for the place. Nothing's worked. Then I read your book."

What did he want? The hot, airless wind moved the leaves on the trees as a huge buzzard held the thermal above the valley, drifting, drifting, until he fell into a smooth glide and was gone over the hilltop.

"So say no if your life's already on track for something else, or you just think I'm plain mad. But would you like to come and live here? Help return this special place to what it should be. Put the nature back into this battered landscape and the wildlife back in its hedgerows. Live here, make it your home. Manage my vision for the place: a biodiverse farm that still keeps a few sheep and makes cider, but puts the environment first. Can you help make it happen? What do you think?"

What did we think? We couldn't think, but sat in the sun-burned grass. There was a silence in the air, no bird calls, or insects buzzing, not even the gentle rustle of the seed heads of grass moving in the wind. Just a hot, still, wild silence. The silence of an empty land where no wild thing lived. Below us lambs were penned under the apple trees, confined by metal hurdles into a corral of dry earth, the grass eaten away to stone and tree roots. Fleeces brown with dry soil, they scratched at the fence, hungry, waiting for food to come. The buzzard had circled the hill and appeared out of the sky behind us, weaving his way down the valley, his long plaintive call filling the silent empty landscape. What did we think?

"Do you mean you want to rewild the farm?"

Rewilding can be a divisive term in farming circles. Most people take it to mean leaving nature to its own devices, opening the gates and allowing free roaming herbivores—domestic and wild. Many farmers see it as something pursued by conservationists and tree-huggers, a way of land use that leaves no room for enough food production to feed the country and hardly any profit for the farmer. But biodiversity can be returned in a way that balances the argument, by cutting the pesticides to only emergency use, not using nitrate fertilizers and reducing stocking levels, you can still produce food *and* allow biodiversity to return at the same time. It's like rewilding-lite, the best of both worlds, but unfortunately without a catchy term like rewilding.

"No, not to totally rewild it per se, more a case of keeping the rewilding gate open and nodding in that direction."

"Okay, so something more like restoration, restorative farming?"

"That's it, that's it exactly."

We didn't know him, or anything about him. This could be the most amazing offer, or the wandering thoughts of a madman. He'd obviously read something about us online, he'd read the book, he could have any number of ulterior motives. No, we were safe at the back of the chapel, hidden, dark, quiet, *safe*. But the earth was warm beneath my hands, the short grass sharp, brittle and smelling like hay. The dark, musty, deep-sweet smell of the hay barn of my childhood. And for a moment I felt my feet catch against the baler twine and the wind begin to ripple my shirt. No. No. No. We'd learned so much, lost so much; we would never allow ourselves to trust anyone again. How could we? I looked over at Moth, hunched, dizzy, forgetful. He needed a wild green life, but not stress, or complexity, or problems. Just the simplicity of a life in nature.

"We'd have to think about it."

"Of course, but I just know you're the right people for this place. I feel as if this was meant to be."

The bright white lights were pointing straight at the stage, so dazzling I could barely see beyond the first two rows. But through the dimly lit sides of the church, behind the columns, I could see full seats all the way to the back. I tried not to look and kept my focus on the woman asking the questions. A strange jumping, pounding sensation in my chest distracted me and I stumbled over the answers. The other author was talking, but as I sat under the spotlights my mind ran in panicking circles. My phone was on silent, but still vibrating in my pocket. Him again. I knew it was him. Stop calling, I don't know what I think, how can I possibly tell you what I think, especially when I'm in this alien place, dazzled by the interrogation lights. I suddenly realized why Bono always wears sunglasses and my thoughts disappeared down a rabbit hole of U2 songs, my mind running like a river to the sea.

"Ray, would you like to read an extract from your book? Ray, Ray?"

Even Bono's sunglasses didn't stop my hands trembling on the pages, but as I started to read a strange calmness descended. Trust the words, trust the path, it's got you this far. And as I read on, I wasn't on the stage, but back on the beach as the tide rushed in, breaking over the sand shelf, racing toward the tent. Moth running through the soft sand in his underpants carrying the tent above his head, and there was laughter, and possibility. As I looked around the audience they were there too; they'd run up the beach with me. We'd all put the tent down at the foot of the cliffs together, and there was hope, and a future, and life still to be lived. I knew I wanted to say yes. Yes, Sam, absolutely yes. But that's rash and foolish and learning nothing from hindsight. Hadn't we learned that nothing can ever be that simple, that no one's to be trusted, that there'll always be a problem waiting in the wings, waiting to catch you out when you're off your guard?

"Well, it's been so nice listening to you both talk about your books, but I think it's time to turn to our lovely large audience. Does anyone have any questions?"

As the lights dimmed the crowd came into view and I could see him, beyond Moth, standing by the column. The greenkeeper.

"So, I'd like to talk to you about camping on the golf course . . ."

18. One Deer Passing

As we took the photo it captured our outlines reflected in the bookshop window, behind us the shops on the opposite side of the cobbled street and above, in a blue sky, the spires of Truro Cathedral. But as we took it we saw none of that. All we saw was a pile of pale blue books with swallows flying from their spines and a hand-drawn poster with quotes from the book. My words written among drawings of waves and gulls and draped in bunting. Dolphins and birds hanging on triangles attached to blue ribbon.

"Can you believe this?"

"No, not at all. Don't you think the picture on the cover looks just like that spot where we camped at Land's End?"

"It really does. Who'd have thought, when we put the tent up that night at the end of that horrendously wet day, that a few years later we'd be standing here?"

"Take another photo while I pose by the books."

"Shall we go upstairs to the café, have tea and a teacake to celebrate?"

We poured tea while people walked along the street below, still in T-shirts and shorts in unexpected early autumn warmth.

"You know if we say yes to this man, it'll be as if we haven't learned anything. Putting our stability back into the hands of someone else. And look where that got us before. Homeless." Moth scratched at his teacake with the thinnest smear of butter.

"But this isn't the same. We're not putting money into this, so what do we have to lose? Anyway, that's what renting is: you're only ever as safe as the landlord lets you be. We're on a rolling contract now, so any month Anna could give us our two months' notice and that's it, we're out. I'm sure she wouldn't, but things can change. So I don't think we can look at it from that angle." I buttered my teacake, using all of the small pot of butter. I've never understood why confusion makes me eat so much.

"That's true, but it's going to take a lot of work to clean the place up, before we even start any repairs, or consider how it could make a turnover, never mind a profit. And we could get the place back in shape, then he could ask us to leave."

"Can't stop thinking about the bunting in the window. When we were in that gale at Land's End we'd have given anything to be in this position. Trying to decide if we dare to give up one roof to go to another. I know it's a risk, and it could go wrong, but I think we should at least consider it." Clouds had moved in and people in the street were putting jumpers on. I shook the last dregs of tea from the pot. Despite my brave words, I feared Moth was right, as always.

"But the difference is, when we were at Land's End all we had was a Mars bar, so nothing to lose at all. Now we at least have an apartment and we can't walk away from that lightly. And Anna helped us when no one else would, so I feel a loyalty to her. But it's the land. I watched that buzzard as it held the air, almost caressing it as he followed the contour of the hill, and I wanted to be there more than anything else. But I can't let us be hurt so badly again, to put all our efforts into something then have it taken away. I couldn't go through that again. And I have to think of you. If my health carries on going downhill at this rate I won't be able to do any of the work—I don't know if I can now. And I have to just say it: if I die in the next few years you'd be left in a really difficult position."

"Don't say that, don't. I can't let that happen."

"Ray, we've been through this. Some things you can't control."

Umbrellas were being put up in the street, people rushing into shops, sheltering from the unexpected rain.

"I'm sorry I didn't have the key with me when we met, but I'll post it to you. Go and have a look around the house."

How much longer could we procrastinate before he gave up on us? We'd go back to the farm and look again, on our own, and see how we felt when we'd seen inside the house.

The sun was lowering on the horizon, the nights getting longer, but still the days hung on to their warmth. Standing out-side the farmhouse, the wind blew up over the abandoned orchards from the creek below. Before we went into the house we felt drawn to explore through the long grass and tangled branches. Monks had rowed to the shore of the creek centuries ago, getting out of their boats with sacks of grain and bottles of rum of unspecified origin, and storing them in the priory that had stood on the edge of the mudflats. A handful of men, living a strange and isolated religious existence in a wooded valley. And quite possibly planting apple trees. Sam had found reference to the farm being in cider production at the time of the signing of the Magna Carta: hundreds of years of apples being made into cider on this one spot. Quite possibly those monks, with very little to do with their days other than pray and fish, would have wandered up the sheltered valley and thought, What an ideal spot to plant apple trees. And hardly surprisingly, living such a quiet life by the water, their thoughts might have turned to cider. Some historians would say that cider was offered in exchange for illicit goods brought in by sea, and their monastic life was far from quiet. But that could just be a Cornish version of history. The priory is long gone and a Georgian house now stands on the site, but the history remains, and looking at the apple trees on that autumn afternoon, it seemed quite possible that some of them were actually the ones planted by the monks. Gnarled and filled with canker, branches weighed down and broken with ripe, unpicked apples. At least we knew the source of the mysterious falling apples in the river: not children in the woods at all, but crows collecting a feast from the orchard and carrying the fruits away, then, distracted as they crossed the creek, dropping their lunch on passing canoeists. Heading back to the house, we found one ancient tree stood out among the others, its roots broken and twisted, leaving the tree lying on the ground where it had clearly been for years. The branches on one side were dead and crushed in the waist-high grass, but the ones that remained growing stretched vertically up to the sky, hanging on to the last gasp of life, still reaching for the sun. And along the length of the fallen trunk was a scattering of perfectly symmetrical holes as if they had been bored out with an electric drill.

"That's weird. Someone practicing with their new drill maybe?"

"Or bugs? Some kind of wood-boring bugs?" We stared at the holes for a moment. "Enough of looking at bug holes. I can't wait any longer—shall we go and look inside?"

The house was built of a gray Cornish stone that looked like narrow blocks of flaky slate, but with two sides rendered and painted in the same peach I'd seen in lots of 1970s bathrooms. Although livestock would still be on the land for a few more weeks, Sam's plan to sell the farm had left the house standing empty, the doors locked and windows closed for months, so we held our breath as we turned the key. The plastic front door led into a peach corridor, lined with a wildly patterned carpet that oozed damp when we trod on it. In one of the main living rooms the plaster was cracked and hanging from the walls, held back only by layers of peach wallpaper; in the other there was a wood-burning stove and patchy rugs, with sodden, rotting cardboard underneath and water collecting in a pool in the corner. The kitchen was a brown box, brown tiles on the floors and the walls and only a tiny outside window, making it hard to see

anything in the early evening light. A corridor formed by sliding hardboard doors led out of the kitchen, hiding a stairway
and the entrance to another small room, where a small wood
burner stood out of the fireplace, attached to the wall by a piece
of flexible flue-liner that curved across the tiled floor and up the
chimney.

"So, why are we here? There's obviously been no one living
here for ages, but when there was . . ."

"When there was, they loved peach?"

"They really loved peach."

Upstairs the smell of damp was overwhelming, the carpets
clearly holding the wet air that rose from below. The damp had
collected at the highest point, leaving the Artex ceilings swathed
in black mold. The seal of the double-glazed plastic windows
had perished over time, turning the gap between the two layers
of glass into a trap for condensation, mold and dead flies.

"Jeez, I don't know if I can bear the smell up here." The pun-
gent smell of damp was burning my throat.

"Let's open the window, see if it makes a difference."

"It's going to take a lot more than fresh air to make this okay."

"You're right, this is grim." Moth hung his head out of the window, the plastic sash hanging over him like a guillotine. Could
this be a life sentence for anyone mad enough to accept Sam's
offer? "Oh wow, Ray, get your head out here and look at this."

I leaned out of the window next to him. Through the apple
trees, beyond the barns and heaps of cow-muck, was a view to
the creek. The late-afternoon sunshine caught the water, reflecting the autumn colors from the trees lining the banks. Then in
the distance, faintly, softly on the wind as it lifted, dry and cool,
carrying the sounds of the creek up the hillside and across the
quiet dead fields, the calls of oystercatchers on the mudflats.

"I bet you could almost see the curlews from here." A flicker
of possibility lit Moth's face.

"Maybe, if the grass was managed differently, the fields might become their feeding grounds."

"I don't know if you could get this grassland back to a state of biodiversity that would attract them. It might have gone too far."

"It would take a lot of work."

"Too much work for us."

We hung out of the window as the day cooled toward dusk. The house was becoming cold, intensifying the smell of dampness. A mist began to rise from the creek, creeping through the trees of the riverbank and following the valley up to the orchards. We gathered our things, preparing to head back to the chapel, but as Moth turned to close the window there was a movement in the hedgerow on the other side of the narrow road. Almost without sound a roe deer emerged on to the road and walked slowly and calmly in front of the house, along a path she clearly took every night. She hesitated at the edge of the stone yard, glanced around, checking she was alone, took a mouthful of short grass, then vanished into the tall vegetation, a mirage disappearing into the dusk. No other sounds. No roosting birds, no owls emerging to call across the valley, no blackbirds with their late-evening song. Just one deer passing into the night.

We closed the window, locked the door and drove back to the chapel. There was no need to speak, no need to examine the sanity of the choice. We'd been through the best and the worst of life together, had made choices that had turned out well and others that had been disasters. But we had reached a point where we understood that nothing was permanent, anything could or would change, that the only stability in life was my hand in Moth's and our children's voices on the phone, that risk only has meaning when there's something to lose. We stood outside the chapel on a cold evening, about to go down the dark concrete corridor to the door at the back, but our feet were shuffling on the warm soft hay of midsummer. Trust was still elusive, we might never find a way to truly trust other people again, but we had something bigger than that. The South West Coast Path had led us out of anguish and despair to a place of hope and possibility. And now, by walking it again on paper, *The Salt Path* had led us to the farm. Our feet stepped over the baler twine as a warm wind blew against our skin. We held hands, put our trust in the path and jumped.

19. Weasels

Fearful, nervous, excited, hopeful, unsure and yet definite, I took the pen from Sam and signed my name on the tenancy agreement. Did this finally mean that there was no doubt about where we would sleep next month, next year, that Moth wouldn't need to worry about homelessness entering his life again? I crossed my fingers and hoped that this would give him time to focus on the farm, put his degree into practice and create a sustainable project. Time for him to spend his days on the land and for me to watch and hope.

The house was oozing like a sponge, sucking up water when it was raining and squeezing it back out when it stopped. We couldn't move in immediately; we had to find a way of drying it out first.

"The carpets, we have to get rid of these stinking carpets."

Late October sun warmed the walls as we dragged the dripping rugs into a pile outside, peeling up pulpy cardboard from a lime floor that had no damp membrane. We lit the stove, roaring hot fires turning the room into a sauna as the floors steamed and the walls bubbled with damp that dried to a salty dust.

Peach wallpaper burned on a bonfire that smoldered for days, peach smoke spiraling over the valley. And still the floors steamed. Days passed as we scraped at wallpaper and scrubbed black mold from every crevice. Leaving the house every evening to collapse exhausted in the chapel, doubt creeping in with the dark nights. Finally, as everything that held the smell of wet fungus was stripped out, the floor began to dry. The windows were scrubbed and a plant stood by the gate. As we closed the door to return to the chapel there was a sense of maybe. Just maybe it could be possible.

I woke to the sound of the horn of the pilot boat as it guided a ship out of the mouth of the estuary. Cold in the early light, I put on a thick jumper and slippers and went downstairs to make tea. I checked my phone for the morning message from Rowan on her way to work, the normal start to the day. "Hi, Mum, I'm late but have a good day, call you later." Today there were two other messages. A small independent publisher of beautiful nature books telling me that they were republishing a series of classics with introductions by other writers. "I have a book which I'd love you to consider writing an introduction for. It's called *Copsford* by Walter J. C. Murray." My breath caught in my throat and I could smell antiseptic and mashed potato and nail varnish and hairspray and commodes and bleach and finality. I was on my knees, sobbing. Gasping in gulps of air in a flow of emotion rising from a box on which I'd kept the lid for so long I'd thought I was safe. I'd tightened down the screws of self-hate, and regret, and loss, and just undeniable, unquenchable sadness, to the very end of their thread, but now the lid blew, carried away by a storm-force wind of pain. Crawling under the blanket on the sofa I tried to swallow the hot tea, rocked by the unexpected gale that had blown through the morning. To write an introduction would mean rereading the book. Could I do that? Just the thought of the text took me straight back to the hospital. Was I strong enough to face that all over again? I drank the tea, then made another, shuddering with aftershocks.

One message remained. From Sam. As soon as I opened it I wished I hadn't. I closed my eyes and looked away, trying not to let the words find a space in my battered thoughts. But once they're in you can't take them back; the words are there. "Ray, so sorry to send this, but I thought I should tell you before you see it for yourself." I closed the phone. No, no more, please no more. But too late, the words were in. "There has been some vandalism at the house, a neighbor spotted it and called me. I don't think it's permanent, a pressure washer and some paint should put it right." I pulled the blanket back over my head and gave in to the spasms. It was all my fault. I had let Mum die; I'd sat there in the doctor's office and willfully let her go. And I'd dragged Moth to the farm, when we should have stayed at the chapel, safe, warm, dark, and just let it be. Let CBD take its own course and stopped pushing him forward; just let him be. Safe, warm, and slipping away. It was all too late; I'd ruined everything. I'd as good as signed Mum's death warrant, and in signing the tenancy agreement, I might as well have signed Moth's too. I put the kettle back on. I would have to tell him about the vandalism and he would say, "I told you we shouldn't have done it, it's all your fault." And he'd be right. I took the tea upstairs.

"Well, I don't know why you're so upset. We haven't seen it yet—it might not be that bad."

We saw the green before the red and it made us stop the van. At the top of the hill, on the rim of the valley, it was green. We hadn't spotted it on the dry sunny days, but that day, in rain that didn't fall but hit our faces with the force of a power shower as we got out of the van and walked into the field, it was green. The brown stubble had gone and a faint wispy growth of grass had emerged. Even in the autumn as the leaves on the hedges were changing color there was a simultaneous tentative regrowth on branches that had been stripped clean. After only two months with no human or animal interference, the land was moving again. Shaking off the shackles of overuse and standing up. It might be years before any sign of biodiversity returned to these overused fields, but if there was green there was hope.

If green signaled hope, then red should have been the signal to stop, turn around and go back to the chapel.

"Can you believe that?"

"What a mess. What sort of weasels would do a thing like that?"

"Weasels?"

Surely the fact that it had happened before we even moved in would be enough to get us out of the tenancy agreement. Across the peach-painted render, over the doors, obscuring the glass in the plastic-framed windows, covering the crazy-paved yard in front of the house, over the low wall that enclosed it: red paint. Sticky red car paint. Graffiti from a spray can, but definitely not a visit by Banksy. Then red paint of a different consistency running down the walls in the rain. Like the red stain from a can of antiseptic spray used for animals. On the front of the house, with a slight curve in a hopeful rather than expectant angle, a ten-foot-high dick. The artist must have stood on the small wall to create the masterpiece. But on the gable end facing the road, the artwork that felt like a body blow, in capital letters three feet high: "SCUM."

I picked up the broken pieces of the plant pot by the gate. The plant was nowhere to be seen; maybe someone had taken it home as a souvenir.

"Oh fuck, what a mess."

"Well, at least the dick's washing off in the rain." It was losing its height already, shriveling in the cold water.

"Wish I hadn't bothered cleaning the windows."

"Let's go in and make some tea. Think I might light the fire." Moth tried to turn the key in the lock but it wouldn't work. A dribble of glue had dried down the brown plastic.

"Little shits—they've glued the locks. Let's try the two at the back." An outhouse extension at the back of the building had two outside doors. The one facing the road wasn't brown but completely red, with a bulging bubble of dried glue encasing the keyhole. Facing the garden and hidden behind the shed, only one door left to try. The key turned and we went in.

The fire flickered out its heat and within an hour the floor began to gently steam. Two mugs of tea and a packet of fig rolls had been consumed with very little said.

"I had an e-mail this morning, asking me to write an introduction for *Copsford*. I don't know if I can. It feels so personal—I don't know if I can disconnect myself from it."

"Wow, that's a weird coincidence. But you were the one who thought every little coincidence on the path was a sign, so maybe that's what this is."

"A sign of what?"

"That enough time has passed and you have to deal with how you feel and move beyond it." Moth put another log on the fire and I put the kettle on for a third time.

"Scum—is that how people see us? I'm so sorry I encouraged you to come here. It's all my fault."

"What are you talking about? It's nobody's fault. Just stupid kids on a Saturday night: too many beers and they think the house is empty. Well, it is empty. Wish they'd left the glue at home though, that's really annoying."

"I'm sure this would be enough to get us out of the contract and just forget we ever saw the place."

"Don't be ridiculous. I'm going to get the sweeping brush and scrub it while it's still raining."

The stiff bristles bit into the red paint, taking the peach layers off with it, leaving the walls in patches of peach and bare render as the red washed down the road.

"That's got rid of the thin stuff. Don't know how we'll shift the rest—it's like a sticky lacquer."

"At least the dick's gone."

"Should have kept that, it was the best bit."

"But 'scum,' though. Someone must have read the book; they know we've been homeless. That's why it says 'scum' and now it won't wash off. I should never have let it be published. This is what happens when you let people see into your world. It's like the water voles."

"Ray, you know I love you, but sometimes I don't know what the fuck you're talking about. If it bothers you that much we'll scrape it off with the paper scrapers."

A wet hour later and the red paint was gone, leaving "scum" etched in bare render against the peach background.

"Okay, I'm done: my shoulder's killing me. If we'd got a bed here, I'd just go and lie down. I'll have to go back to the chapel now."

Moth and the land in submission. Both at their lowest ebb, just flickering pinpricks of light shining through an enveloping blanket of darkness. I stood beneath an apple tree as Moth switched off the lights and locked the door of the house. The rain had finally slowed to waves of heavy drizzle, blowing over the hill in banks of dark gray cloud rolling into the late afternoon. Water dripped through the last remaining leaves and dried cold against my skin in the high wind. Wet metal and plastic caught the fleeting shafts of low sunlight, piles of it everywhere, bent and twisted, grown through with brambles and nettles, leaking rust and oily residues into the poisoned ground. A group of sparrows squabbled over a few hawthorn berries in the tall, bare branches of the hedge as two crows flew in to roost in the top of a sweet chestnut tree. The ground beneath was littered with the spiky green balls of the nut cases, but inside them only tiny shriveled nuts. No food for birds or mice there. But in the orchards apples were falling into the waist-high grass, lost to humans but available to be eaten by whatever lived beneath the waving sea of brambles. The crows hung on tightly to the high branches of the tree. The only birds in the area that seemed to have found the rare feast offered by the apples, they held their ground, dancing with the high wind as it broke the mass of cloud into angry islands of gray, scudding furiously east.

We could get in the van, drive away and forget we'd seen this place, carry on as we were before. Walk a little when Moth felt able, wait and watch as his lights slowly went out. The obvious thing to do. But I could still hear it, the voice, whispering from a land that had suffered, muffled still but rising in green shoots of hope and falling with the apples ripe on the ground. A sound, a rhythm, a call. Strengthening in the wind as it swept over the hill, pushing down into the silence of the valley, a low tone behind it all. The sound of connection.

Moth walked slowly back to the van, stiff and awkward, tiredness forming in gray lines across his face. I got into the van next to him, the voice still humming its faint, quiet song.

"Shall we pick up a can of paint on the way over tomorrow?"

20. Rats

I opened *Copsford* again. With tea in my hand, I thumbed through the pages, ignoring the faint smell of disinfectant. Rereading familiar passages, looking for the real Murray hidden in the pages. I couldn't find him: the writing felt somehow empty, as if I was looking at a naturalistic painting by Constable. Accurate and perfect in so many ways, yet missing the true essence of life, the darker, harder, painful edges that you know are there, hidden under the sunlit branches and sparkling waters of *The Hay Wain*. I closed the book. What could I possibly say other than it was a portrait of a young man's experience of a year in the country?

Back in the farmhouse, scraping moldy wallpaper from the walls became a task without end. A seemingly pointless endeavor when so much of the house needed repair and heat to win the battle with the damp. But it was almost impossible to prioritize where to start with the problems the house presented.

"I think we should take out the hardboard walls and the sliding doors. If we rip them out and open up that room to what it would have been, take it back to the stone walls, it might help the air movement in that side of the house and get rid of some of the damp."

"Are you sure? Shouldn't I finish that wallpaper first?"

"There's so much to do it doesn't really make a difference, does it?"

Half a day of hammers, screwdrivers and a large bonfire pile later and we sat in a dusty empty space with an open staircase and exposed original banisters. Everything was still, the commotion had stopped, but somewhere in the house a faint noise of scratching continued.

"What is that?"

"You don't think we've dislodged a water pipe, do you? It could be a leak."

"No, listen, it's moving. It's gone into the other room."

We followed the noise, not just a scratching now, more a running of many tiny feet.

"What do you call a group of mice?"

"A herd, a flock . . .?"

"A lot of mice—no, a nest."

"That's not a nest; it's a whole village. Do you think we've disturbed them with all the banging?"

The hatch to the roof space was just a plank of plywood wedged in the hole into the loft. As we pushed it out of place a shower of mouse droppings fell into our hair and across the landing.

"No, not a village, a town of mice."

The tall airy roof space was hung with cobwebs; rolls of insulation were partly unfolded in patches across the center of the room. Two sparrows flew around in alarm and then out beneath the open eaves. A carpet of mouse droppings lay thick across the insulation, but the roof was silent. The mice had heard us coming and frozen on the spot, hiding in their pink fibrous nests. We retreated from the space, carefully replacing the plywood and dusting the tiny brown pellets from our hair.

"That's a lot of mice."

"What do we do about them?"

"I don't know. Check there's no way they can get into the house from the loft first, I think. Let's seal around the waterpipe holes, then make sure there's no other way in."

★

I stood on the railway platform in Par, waving to the train as it pulled away east, choking on tears like a child parted from its favorite toy. Moth's degree had consolidated a lifetime of knowledge, adding a layer of design skills that were now needed by an unexpected client two hundred miles away. We'd agonized for days over his decision to go. Could he make the journey alone? Would he remember where to go? Could he do the work when he got there? Should I go with him? He'd finally packed his bag and written out a list of train changes and phone numbers, addresses and names, deciding that if he couldn't do it alone he shouldn't do it at all. And now he was on the train, gone, out of reach already.

I headed back to the farm. Walking through the door, I realized it was the first time I'd been alone there and a strange damp-smelling sense of isolation hung over the place. Rooms that seemed full of possibility when Moth filled the space were now stripped of any veneer and displayed themselves for what they truly were. Cold, damp, dreary containers for mold. I wanted to leave, to return to the warm familiarity of the chapel, shut the door behind me and stay there until Moth returned. But I wasn't alone. They were here: running, scratching, scuttling through the roof space; the house was alive, or at least the roof was. I put my bag down and found some kindling to light the fire. I was far colder downstairs than the mice in the roof, cozy in their home in the pink insulation. The fire burst into flames as a cup of tea warmed my hands and the mice settled down for a nap—or the smoke from the leaking chimney sedated them; I wasn't sure which. I took the copy of *Copsford* from my bag, quietly turning the pages again, letting Walter's summer days in the hedgerows push aside the memories that the book held for me. There at last, in his early days in the cottage, before his forays into herb-collecting, I began to see something of who Walter really was; something of the grittier edge of the young man was hidden in his battle with the ruined house.

Entering Copsford for the first time, Murray describes a feeling of absolute isolation, a sense of the cottage rejecting him. He'd stood in the house, frozen by a deep loneliness that pervaded the ruined walls, unable to shake the feeling. I put another log on the fire. I couldn't let that happen here. No, while Moth was gone I would get a hold on my feelings of doubt about the move and strip everything from the house that felt unwelcoming. I wouldn't be Walter, in the icy grip of a house that seemed to resent our presence. But he'd had more to deal with than a roof full of cute but smelly mice. Copsford teemed with rats. Rats that climbed down the walls and out of the fireplace, that ran across his bed at night and lit the room with a thousand eyes reflected in his torchlight.

Dealing with a few mice shouldn't be a problem. We'd had a rat infestation on the farm when I was a child, rats that were invisible in the daylight but came out like a plague as soon as the light began to fade. Attracted by the grain stores full of wheat, oats and barley, they thrived in their thousands. Eating the corn, spoiling the animal feed, growing fat and lazy until they didn't bother to hide during the day but sat defiantly on the beams of the barns and watched. I followed at Dad's heels as he laid traps and rat poison, and then encouraged an army of cats to live in the grain barns. Yet still the rat population didn't reduce. Despite my protestations he became convinced that the rats came from the holes in the riverbanks and poisoned every furry thing that moved. He resorting to hunting them with an air rifle at night when they came out in hordes. Always by his side, I would shine the torch to target the rat while he shot and reloaded, and reloaded, and reloaded. Eventually his poisons became stronger and he laid them out in greater and greater quantities, until the rat numbers reduced along with some of the cats and a dog. So surely I could get rid of a family of mice?

Walter solved his problem by getting a dog. A borrowed dog

called Fluff who ended his rat invasion in a night of noise and bloody execution. That wouldn't solve my mouse problem, but neither would poison. We were aiming to increase the wild-life here, not poison it out of existence. There had to be another way. I replied to a message from Moth, reminding him where he'd put the list of train times. I had to do something, or I'd spend the next week checking my phone and worrying. I scraped more wallpaper until the light began to dim, finally heading out into the cold air and straight into the evening flight of the first owl I'd seen at the farm. His broad wingspan seemed to frame his pale round face as he flew straight toward me. The owls, of course! The answer was obvious: the mice just needed to be out-side. But how to get them there?

"I've almost made it through this, but I can't wait to get back on the train. I fell over this morning. I was surveying the final sec-tion of the garden, standing still on a patch of completely flat grass, and without warning I just fell over. I couldn't stop myself."

"Do you want me to come and pick you up? I'll leave now."

"No, I'll be okay. Anyway, I've got a return ticket. I'll be back tonight."

I sat on the small wall outside the house, suffocating in the silence. Not a breath of wind, or a bird call. Not a voice. Not his voice. This is how it would be without him, without his con-stant conversation and ideas and action. CBD was changing him. Not with the instant destruction of an illness that spread like wildfire, but with a slow loss of form and connectivity. Imperceptible until you compared him to how he was before. Less wildfire, more a slow, insidious, climate change of lost functions. His was becoming a flatter, emptier place. His body a world of hedges without birdlife, of rivers without fish and orchards without insects, as his tongue forgot how to taste and the feelings slipped from his hands. I shivered in the winter sun. I had no interest in a life without him providing the backing track. A silent void of existence.

I had a few hours before he came back; I couldn't spend it sitting on the wall waiting. No, I'd solve the mouse problem instead. Killing them wasn't the answer when raptors were outside in need of food; no, they just needed to be removed. I stood in the loft with the head torch and a face mask on. I could remove all of the insulation and shake them out, but that would probably result in them falling out as I went down the stairs, so filling the whole house with them instead of just the roof. I'd roll them out instead. Walking across each beam, I shook the previous piece of insulation on to the next, occasionally spotting a brown body falling on to the next layer of fiber, until I reached the final stretch. I dragged the end of it to the eave, pushing it out into the gutter, then rolled it from the other end, shaking it as it I went. Brown furry forms spilled out in all directions until the gutter was full of mice that slid to the downpipe and on down to the ground. I ran outside as nests of mice scattered across the grass and disappeared into the nettles. Smug that the mouse problem was solved without a granule of poison, I put the kettle on and went upstairs to the bathroom. The house was quiet again. Quiet, until a faint shuffle of tiny feet passed above my head. They were still there. Maybe we'd just have to learn to live with them. I found the silicon gun and resealed the holes around the water pipes. They could live in the roof, but nowhere else.

I tried again to find a way to write an introduction for *Copsford*, but there seemed no way in. Murray describes the young Walter as a believable, almost recognizable twenty-something, embracing an adventure as he tried to find a way to live in the ruined house. But when he moves on to Walter's new career collecting herbs to sell to manufacturers, and takes him into the fields and hedgerows, he gives the young man an almost spiritual quality as he flits through the countryside of post-war Sussex. A landscape where herbs, flowers and butterflies grow in abundance and peace and tranquility override all else. What was there to write about? I couldn't do this; there really was nothing of any depth to say. I could hardly write an introduction that said, "Walter was luckier than most because he barely saw the war, then he had a lovely time in the English countryside picking flowers."

I drove to the railway station with almost teenage excitement. Paced on the platform in anticipation until the train pulled in. There he was. For a moment I'd expected the young man who'd waited for me at the station the first time we'd been apart, when I'd been the one on the train willing it to go faster, to take me back to him a few seconds sooner. Who'd grabbed my hand as we ran from the station, vowing never to be apart again. But I couldn't see him.

Moth stepped from the train, tired, hunched, moving slowly and deliberately, his uneven walk more pronounced, his face gray and tired.

"I'm so, so glad you're back. Give me your bag."

"Am I actually here? I thought that journey would never end."

"Yep, it's you, you're definitely here. Let's get back to the chapel and put the kettle on." The young man who had held me so tightly that afternoon that I thought no air would ever pass between us again? He was still there. Somewhere.

"Let's not move into the farm until after Christmas. We're never going to get the place dry enough by then, so let's just enjoy Christmas with some heating and then move. Can we afford to pay two rents for another month?" Moth was exhausted after his journey; he needed to rest not move house.

"Just about." Suddenly this was feeling like the most ridiculous decision we could have made. When we'd signed the tenancy agreement we hadn't accounted for it taking us two months to clean the house and get rid of the damp. Two months of paying two rents. The advance on the book couldn't last forever and there was no way of knowing if the sales would increase, or if it would disappear into obscurity. "But by mid-January we have to be in. We can't do this for much longer."

"Good. I've had enough of painting—I'm going to strim. If I can remember how to get this started." Moth was fiddling with an old strimmer that we'd stored in a friend's barn, dusting off straw and cobwebs and refilling it with oil.

"How are you going to be able to use that? It's going to really hurt your shoulder."

"I don't know, but I'm going to try."

I walked away; I couldn't bear to watch. I went back inside to continue scraping wallpaper. The ring of an email arriving on my mobile broke through the familiar thrum of Moth trying to start a pull-motor that refused to work. The reluctant chugging noise that, if I closed my eyes, would take me straight back to our home in Wales and sunny afternoons when the beech trees were full of bees and swallows filled the air. I kept my eyes open and read the email.

"Hi, Ray, just wondering how the introduction for *Copsford* is coming along. It's going to print soon, so when you're ready . . ."

Had I absolutely agreed to do this? Somewhere in the confusion of book events and coming to the farm I'd obviously committed to it. But how could I? What could I possibly say? I'd recently bought a small, obscure biography of the life of Walter J. C. Murray; maybe if I actually read it I could find something more to *Copsford* than it superficially presented.

The strimmer was humming and Moth disappeared into the undergrowth leaving a mown path behind him. The biography was in the kitchen cupboard. I'd had it posted to the farm, expecting to have moved in weeks before, so I put the wallpaper scraper down, switched the kettle on and found the book. Written by a man who clearly adored Murray's writing, the pages explored the events of his life and his Christian beliefs. A life in which he loved nature but didn't allow that feeling to surpass his religion. I couldn't quite see what it was, but there was a contradiction between the man in the biography and the young man in *Copsford*. An impression that I wasn't reading about the same person. It made no sense, but I continued reading anyway.

An hour later Moth stood on a broad patch of cut grass. A muddy, scrappy expanse covered with the cut stalks of nettles, thistles and tufted grass. An expanse of possibility; a garden in the making. He came into the house, took off his goggles, sat on the deckchair in front of the fire and went instantly to sleep. How could I possibly have thought coming here was a good idea? I watched him sleep, his chin resting on his chest, his head moving rhythmically with his breathing as I closed the book. I realized I'd found them: Murray and Walter, the writer and the young man he wrote about. I finally understood they were one and the same, and entirely separate. I opened the laptop. Darkness fell and firelight flickered colors across the walls as I began to write the introduction.

21. Moles

The pale underwings of the buzzard were barely distinguishable against the flat gray backdrop of unbroken cloud, stretched out across a late-winter sky. His dark-edged wings, tail and head gave him a deep brown outline, making his body seem nearly translucent. This was his valley. Each morning he flew north to south across the farm, following the line of the old deciduous trees that hid the stream, before banking to the west to come to rest on a fence above the new orchard or the telegraph pole by the cider barn. But this morning he was distracted by something moving in the small field behind the house. Voles probably, their tunnels spread under the grass in a hidden network of rodent highways.

Just a few weeks earlier we'd closed the door of the chapel for the last time, leaving behind the safety and easy security it represented, and moved full-time into the farm. A wild, improbable leap of hope to a neglected farm in need of committed attention. Unaware that in a few short weeks' time *The Salt Path* would go into paperback, the demand for book events and interviews would escalate and my time would be spread paper-thin. I wanted to attract Moth's attention to the buzzard hanging almost motionless in the still air, but he was beyond reach. Lost in the enfolding undergrowth of the long-neglected orchard, where cankered branches hung twisted and gnarled to the ground, grown through with long tufted grass or overgrown with brambles into mounds of thorns fifteen feet high. Struggling to get moving each morning and sleeping twelve hours a night, Moth's days were short, but filled with sawing, stacking, strimming and mowing. Slowly, slowly, the trees were beginning to emerge behind him as he made more holes in his belt to hold his jeans up. Trees stripped of old dead, broken or diseased wood began to lift a little higher, as if straightening after years of stooping. And he strimmed on. Rhythmically swinging the machine from side to side he made tunnels through the wild growth, letting in light where there had been none for years.

With the light came more life. Small birds were finding their way into the trees. And with the shorter grass other life was moving in. Molehills appeared, following the green paths out of the trees, clustering at the side of the hedge, but then reappearing on the other side and away up the hill. Commercial agriculturalists would list moles as pests of the highest order, digging through the earth at a rate of up to twenty meters a day, producing mounds of earth as they go and spoiling huge areas of grassland. For generations farmers have dug them out, poisoned and gassed them out, all in pursuit of perfect grassland. But moles eat grubs, bugs, slugs and all manner of underground life that can equally destroy crops from the root upward. Pests that, if they're not eaten by moles, would be destroyed with poisons, poisons which can then kill the birdlife that might feed on the pests. Poison the pest, having poisoned its predator the mole: obviously the logical course of action. The buzzard fell like a dart from the sky, hesitating for a while in the grass before lifting off, a deep-black mole grasped in its talons. Plucked from the earth as its nose broke the surface of a molehill, its feet still digging hopelessly through the air. A predator chain in action.

Walter Murray would have embraced that moment in both his incarnations: as a young man and an older writer. As the months went by and Walter's herb stores began to fill, he found himself learning to be still, to embrace nature in a way that was "closer contact than touch, it was almost union." Murray wrote about this younger version of himself as his "nature spirit." Something innocent and naïve that he replaced in later life with a deeply Christian man. As if embracing nature in such an absolute way was something to be put away in the toy box, not carried through into adult life. I'd watched my own children running through fields of buttercups, standing knee-deep in muddy water trying to catch elvers as they ran downstream, or sitting in trees idling away an afternoon. Their wild, uncontrolled union with the natural world had been a normal part of their lives, not something to be put away as childish, but the foundation of the adults they became. Murray became a nature writer, thought of as a forerunner to Deakin and Macfarlane, and yet none of his other writing holds that elusive connection that he writes of in *Copsford*. I'd finally found what informed that book, what gave it the depth and light, what it was he was searching for in the descriptions of herbs, something he didn't even hint at in his other books.

Murray wrote about Walter long after he'd left Copsford, but very shortly after the death of his only son, Dick, when the boy was just fifteen. He doesn't mention his son in the book; he barely talks of his emotions other than his response to nature, or of death other than recording the extinction of a butterfly. But it's impossible to believe that as he wrote those words his son wasn't ever present in his thoughts, guiding his pen, filling the pages. It's as if he used *Copsford* to give Dick the youth he didn't have, to re-create the life he'd lost. The words don't just capture the spirit of his own youth, but hold his son within them too. Within Walter's year at Copsford, Dick lives on. Permanently on the page in the herbs and flowers of the hedgerows of postwar Sussex.

As Moth walked back to the house I realized why I was so drawn to *Copsford*. It was more than sharing Walter's sense of union with nature; it was an understanding of Murray. How, maybe without even consciously intending to, he had put Dick in a place where he could always find him, a place Murray could always return to.

"Fuck me, I'm totally knackered and I've run out of petrol." Moth put the strimmer down on the concrete. Hot and sweating under the plastic goggles and earmuffs despite the cold wind, he unbuckled the strimmer harness and peeled off his jumper in one smooth action. "Is the kettle on?"

In the pile of books on the table waiting to be signed, Moth would always lift his rucksack and turn his face to the wind, never fading, never lost, always beckoning me on to the next page, the next adventure.

"We're just crossing the fields to check the osprey nests, hope that's okay?" A man in a National Trust T-shirt sat on a quad bike in the farmyard; another stood at the door having just got out of a four-by-four that was loaded up with small tree trunks and wire.

"Osprey nests, what osprey nests?"

"Well, they're not nests, not yet. They're platforms."

"Where are these platforms? I haven't seen them."

The man at the door pointed to two poles in the field on the far horizon. Two strange contraptions that I thought were abandoned, misplaced telegraph poles.

"I thought ospreys went back to the same nest every year, not to a new one?"

"They do. The idea is that any young osprey looking for their first nesting site will see the platforms and think they're old osprey nests and choose to reuse one. We're going up there to attach some new branches, replace the broken ones."

"Have they used them yet?"

"No, we're just hoping to attract one that might be passing on its migration path back from Africa. The herons are near there, so we know the river's a great food source for fish-eaters."

"I thought herons were just waders." But the quad bike was already revving to leave.

We followed the rounded ridgeline at the top of the hill, across the fields that formed the highest part of the farm. From there the farm sloped on both sides: on one, to the river where the tide was out, leaving deep brown mudflats glistening in the low light, and to the valley on the other, where the house sat alone above the bare branches of the orchard. From the highest point near the would-be osprey nests, we headed steeply downhill to a broken gate and a field waist-high in thistles and nettles. A field so steep it was difficult to walk down, so we dodged the thistles and climbed the fence into a dark, dense strip of woodland that descended to the river. We followed the trees down, precariously holding on to the trunks of saplings to prevent a fall, stopping repeatedly to rest, or decide if we could go on, until we reached the edge of the wood and turned to follow the level ground along the boundary between the field and the mudflats at the creek's edge.

Gnarled oaks and sycamore lined the creekside, but among them rose a group of old twisted trees that must have stood in that spot with their roots in the mud for hundreds of years. A familiar spot; we'd definitely seen a picture of that muddy brown riverbank in print. Closed in and overhung with willows, the creek winds its way straight off the cover of Sam's book. There were no signs of Ratty or Mole, but high in the trees huge nests sat solidly in the branches, unmoved by the strong wind from the water. Scattered along the bank an occasional solitary heron stood silently observing the mud. Necks outstretched, ready to snatch anything that moved. We hadn't known, until we'd looked into it after the National Trust men had left, that we were on land that bounded what is thought to be one of the largest heronries in Cornwall. It's true that there were many nests in the trees—not as many as the river-watchers think, but more than I'd ever seen in one place. Yet there were only three herons here. Herons spread out after the breeding season, dispersing across the countryside to live their solitary lives, but coming back to the nests in February for the start of three months of communal living. Mid-February now, they should be here, the males repairing their nests and putting on their best displays for the females. We scoured the area with the binoculars, but there were no more to be seen. Maybe they'd gone down the river with the outgoing tide? Possibly not all the nests were used, or maybe some were migrants flying in to the heronry in the spring from Ireland and France, held up somewhere across the Channel waiting for the right weather conditions? Or maybe they were far fewer in number than the nests would suggest, and the twiggy platforms were more resilient than the species that inhabited them.

"We'll come back in a few weeks. It's still early, but by then we'll definitely see if they're nesting."

"I'm not sure if we will. We've got to climb back up that hill somehow."

"Shall we come by boat next time?"

Throughout history birds have been seen as auguries, messengers and omens. In the *Iliad* Athena sends a heron as an omen to Odysseus as he carries out a risky night mission into the enemy camp. Supposedly the call of the heron offered comfort to the night raiders. If the empty heronry was an omen of anything now, it undoubtedly wasn't of comfort.

In the early light of a late February morning, an omen sat on the telegraph pole just outside the house. The mist from the river had engulfed the orchards, but as the light lifted the mist began to clear, showing a new trail of molehills stretching out of the trees. Not just one creating mole highways under the grass then, but a whole family of them. Above the trail of soil mounds, on the telegraph pole near the house, a huge bird sat quietly looking around. A tall bird with a white chest and darkest brown back. Could it be an osprey? I wanted to google to check, wake Moth so he could see it, point the bird in the direction of the would-be nests, but I daren't turn from the window in case the slightest move alerted him. He casually moved a few feathers with his hooked black beak, stretched out an immense wingspan, lifted slowly from the pole and away, his huge wings arching in an undeniably osprey motion.

"Wow, Moth, you should have seen that. Quick, get up before it disappears."

Moth sat up without help, swiveled round on the bed and was by my side in seconds as the osprey looped across the barns, over the hill and headed inland.

"Fuck, was that an osprey?"

I looked at the empty bed and at Moth standing by my side in a baggy T-shirt and shorts now two sizes too big. Standing alone in the early morning, without my help.

"No, I think it was a sign."

22. Badgers

In the late afternoon a large fox wandered around the slope of an empty field through grass up to his belly, his rich auburn coat catching the light, a burnished body pushing through the thick green growth. He criss-crossed the field, abstractedly following an unseen path, his head down and out of sight, then up again and smelling the air.

The fox's main food sources are small rodents and rabbits. But foxes are opportunistic hunters and if their natural food source has gone, they'll take food where they can find it. It's well known that they will occasionally kill young lambs—born in the spring, just at the moment when the fox has a den full of cubs to feed. I'd stood in our field in Wales and watched two foxes rip a lamb apart. A hideous sight. I'd chased another as it jumped through the hedge with the last hen in its mouth, after it had spent the night emptying the hen pen. But I'd also followed Dad through the fields as he shot rabbits that had exploded in numbers and were decimating the cornfields in the years after every fox in the district had been removed. I'd watched him poison the rats too, and the mice. And the water voles.

But far more persecuted than the fox or rabbit is the badger. Bovine TB is an ever-present disease among the cattle population of the UK. Cattle are regularly tested for the infection and any animal testing positive is slaughtered—leaving farmers to endure the financial and emotional heartache of losing their livestock. Alongside humans, badgers can also contract TB, a disease that's equally deadly for cattle, humans and badgers alike. Most of us have been vaccinated against the disease, but to combat the spread among cattle we don't use vaccines, we cull badgers instead. It's commonly thought that badgers spread TB to cattle, so the government approves culls across an area of this country larger than Israel, causing localized extinctions of an animal that has inhabited this island since the Ice Age. As a child our pedigree herd of cattle was termed "accredited." In the 1960s and 70s that meant the herd was tested and proved to be TB-free. Free to live and roam the fields that were surrounded by woods. The same woods where badgers lived, silently getting on with their lives. TB-free. A bovine vaccine exists and yet we don't vaccinate cattle, as apparently it's impossible to develop a test that will differentiate between a vaccinated cow and one infected with TB. We encourage mothers to vaccinate their child against every possible disease and yet a cow that is tracked and traced from birth can't be injected with a vaccine that's readily available, a vaccine that could be visible and readable on their record, like any human medical record. So the cull goes on, and yet the numbers of cattle with bovine TB don't fall. Possibly they're not catching TB from the badgers after all, but, like the common cold, from each other.

Rarely seen, other than as roadkill on the side of the motorway or playfully running around their sett on an episode of *Springwatch*, the badger stays low, hidden in the woods and hedgerows. Safe in their world of undergrowth, on their diet of grubs, mice and ripe fruit, only ever venturing into the fields in the dark of night, vulnerable to any infection that might be lying waiting for them in the grass.

At what point in our lives does cynicism take over from instinct? When we stop feeling the softness of rain on our face and start worrying about being wet? Stop marveling at the wonder of a badger rooting through the grass in the twilight, stop listening to the sounds carried on the wind or the echo of ourselves inside it? Or when we hear the young voice of an activist on the radio and doubt its validity? When do we make that switch from being part of the natural world to being an observer with an assumed right to control it?

As Murray was writing *Copsford*, he looked back at Walter, a naïve twenty-something, wandering in the fields picking herbs, and painted a picture of a discovery of life and nature in a landscape that has gone. There are few areas now where you can walk through meadows and collect armfuls of foxgloves and centaury. There are few people who have heard of centaury, fewer still who have seen it in the grass and heathlands it used to inhabit in abundance. Even as Murray wrote the lines in the years after the Second World War, decades after he hid in the bushes watching the girl he loved picking blackberries, he could see that the countryside was changing, that plants and animals were disappearing, unnoticed and unseen. Simply fading from sight as people lost their connection to nature and became mere observers.

As we walked across the farm in the early spring, the empty fields shone with a new green carpet. The last of the previous tenant's sheep had left the land at the start of the winter, allowing the land to recover over the winter months. But there were no badger trails through the grass that was tentatively beginning to grow, or beneath the hedgerows showing the purple spring haze of buds about to break. Sparrows argued among the branches and overhead the buzzard circled his territory, calling into the distance, yet if there were badgers in the area they didn't cross the farm. We stopped to look downriver, the water catching shafts of sunlight on the high tide, to a church tower and the woods beyond.

"Do you remember how much equipment and livestock it took to farm a place this size?" Moth was now lying on his back on the damp grass, watching clouds mass and then separate, but obviously his thoughts were far away.

"Not really, I think I've blocked it out. When we were walking I tried not to remember because thinking about home hurt too much, and now if I try to remember I can't."

"I can, I remember it really well." I turned to him and watched his face, eyes closed, concentrating, as he listed an inventory of machinery and livestock numbers that I couldn't recall if I tried. "The grass is growing now, it can't be ignored, and we're in no position to buy livestock."

"But do you remember that day on the beach on your fortieth birthday when it rained all afternoon?" How could he remember livestock numbers?

"Of course, and we played cricket in our wetsuits because it was so wet, but the kids didn't want to go home. But what's that got to do with it?"

"Nothing, but you remembered." I lay back on the grass. He remembered.

"I think we're going to have to talk to Sam about finding someone to use the grass. We can focus on resurrecting the orchards, making cider and overseeing a biodiversity plan for the farm, but I can't see us being able to actually physically farm the whole place ourselves." He stood up, looking around the fields and down to the wood. Sure about what he was saying, clear in his reasoning. "And I need the freedom to do other things too. If we own the livestock that graze the land then we're tied to the place, every day of the year. I need to be able to come with you to your events and do other things too."

"What sort of things?"

"I've been thinking about another walk."

I followed him as he wandered down the hill, back toward the farmhouse. His stride still a little lopsided, but his feet finding the ground with certainty. The sun broke through the clouds, the grass grew a little greener and at the base of a hedge, untouched by man or machinery for months, a patch of snowdrops pushed through the ground.

On a dull, flat morning when the air was still and even the spring light didn't seem to lift over the hill, I followed the newly created paths in the orchards where apple blossom was showing the first signs of swelling on the branches and in the long grass something stirred. A roe deer, a doe, clearly pregnant, trotted slowly down to the stream, disappearing into the darkness of the old deciduous trees that followed the water downhill. I reached the tree I'd been looking for. The fallen tree with the drill holes. Flicking through a magazine in a waiting room my attention had been caught by an article about the larvae of a moth that eats holes in trees, and the picture of the holes had looked identical. In the new growth of the tree, where branches covered in the buds of new growth pushed skyward away from the fallen trunk, a sticky sap oozed from the randomly drilled holes and a few insects buzzed around the spring food source. An early red admiral butterfly folded its wings, unable to tear itself away from the all-you-can-eat breakfast, but on the lower dead side of the tree the sap had dried to a hard resin around the holes.

The goat moth is huge, one of the largest moths in the country, and increasingly rare. Its main habitat is in the south of the UK, though it's rarely seen this far west. The adults lay their eggs in a number of wetland trees, ash, birch, alder, but also apple trees. The larvae can live in the tree for as long as five years. Five years of munching and digesting the cellulose in the wood before a bright red caterpillar nearly ten centimeters long crawls out into the light of late summer. It will then quickly disappear into the grass to pupate over winter before emerging as a fully fledged moth, so well disguised that it's barely distinguishable from the bark of a tree. Five years of hiding away from the light, of collecting its strength and preparing for life. There'd be no way of knowing what insects were in the tree until they emerged, maybe tomorrow, maybe in five years, emerged blinking into the light, ready to shed an old form and embrace the new. Five years is a long time, long enough for even the most reticent insect to transform and finally spread its wings.

The sound of a vehicle pulling into the yard gave me the familiar sense of nervous reluctance and the almost overwhelming desire to stay hidden in the orchard and hope that Moth was awake to go and see who it was. I was still struggling to shake the deep-grained mistrust of others. Few people ever called at the farm—occasional visitors from Polruan, but more often just someone whose satnav had sent them in the wrong direction. I took a deep breath and headed toward the house. How long would I need to be here, hiding from the world, before enough time had passed to allow me to spread my wings and transform?

23. Toads

The moon, white and dimming, still hung nearly full in the sky as the cloud began to break. An owl called from the dead oak behind the house, a last call before heading into the trees to sleep through the day. The last of the apple blossom had fallen in the orchard; tiny apples had formed in its wake, filling the air with the faint scent of summer. I sat on the fallen tree and watched the holes in the wood. Nothing stirred. So I spread the letter across the trunk. There'd been so many letters. So many people.

The first letters came when *The Salt Path* had been out in hardback for a few months, but after its release in paperback they began to come every week. Letters from people whose lives had taken a wrong turn and fallen apart, people who'd lost homes, families and businesses. Letters from the sick and dying, people struggling with disease whose fears were not for themselves but for their families and how they would cope. And from the families trying to cope without their loved ones. But all of them holding out hands full of care and concern for Moth in a mass exhalation of hope. Each letter I opened held words of compassion and empathy, offers of help and homes. I breathed all of them in, each envelope adding a layer of restored belief. But this letter was different.

Invitations to speak at events were coming thick and fast. More stages to be sat on and audiences to be faced. Fear gripped me every time the lights shone in my face and the first question was asked. But in the queues that formed after the talks, queues of people waiting to have their book signed, there was no fear.

Just stories. Stories of lives lived, loves lost and walks that changed beliefs. But something else was happening in the queues. Not for those waiting patiently with their copy of the book, but for me. As I signed my name again and again among the birds that flew through the endpapers, the shared stories joined my own in a unity of hope, fear, trauma and pain. Feelings as unfathomable as humanity, as old as the cliffs we'd walked on, part of the complexity of existence, but feelings that united us all into a collective hand, gently moving the sofa away from the wall and lifting a small girl out into the light.

Moth wandered through the trees, a mug of tea in his hand, picking his way through long grass and cut thistles, past fallen branches and a bed of nettles covered in butterflies that had appeared from nowhere, hatching in their thousands in the morning light and clustering over the seed heads of the tall grasses. The meadow brown is possibly the UK's most common butterfly, small and faded brown with a flash of orange on their white-edged wings. As the air turned brown it was easy to see why these grass-feeders could explode in numbers if the grass stands far enough into the summer for the seeds to ripen.

"What are you doing down here? I was going to make some toast, but I thought I'd find you first."

"I'm waiting."

"For what."

"A goat moth."

"You're waiting for a moth? What are you talking about?"

"It's a moth that has a five-year larval stage and I think it could be in this tree."

"So you're going to sit here for five years?"

"Might have to."

"Just come and get some toast before the teapot's cold."

I spread the latest letter on the table while I buttered toast. Reading it to Moth between mouthfuls. ". . . I knew I would be arrested this week, so in preparation I looked for a book to read in the cell, and yours seemed the obvious choice . . ."

"I'm not sure but reading on I think it's about taking the wild with him into a closed space. You know, looking at it now, I don't think I was really writing about nature at all."

"I'm not sure about that; it's a multilayered book, perfect for book clubs, hospital visits and prison break-outs. If it wasn't nature then what were you writing about?"

"You. It was always just about you. As I was writing it I thought it was for you, so you wouldn't forget our path, but now I think it was more than that. I think I was putting you permanently on the path for myself. Like Murray did with Dick. So I could keep that time, keep you in that time with me. Always, even after . . ."

His hand reached past the toast and held mine.

"You're an idiot—you've reread *Copsford* far too many times. I think we should do it again, another walk—maybe not quite so far this time though . . . What's that noise?"

"Probably the mice."

"No, not mice, something else, more like a croak."

"Where, in the house?"

"Not sure, it's gone now."

"Where do you want to walk? Have you thought of any-where?"

"Haven't really thought about it in depth, but maybe we should go with someone else, you know, just in case."

"In case of what? And who? I can't think who would want to go with us."

"What about Dave and Julie? It'd be great to be on a trail with them again."

"There it is, I heard it this time, definitely a croak."

The reddish-brown color of her coat blended almost invisibly into the long grasses, but flashes of her white rump gave her away. The roe deer stepped out of the undergrowth on to one of the mown pathways and began to graze on the short grasses that now criss-crossed the orchard. Pathways of green among the nettles and scrubby tufted grass: her ideal home. Easy grazing, easy walking and cover to hide in when she needed it. And she needed a safe place now. Behind her, on tentative legs that sprang and jumped seemingly without pattern or reason, a roe-deer kid. Tiny, red and frail, and yet leaping with life and summer strength. I watched them wander slowly to the stream, wrapped in the hum of insects carried through the air on a breeze of nectar and warmth. A deep glow of noise, moving like a whisper across land freed from pollution, lifting over pollen-filled banks of new-sown flowers. The earth breathing.

One last mound of plastic sat in the barn: buckets and feed bags pulled from the stream where the deer drank, tangled in a heap with rusting wire and other rubbish. One last load to go to the tip, and then the land would be free, its polluted surface cleared. Time now to hope that the earth could regenerate and life would find its own way back.

"What time's Sam coming?" Moth tipped a wheelbarrow of silage wrap on to the heap, the final lot of waste pulled from the soil. We stacked the old tires against it to prevent it blowing away. In the days before big silage bales and wrapping machines, farmers regularly made silage clamps, huge piles of cut grass that fed the cattle through the winter. The clamps were often covered with plastic sheeting to protect the grass crop and weighted down with old tires to stop it blowing away. These tires hadn't come from a silage pit, they'd been all over the farm, emerging from every hole and corner, but the last of them now stood in the barn, waiting to be taken away.

"Can't believe that's the final load. Two o'clock, I think."

"Don't believe it, rubbish keeps working its way out of the soil every day."

"It's not just here though, is it? You can't really blame the last tenants, most farms are the same. Mind you, we never had mountains of rubbish on the farm when I was a child. I think we burned everything and a scrap man always came for the metal."

"But that was before plastic."

"Careful. I'm not that old."

A vintage Triumph motorbike revved at the gate, its rider's hands still on the handlebars, his helmet on but the visor up as he slowly looked around. Still revving.

"I daren't turn it off, it might not start again." Sam revved the engine again. "Wow, I don't know what to say, just wow." Was he going to get off the motorbike, or was that it? "Just got the bike out of storage and the battery's flat. I can't stop. I'll be back later." Were they tears running down his face, or sweat inside the helmet? It was quite a warm day. Wasn't he happy with what we'd done? Did he think we hadn't done enough? The Triumph revved up the hill and was gone.

There's an innate vulnerability in renting the place where you live. To allow yourself to like your rented home too much is a gamble. It's a one-sided relationship, a poker game where the other party holds all the cards and all you're left with is a fear of commitment and the probability of loss.

"That was weird."

"Very."

We didn't need to discuss it. The weeks, months of cleaning, clearing, strimming and mowing had been a huge commitment of time. But finally the land was rising again, straightening its back after years of carrying a heavy burden, clearing its throat and finding its voice. A family of goldfinches landed on a patch of grass where the seed heads had dropped their seeds before being cut. A group of eleven dazzling birds flashing yellow and red as they fed on the seeds, chattering loudly. In the fields grass had been left to grow later into the summer than with conventional farming, offering food for birds and insects that hung over the grass as it swayed in the wind and roe deer that showed an occasional head above the savannah of green, testing the air before continuing to graze. Even the ground-nesting skylarks had had time to rear their chicks and see them fledge before the flailing blades of the grass-cutters came into the field.

"Feeling a bit vulnerable now." I sat on the small wall outside the house, feeling not just vulnerable but suddenly quite foolish.

"We're renting, we've always been vulnerable."

"I know but that's just a house. If Sam wanted us to leave, I'm sure we'd be okay. We've learned enough about surviving over the last few years; we'd work it out. It's not that, it's the land. It's starting to breathe again—I can almost hear it coming back to life. I'm afraid he'll change his mind, say it's not financially viable and just sell it."

"It's not ours, Ray, you have to remember that. Don't let yourself get attached."

"I know, I know."

The roe deer and her kid jumped down from the long grass to a ditch that passed into a lower field, slipping away into the undergrowth.

An iconic pale blue camper van pulled up outside the house. Sam driving, but another three passengers inside. He got out, looking around again, this time without a helmet, so his expression couldn't be hidden.

"I've got to say it again: oh *wow*."

"Is everything okay, Sam? Is there a problem—did you think we'd have got more done by now?" I couldn't hold back and talk carefully or tactfully around my fears. If the idea of a truly biodiverse farm was over I needed to know right now, without hesitation, before I slipped any further under the spell cast by the land.

"Are you joking? I'm stunned. I never thought the place could recover like this, I just hoped. And you've done so much work. Thank you, thank you."

Behind him the goldfinches took off in a chattering cloud to land in a row on the telephone wires. His wife got out of the camper van, smaller, compact, giving me a hug that held a casual, assured resilience.

"Hi, I'm Rachel. These are the kids, Jack and Lottie. Nice to meet you, although I wouldn't have said that a few months ago."

"Oh no, why?"

"I wanted Sam to sell the farm. I was adamant that he should let it go, get rid of all the problems and just walk away. So I was furious when he suggested you should move in. He's been so let down, I couldn't bear to watch him be disappointed again—I didn't think he could take anymore. Since I was diagnosed with breast cancer I tend to just think about the here and now, and the farm, well, it's been a huge financial and emotional black hole. I wanted to live for the moment, enjoy my children, not cling to this place. His dream; my nightmare. I even refused to read your book. But I have now and at last I think I get it. You and Sam, you share a passion for the land and sleepless nights worrying about your partner. No wonder he felt such a connection with *The Salt Path*. That's why I agreed not to sell it. I think I finally understand."

I watched Rachel as she looked across the land, a woman who had the power to end a dream or fan the flames. I could have doubted the permanence of her decision, but as she linked her arm through Sam's I thought I understood why she had opened the stove door and allowed the air to reach the fire.

"Well, okay, that's good, shall we have a cup of tea then?" Practical, be practical before they see that your knees are weak with relief.

"Earlier, when I was on my Triumph, I couldn't stop . . ."

Their two children wandered into the orchard. The younger, the boy, Jack, throwing the ball for the dog; Lottie, wandering behind, trailing her teenage hands through a purple haze of Yorkshire fog grass.

"I know, you said. Have you got a battery charger?" Moth put the teapot on the table, calm, unmoved, as if this was any day and of no importance at all. Was it just me, would the fear of imminent insecurity always haunt me, would I ever truly trust in anything again?

"Yes, but it wasn't that. I couldn't take my helmet off, I felt like such an idiot for crying at the gate."

"What do you mean? Were you upset—did you hope for something else?"

"No, it's perfect, better than I could ever have hoped. As Rachel said, we were going to sell the farm, until I read your book. Asking you both to come here was like a leap of faith. But today . . . today, I'm so glad I took it. And I didn't think the change would be so quick, I thought it could be years before we saw the land come back to life."

The sunlight through the window caught the mirror on the opposite wall, highlighting the pile of letters heaped on the shelf in front of it. Letters full of individual stories all waiting for a reply. Each person's story entirely their own, yet totally the same in their frailties and strengths.

"Do you take milk in your tea, Sam?"

The moon rose, almost full above the creek. Hanging out of the bedroom window, I watched the pale light cloak the hillside in a silver blue haze. Total stillness; not a sound to break the silence. That croak again.

"It's not frogs, look." In the moonlight a huge fat brown toad walked among the plant pots in front of the house.

"Toads! Who'd have thought?"

A faint mist began to lift from the creek, pulled almost magnetically up through the trees in the valley.

"It would be great to be in the tent on a night like this. What you were saying about another walk? Shall we do it? We've got a window between events at the end of the summer—only two weeks but it might be enough time." I'd watched Moth as the weather improved and he spent more and more of his days outside, rhythmically, patiently working in the landscape. The land coming back to life as he began to move a little easier, remember a little more. I'd watched, speechless, as he'd replaced a tiny, tightly coiled spring in the strimmer head, a precise little job that took focus and dexterity to complete. Maybe if we walked again, if only for a couple of weeks, it might give him a resource to draw on as winter came and the darkness drove him inside.

"Yes, let's do it. You know that book you keep leaving lying around the house, *Epic Hikes*? There's a great walk in there. It's in Iceland."

PART FOUR

To a Beginning, in the End

If I breathed the word

that disappeared all people
in the world,
leaving the world

to the world, would you
say it? Would you
sing it out loud?

"so the peloton passed," Simon Armitage

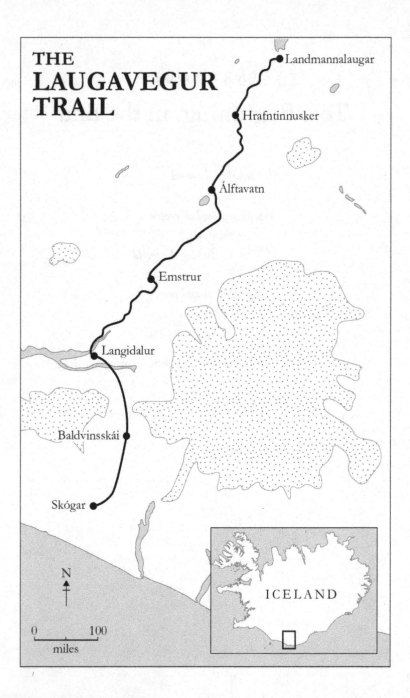

THE
**LAUGAVEGUR
TRAIL**

Landmannalaugar

Hrafntinnusker

Álftavatn

Emstrur

Langidalur

Baldvinsskái

Skógar

N

0   100
        miles

ICELAND

Landmannalaugar

"Hi, it's Dave. You know, Dave and Julie. How're you doing?"

"Dave, fantastic to hear from you."

"We've been thinking, it's about time we went for another walk. Do some camping and stuff like that, do you want to come?"

Dave and Julie were eating ice cream in a car park when we met them. Walking the South West Coast Path, we hadn't come across many other backpackers who were wild camping, and even fewer middle-aged ones. So we'd been immediately attracted by the size of their packs as they lay on the ground; they were obviously camping. Dave, a brusque, Northern, no-nonsense man who worked hard long hours, but in his free time insulated bird boxes, walked alone on the Lakeland Fells, and adored Julie despite pretending he didn't. Julie, externally calm, quiet, unassuming, was under that veneer a tough, remorseless campaigner for the underprivileged. A mirror image of each other. They'd appeared repeatedly as we walked along, our paths crossing and interweaving, until we'd given up trying to avoid each other and walked together along a hot, tranquil section of the south coast of Dorset.

"How weird that you've said that; we've just been saying the same thing. Do you fancy going to Iceland?"

"Iceland? I've always wanted to go to Iceland!"

We stood under the covered walkway outside Keflavík Airport as rain fell in curtains from its domed plastic roof. The lights from the building and car park blurred into an Impressionist painting of night. Waterproofs on, we hoisted our rucksacks, Moth putting one arm through the shoulder strap while I took the pack's weight and helped him maneuver the second strap over his second painful shoulder. We crossed the car park through the torrential downpour, dropping our rucksacks in the lobby of a hotel on the opposite side.

For weeks Moth had known he needed to do this. He was beginning to understand the needs of this new body, the one that didn't always respond to his instruction, that tired without effort and agitated his thoughts. He was learning to sidestep it, to move when it told him to lie down, to shout when it said be quiet and give in. He willingly rewaxed his boots and bought the same model of Vango tent that we had used on the South West Coast Path, knowing that our old tent with its duct-taped poles wouldn't survive the subarctic winds of Iceland. But this trip couldn't have been more different from our Coast Path walk if we'd designed it to be so. *The Salt Path* had unexpectedly sold quite a few copies and we could afford to walk into the airport hotel at midnight and check into a room, rather than put the tent up in the torrential rain on some scrub grass under the flight path of the planes. We opened the blinds and watched the last plane of the night land on the small runway, lights smudged through the water running down the window.

"So, we're in Iceland. Top of the habitable world. Above us, only the Arctic, and below, the green earth curving away in an arc of increasing heat and dust, before cooling to the Antarctic. Weird thought." I had my face pressed against the window, trying to see beyond the rain on the glass.

"Not as weird as getting on the plane in an August heatwave and getting off into early winter. I've read that there's no autumn here, but that summer ends and winter begins. Have to say I thought we'd still be at the tail end of summer."

"How did your pack feel?"

"Not too bad, but I have only walked across the car park."

The same rucksacks that had walked the Coast Path were propped together against the wall of an Icelandic hotel: Moth's looking quite full and mine straining at the seams. I'd packed it so tight that the fabric had split and was now displaying a bright green patch that I'd hastily sewn over the hole before rushing to the airport. Crammed with things we hadn't needed on the Coast Path: a warm jacket and waterproofs that didn't let the rain pour through, a water filter and ten days of dried-food rations. We had no idea if we would be able to access provisions where we were going, but knew that even if it was available the price would be excessive. The island imports the majority of its food supplies, making the cost of food far higher than in Britain, higher still when we reached the mountains. The three-kilogram weight limit on foods brought into the country hadn't left us too much choice about what we packed. We'd considered pre-packed hiking meals, but they were so expensive we might as well have bought them in Iceland. I opened the rucksack and looked for my toothbrush, moving the food pack aside and trying not to think about it. I knew it contained things I'd thought I would never eat again, but that was two days away, no need to dwell on it now. We made tea and ate the biscuits we'd bought in the airport.

"This seemed like such a good idea when I was standing in the orchard in Cornwall, but I don't know if I can do this. What if I get into the mountains and find I can't?"

The orchards and fields of the farm were feeling suddenly distant. After Sam's visit, we had finally begun to feel as if there was a chance of letting ourselves relax, a chance to consider the possibility that for a while at least we could simply *be* without the fear of our time there ending abruptly. But now we had snatched ourselves away to walk a trail in a wild, inhospitable land. A trail we might not even be able to complete.

"We'll just take our time; that's why we've got so much food.

If we need to stop we can and just wait until we feel able to go on. And Dave will be there, he's like a man-mountain—we'll just give him your pack. Anyway, we know who wrote the guidebook for the trek. We'll probably have to cut the sections short; you know we can't keep up with the pace he sets."

Moth marked the page in the guidebook that illustrated the start of the Laugavegur Trail. A small book with a practical waterproof cover that fitted neatly in Moth's jacket pocket. Paddy Dillon's *Walking and Trekking in Iceland*. We could have found a lighter book, one that didn't cover a whole group of trails, or just a map. But there was something reassuring about having a guidebook by the same author who had steered us through every cove and gorse thicket of the South West Coast Path. A sense of knowing there was someone we could rely on who absolutely without question would tighten his bootlaces and show us the way. The friend in our pocket.

"Well, here we are then, in the rain in Reykjavík. Who'd have thought—from the Coast Path to Iceland. But we're here, bloody brilliant." Dave, as large and loud as he had been the first time we met appeared out of a crowd in the main street of the island's capital. As he enveloped Moth in his bear-like grasp there was a shocking change to the view I'd had of the two men hugging good-bye in West Bay on the Coast Path. The weight that Moth had lost became not just something that I could feel, but a large loss made visible by the mirror of our unchanged friend. Suddenly I could see him as Dave and Julie must too. Was his deterioration so gradual that I was taking it for granted? Forcing him into more and more physical challenges that he was fighting to achieve just for me, battling on because I couldn't accept that one day he would have to give in to CBD, to give himself over to the wind and the dust?

"Julie, you're here, can you believe we're doing this?"

"Not at all. We said let's meet in Iceland, but I didn't really expect it to happen. Now look at us, in the rain with walking poles." A gentle-natured woman, not much bigger than her purple rucksack, she couldn't have been in greater contrast to Dave, Northern England to the bone, filling the street with his seventy-liter pack and huge presence.

"What on earth have you got in there, Dave?"

"Twelve days of food and stuff we need, like."

"But we should only be out for six, eight at the most."

"Well, you never know what might happen. It might snow and we get trapped on the mountain, or someone could get hurt and we'd have to wait for help, or we find it too hard and stuff like that. If not I'll just eat it anyway."

Julie looked around the vast pack and raised her eyebrows. We were all laughing at Dave, but he had a point. It wasn't just Moth who would find this hard; all four of us were well past our prime. Standing in the pouring rain just below the Arctic Circle about to start a trail that Paddy Dillon, who walks the South West Coast Path at superhuman speed, describes in part as "steep and rugged climbing, with some narrow, exposed ridges." What were we thinking of?

A sense of nervousness dulled the excitement as we booked the bus tickets to take us to the trailhead at Landmannalaugar. Not really a place that should have a name, more a word on a map that people collect around. An encampment in the southern highlands of Iceland. We would follow the Laugavegur Trail from there to Þórsmörk, which Paddy said would only take four days. From there we would cross the Fimmvörðuháls, a high mountain pass that would take us across the Eyjafjallajökull volcano that erupted in 2010, shutting down airports across Europe and beyond. Two more days. If we'd understood Icelandic weather patterns a little more, we might have been even more nervous. The Iceland tourist offices would assure you that there are four seasons in Iceland, just like any of the more southern countries. But the old Norse calendar knew the truth. Iceland has only two seasons, summer and winter, and the locals know almost exactly when winter's coming. On the first Sunday in September. We put our rucksacks in the hold of the bus with only five full days of August left. Five days of summer.

As the bus left the main road we began to understand why it had such immense tires. Two hours into a four-hour journey and we were off the tarmac on to a stony track that headed toward mountain peaks unlike anything I'd seen before. No gentle hills here, but ripped earth pushing up in near vertical shards from flat, desolate river valleys. Boulders in a stationary landslide from long-dead eruptions and ash everywhere, flowing smooth and black over the hillsides like a sheet of fluid porcelain. The bus forded rivers where small jeeps stood with bonnets up, engines washed out by the cascading river. Small clusters of sheep clung to occasional green patches of subarctic vegetation, their thick fleeces making them look much bigger than their delicate legs said they were.

An arctic fox stood in the open landscape, its front paws propped on a boulder, his back fur brown in its summer colors but his chest and belly white, his coat already adapting to its winter camouflage. He obviously knew Sunday wasn't far away. As Iceland's only native mammal, he knows this land better than any meteorologist ever can. Even on the hot bus I felt a chill and wished my rucksack was as big as Dave's, stuffed full of four-season sleeping bags and Icelandic jumpers and a lot more food than my forty-liter pack could ever hold.

We climbed over a pass between two mountains, where fin-gered combs of rock pointed skywards, on an ever-narrowing track that fell into a valley bottom. Carved by millennia of snow, ice and rain, the valley ran like a river of shale between mountains of mysterious colors. Sunlight catching the peaks of luminous peach, sand and green. And between them, abrupt and violent, the dark angry head of a lava flow. Thrown out of a volcano with unstoppable power, an outpouring of rock, flames and lava had cascaded down the shattered hillside, cooling as it came. Possibly hitting a vast river running over the shale bed, the lava had stopped moving, its energy spent. It now stood frozen in time, a snarling face looking out across the dried riverbed. The Laugahraun lava field came to a halt in 1477, but it feels much older, ancient beyond time. At its head, only meters away from the last fall of rock, was Landmannalaugar. A scattering of sheds and tents, people milling around in the rain between a toilet block and an information hut, or making their way to a collection of old green buses that stood together like a stockade of American school buses about to repel an attack of teenagers.

We got off the bus, stiff from two hours of jolting, and dragged the rucksacks from the hold. Faced with the immensity of the lava head, the four packs lay together on the ground like a row of hand luggage, far too small and feeble to provide a means of survival in this wild landscape. A scattering of tents were erected on the bare stony earth between the sheds and the buses, so we erected ours with them. We piled rocks around the edges, copying the other tents, unsure exactly what we were hoping to achieve. If the wind was so strong that it would rip the tent pegs from the ground, a few hastily placed rocks wouldn't stop it.

And the rain continued to fall.

"They're still in a heatwave back home, you know." I was already feeling a longing to be somewhere safe, green and familiar.

"We could have done the Corfu Trail, just packed shorts and eaten in a taverna every night, like."

Not just me who was feeling intimidated then.

"Shall we take the stoves and make food in the communal tent, rather than sit out here in the rain?" Julie, as practical as ever.

A white canvas tent was secured to the ground behind the toilet block: a strange place to position the kitchen where most people cooked their food. But when we got inside it was obvious why it was there. Tucked in behind the main concrete building and secured to the ground with large iron pegs and winching straps, it was clearly in the most sheltered spot on the site, protected from the winds that are funneled up between mountains and pushed into valleys, ripping in from the sea and lifting cars from the road and hikers from the path. Winds with the force of a volcano that make British gales feel like a gentle breeze. If an Icelander tells you it's going to be a bit windy, you really should listen.

Some wind that night might have been helpful; it might have ventilated the cooking tent. From the cold vertical rain, we passed through the plastic doorway into a hot sauna. Ten picnic tables filled the tent, most of them crowded to capacity with people cooking food on gas stoves. Waterproofs hung dripping from every possible point, water pouring from them and through the decking floor. We found a gap at the end of a table and squeezed on, setting up our gas stoves to add to the wet, steaming warmth. With a sinking feeling I put the food bag on the table. Moth got out a bowl and let out a deep sigh.

"Okay, let's do this."

There had been weeks on the Coast Path when we had eaten nothing but dried noodles simply because we couldn't afford to buy anything else. After the path, when there was enough money to make a choice, we had chosen never to put a fork into a slimy bowl of string noodles ever again. But in looking for really lightweight freeze-dried food that would rehydrate in just a few minutes of immersion in boiling water, there wasn't much choice. In the week before we set off I'd bought sacks of freeze-dried rice, vegetables and soya mince in the hope of being able to create something that wouldn't take a lot of fuss or gas to cook, but found that the rice was cold before it rehydrated and the mince had the texture and taste of a sea sponge. So we'd taken a deep breath and given in to the noodles. I'd unbagged them and added dried vegetables, fruit and nuts in the hope of making them a little more palatable. We emptied the Ziploc bag of dried shreds into the bowl, poured on the water, covered them and waited. The tent was full of people chattering and excited about the trek to come, comparing equipment, stirring food, drinking. But we sat in silence and stared at the noodle bowl. For a moment, we were back in another country on a windy headland as the sun set on another day of living in the wild landscape at the edge of the land.

"Do you remember—we were so hungry each night we didn't care what we ate."

"We were so hungry it hurt."

"Let's just eat them then." I put my fork into the bowl of slime, part reluctant, part in anticipation.

"Not so bad . . ."

"Actually, so much better than I remember. Maybe it's the dried figs."

The biggest hurdle of the trip was crossed and we could focus on the room while the water boiled for tea. Dave seemed to notice the same thing that I did.

"They're all kids, like, twenty-somethings. Where're the grown-ups?"

As we all scanned the tent we couldn't see anyone over thirty, and as the room began to empty they gravitated away from us and clustered around the tables on the farthest side of the tent.

"What do you think it is? Do we smell already, like?"

"No, it's simple." Julie, always quick to pick up on the mood in the air. "We remind them of their parents. They're gap-year kids, or away from home on an adventure; we represent repression, control and conformity. Like the teachers on a school trip."

"Well, by the sound of it a lot of these will be trekking the same route we are—we'll break through it, I'm sure." I could see the confusion on Moth's face. I haven't met many people, old or young, with a lower conformity threshold than him. He'd spent his life turning left when he'd been told to go right. "Anyway, fancy a bath?"

"A bath?"

"In the river. It's a hot spring—that's where everyone's going."

Taking your clothes off in the darkness of a subarctic night doesn't feel like the most natural thing to do. But after the cold we'd felt since arriving on Iceland, to slip into the warm, shallow water of the river was an unexpected relief. People gathered in a line where a hot stream fed into the cooler river water, forming a pool the temperature of a hot bath. The group milled around, a line of fish waiting for an invisible barrier to be lifted before they could rush upstream. A rising chatter of unknown languages bubbled with the water. Beyond the line the water was too hot, but in the spot where the hot met the cold it was perfect. It felt faintly ridiculous to be sitting in chest-high water on an open valley bottom, the lava flow rising high above us and the mountains outlined beyond, black against a cloudy sky, in what was really just a hot puddle. But as the night became darker and the warmth eased away all the aches of the long journey, the other swimmers began to drift away and the river became a wild place again. Dark, syrupy, sulfurous water pushed hot steam through the sparse, spiky grasses of the riverbank. We floated in two feet of water, silently moving like water skater insects on the surface of a spring pond, as the dense cloud cover became a little brighter, fingers of faint light from somewhere way above highlighting the boiling, massing movement of heavy cloud over serrated mountains.

"So we set off tomorrow?"

"What if it's still raining as much as this?"

"We could stay here for another day, we have time."

"We could just stay in the river."

I should have said no. No, Iceland in the seasonal cusp between summer and winter is not the place for someone with a terminal neurodegenerative disease. If we wanted to walk a long path in the hope that we could replicate some of the physical benefits we'd found on the South West Coast Path, then maybe we should have looked at the Pennine Way or one of the many other long-distance paths in the UK. Paths that you can easily get off and catch a train back to a house with a bed and warmth and ordinary comforts. Not take him to a foreign country, to an alien landscape with wildly unpredictable weather systems and a path with relatively few points of escape. Or had that been the point? Had that been the draw for Moth, that sense of forcing himself into something without a safety net always close by? I helped him out of the tent into raindrops that rebounded from the flysheet with the force of ping-pong balls and watched him walk awkwardly to the toilet block, shouting as he went.

"Meet you in the kitchen tent. Get the porridge on."

I knew him too well; he didn't have to explain it. There were days when he would answer a question I'd barely formulated in my head and certainly hadn't spoken out loud. He would sing a song that I was humming internally, or pass me something I needed before I asked for it. A silent enmeshing of lives lived in unison. "Get the porridge on" carried so much more than an instruction to start breakfast. It meant "I feel like shit, but don't even suggest that we don't do this. I'm doing it regardless. Just give me the support I need. And don't, under any circumstances, let Dave and Julie think I won't make it."

"Okay, see you there."

Rain poured from the food-tent doorway in a curtain of water. Inside a throng of twenty-somethings huddled, stoves lit, cereals being eaten, last-minute adjustments being made to full, heavy packs. I unpacked porridge on a table in the corner and watched the melee of action. A group of young Finnish people poured a last round of coffee from a communal pot before packing it away, along with wooden hand-carved mugs and the reindeer pelts that they sat on. I quite envied the pelts. Even dressed in most of my clothing, with waterproof trousers between me and the bench, the seat was still cold. I boiled water as two men squabbled over who would carry the frying pan and a woman walked past in a yellow bikini. Dave and Julie fought their way through the crowd and sat at the table.

"More rain then. She's either got no dry clothes, like, or she's off to the river before breakfast. Preferred it in the dark, me, can't see all that flesh."

"Yep, must be an age thing."

Moth ducked through the curtain of water, took his hat off and looked around the tent.

"So are you all heading off this morning then?"

A bedraggled scattering of responses came back in a wide selection of languages. Clearly they were all leaving to start the trail, pulling on waterproofs and tightening rain-covers around their packs. Moth sat heavily down on the bench at the end of the table, bouncing the water on the stoves.

"Most of the tents are packed and they're all off in the rain. Don't know about the rest of you but I'm happy to hold on here for another day and see if it's any better tomorrow."

"Absolutely." Without hesitation Julie was in agreement, which

meant Dave would have no argument; his larger-than-life char-
acter was always modulated by her reasoning.

"Porridge then?"

Iceland sits on the Mid-Atlantic Ridge: an underwater mountain range that runs through the Atlantic for thousands of
kilometers. In the north it rises where the North American and
Eurasian tectonic plates meet; on Iceland they come to the surface in an open fissure that moves a measurable amount each
year. Where these plates meet the pressure and power forces the
plates to the surface, creating an eruptive land, where the old is
pushed outward and a raw uncontainable energy creates a new
earth.

As the day wore on, the rain eased and we were drawn up into
the lava field. One of the points where the earth had boiled out
from below the surface to begin its cycle anew. Black crusts of
rock shattered into millions of jagged, crystalline shapes and
then re-fused, caught in a matrix of molten magma. But now,
only a few thousand years after the earth spewed out its devas-
tating contents, the torn landscape is changing, slowly calming.
Stone and ash breaking down in the rain and sun. At a speed so
slow it can hardly be recorded, the land is being re-created. Ash
and mudstone almost imperceptibly becoming the building
blocks of a black, slimy, peat-like soil. And in that soil, tough
short grasses and moss grow from spores and seeds carried on
the wind. Moss draped over rocks, a bright green cushion of
growth, a basic starter pack of life. We picked our way through
on a path that wound around, over, up and down until it flattened into a riverbed where a central rush of water forced itself
into a narrow gorge. This deep gash of land had been formed by
the edge of the lava flow on one side of the water and a confused
up-swell of rocks on the other, where over time layers had lifted
and mixed in an amalgamation of ages that jangled the senses

and confused the eye. Black, polished, smooth obsidian lay over mudstone and shale and beneath jumbled outcrops of basaltic and rhyolitic magma. Over it all, smooth and slipping, a dense cloak of ash dust. The remnants of a land in transition. And rising above it in a contrast of ochre, cream, blue and green, the exposed hills coloring the horizon like unpolished gems against the gray sky.

The backpackers were all gone; only a few tents remained alongside ours. The bus trips had been, their passengers had used the toilets, walked around for a while in plastic ponchos, taken photographs and left. We stood in the wide-open glacial valley with a herd of horses. The sun lowered on its axis, blending their chestnut coats and long blond manes to the same color as the rhyolitic hills. These hills were formed beneath glaciers millions of years ago, but now sit open and exposed to the light. The brilliant, undulating colors of the mountains changed with the sun as it emerged weakly, brightening as it found breaks in the clouds, then deepening and darkening with the coming evening. Plumes of sulfur cloud emitted from vent holes rose into the air, steam from a boiling land. A sense of the earth breathing. We breathed with it, inhaling sulfur and dust, four people alone in an alien landscape. A place where the earth is born and life begins.

It seems not all noodles are the same. Some aren't just yellow mush, but are practically edible. I emptied some nuts into a bowl of teriyaki noodles and they almost smelled appetizing. Moth sat guiltily at the end of the table waiting to use the pan, his tin of baked beans waiting to be opened. I glanced up the table, unsure whether to laugh or be annoyed. He was finding it impossible to convert the value of the Icelandic krona into pounds sterling and had unwittingly paid five pounds for the tin in the tiny shop in the school bus. Next to us two young Germans had the contents of their rucksacks hung from the roof of the food tent and draped across their table.

"Just drying out?"

"We went to Hrafntinnusker, but the weather was so bad we turned around and came straight back."

"You walked all the way there and back in a day? Why didn't you just stay there?" The next huts were at Hrafntinnusker, eight miles away across the mountains and mainly uphill. I couldn't imagine why they would go all the way, then just come back again.

"The path from there looks really hard and this weather is so bad. We're going back to Reykjavík to hire a jeep for a week. No more hiking for us."

"Crikey, that's a long way in a day. Well, have a good time in the jeep."

"Thank you, we will. We're very happy not to be hiking."

Moth rolled the bean tin between his hands. If it was too tough for young, fit, well-equipped hikers, what chance did we have?

"You shouldn't go up. It's not safe for people like you up there."

The bean tin was gently placed on the table.

"Like us?" He pushed it slightly away.

"Yes, old people: it's not safe for you."

I passed Moth the pan so he could empty his beans. Obviously we'd be starting the trail tomorrow, whatever the weather.

The few remaining campers gathered in the river as the evening became colder, a multilingual shoal in the steaming warmth. The rain had stopped and two curious sheep grazed close to the water, sitting down to chew and watch the odd behavior of the humans. Hours passed, our skin shriveled and slowly all the others left. I sat back to back with Moth, propped together at the extreme of our heat tolerance. Dave and Julie headed to the tent and we were alone in the water, just us and the sheep, watching the clouds change color as if backlit by volcanoes. Drifting in and out of sleep, warmer in the river than in the tent. Even with down-filled three-season sleeping bags the nights were already proving to be too cold to sleep through. I had no idea how we'd stay warm in the mountains, or if we would make it up there at all. No need to discuss it; we'd find a way, or not. Just a few years earlier the possibility of us sitting in a hot river in Iceland had been as unlikely as us walking the South West Coast Path, or living in an orchard. But we'd learned so many things on that long, long walk. Things that we'd carried with us like precious jewels into the life that came after. So there seemed little point in worrying about whether or not we were capable of climbing the Eyjafjallajökull volcano or passing through the Fimmvörðuháls mountain range. We knew that time would answer most of our questions, so didn't bother asking them, but sat in the river instead. Shriveled but warm, breathing sulfur fumes until we fell into a deep sleep and woke underwater.

Hrafntinnusker

A morning wind rippled the flysheet in early green light, but as I lay in the down sleeping bag, swaddled in three layers of clothing and a woolly hat, I couldn't hear any rain. I took the hat off. No, definitely no rain. I crawled out of the tent flaps through a tangle of boots and the gas stove on to the stony campsite. The new tent had a different opening construction to the old one. One zip to either side of a central fixed panel, leaving two small triangles to get out of, one either side. Impossible for rapid early-morning exits. It's hard to run to a toilet block when your legs are still so stiff that they won't move in the right directions. But I waddled in an arched-back, thigh-clenched scurry, crashing through the doorway and straight into the first open cubicle. Breathing finally, I came back out into a shed lined with cubicles and showers with a central row of sinks and mirrors. Dripping bathers and towels hung from washing lines through the shed and looking into virtually every mirror was a clear-skinned, smooth-haired twenty-something, perfecting her appearance. I caught a glimpse of myself, already looking as if I'd spent a month at the North Pole. Hair in a random, frizzy knot on the top of my head and my skin beginning to pinch into unfamiliar lines across my cheeks. I'd only been there for two days and hadn't even walked anywhere; I clearly wasn't going to wear well aesthetically on this trip. I cleaned my teeth with my back to the mirror as the girls adjusted their clothing and brushed their immaculate hair. Then I left the shed as quickly as possible, before the complex had time to develop.

Moth was awake, but still muffled under layers and talking to me through his sleeping bag.

"I can't hear the rain."

"No, it's dry. Broken cloud, blue sky. I think we've had our last night in the river."

"Drag me out then."

I leaned into the tent and hauled him upright so he could wriggle out of his bag. Dave stepped out of his tent in one smooth action. A much smaller tent than ours and a much larger man. How did he do that?

"Looks like this is it then. Are we up for it?"

"That's why we're here, I suppose."

"Aw, c'mon, a bit more enthusiasm please."

"Where's Julie? Has she gone to make porridge?"

"No, I'm in here. I'm not getting out—I'm too cozy."

"Not just me then?"

We ate our breakfast slowly, watching the few young people that remained in the camp as they packed their cooking equipment and headed off. Then, hesitantly, we took the tent down, reluctant to give up the relative comfort of the site and head into the unknown difficulties in the hills. Moth was collapsing the tent poles, absentmindedly folding each section before packing them away, but his eyes were on the horizon. His look held all the forgetfulness, painful mornings and stiff awkward walking of the last few years. A look of self-doubt and hesitation. I took the poles from him and caught his eye. And hope: there was hope in his face too. The faint, barely breathable possibility that this wasn't just a trip to a place he'd always wanted to visit. That this was so much more than a bucket-list expedition. He was here in the hope that he could kick all the fear and pain aside and push his body as he had before. Force himself through the invisible barrier that CBD had encased around his thoughts and movements, shrink-wrapping his life like a fish sealed in a package on a supermarket shelf, viewing normality but unable to touch it. As we passed the huts a voice called to us from the small shed that took payments for the campsite.

"If you're heading to Þórsmörk you need to hurry."

"Why?"

"The buses stop running on Saturday evening."

"Why would they stop?"

"Because winter's coming."

"When, on Sunday?"

"Yes, it will be winter on Sunday."

I lifted Moth's rucksack as he put his arm through the strap, took a photograph of the starting post and a deep breath of hope. There was no going back now. We left the river behind and headed into the sulfurous heart of the southern highlands of Iceland.

I looked ahead and traced the path through the lava flow and the streaking colors of the mountain ahead, trying to keep my focus on the strangeness of the landscape and away from the bite of the rucksack on my shoulders. We'd never needed to carry so much food before and it added weight to the pack that wasn't familiar, creating a sagging, stretching feeling in my neck and a sharp tingling sensation between my shoulders. If I was feeling this, Moth must be too, even though the only extra weight he was carrying was breakfast. I vowed to take some of the things from his pack, just as soon as we'd eaten some of the food in mine.

Rising out of the hazy mist of the valley floor, the sun cleared the last of the clouds and the mountains were illuminated in catwalk colors. Behind us, across the wide expanse, rivers of bright water separated and rejoined in a confluence of dazzling threads. And ahead, white, blue and green patches of slimy chalk-like molten earth steamed and hissed with plumes of gas and water vapor. A bus parked at the campsite below ejected a group of people in long, waterproof, brightly colored ponchos, who wound their way up the hillside, stopping after every few steps to take photos, then rushing past. Hurrying uphill to reach a vantage point and take more pictures, before running back down to catch the bus before it left. A group of volunteers in orange coats bent over picks and shovels, digging chunks from the hillside, creating stone steps to cater for the footfall from the bus trips. A man in orange filled a net with three cans of soup and dropped it into a pool of boiling sulfur water, trapping the net with a rock before returning to the stones. Nearly lunchtime.

At a junction in the path, the last of the bus trippers hurried past and we dropped the packs for a moment. Two backpackers passed, slowly walking over the brow of the hill, stooped under rucksacks so vast that they caused their legs to move with knees bent and their feet turned outward. The boy had a shock of ginger hair, making him look oddly like Ed Sheeran carrying his own luggage. The girl, small and dark, seemed vertically compressed under the weight, her rucksack so large she could rest her head against the top while the bottom prevented her from sitting down.

"Wow, what do you think they've got in there? Thought we had a lot!"

"If that's Ed Sheeran maybe it's a guitar."

"And a drum kit."

"Of course it's not Ed Sheeran. He'd be dropped in by helicopter."

Ahead of us the mountains opened into an undulating carpet of color stretching in every direction. We continued along a slowly rising path as every turn and dip and climb opened a new view to another mountain range. A landscape without borders; mountainous horizons without end. Peach, yellow and ochre hills glowed in the afternoon light. Black ash-falls holding the only signs of vegetation dazzled in streaks of bright fluorescent green: moss and primitive grasses creating the start of life on dry mountains that seemed to still glisten from the dampness of millennia under ice. Sharing cereal bars and raisins, we stopped to take photographs so often that the afternoon was rapidly disappearing. As Dave lifted Moth's pack on to his shoulders a girl stopped for a moment nearby.

"Hi, great view." I'd already fallen back into the hiker rhythm of saying hello to everyone who passed. Responses came in languages and accents new and unheard before, the casual acknowledgment of passing through a wild space. No need for more, the common language was in the air around us. But this girl didn't respond. Just took an enormous camera from her pack with a lens the size of my boot, took a quick snap before packing it away and striding on, her bright red trousers flashing across the landscape in rapid time. We walked slowly on as she disappeared from view.

"Glad I did some training. Could keep up with her if I wanted to, like. Just holding back for the rest of you."

"Course you are, Dave, thanks for that."

Gray patches began to appear on the hillsides as the temperature dipped and we walked in waterproofs despite the sun.

"Do you think that's ice? It's a bit gray for ice." Julie was pointing to a gray patch in the hillside ahead.

"The remnants of last winter's snow. Turned to ice, I think." Dave was closer now, so had a clearer view ahead.

Dropping down from the crest of a small ridge we came to the first ice field, where a deep ravine of snow had turned to hard-packed ice that was now melting in the sun. Beneath, a river visible through arches and caverns in the ice carved its own passage. The ice formed a bridge over a small gorge. I'd expected the ice to be white and pristine clean, but this was darkly streaked with black mush. Moth stood on the ice next to me, kicking into it with the heel of his boot.

"What do you think this black stuff is? Do you think it's blown ash?"

"Could be, in part. But possibly it's cryoconite."

"What?"

I watched Moth walk hesitantly across the ice, taking care that his feet stayed where he placed them. At moments like this I realized that while I'd lived at the chapel, spending so much time inside my own head, I'd really had very little idea what he'd been doing at uni. Cryoconite, what was that?

It seems cryoconite is a substance that's causing glaciers across the world to melt even faster than we expected. Dust, ash, soot, bacteria and microbes picked up by wind and rain fall on the glaciers and ice fields, mixing with the meltwater on the surface and forming black patches. Just like anything else on the earth's surface, a black glacier will absorb more heat than a white one. More heat absorbed into ice can only mean one thing. Melting. Cryoconite is a natural phenomenon that will have occurred across the glaciers for as long as they've existed, especially here where the land throws out clouds of ash on a regular basis. But now rather than ash-fall being an occasional occurrence, soot from the world's carbon emissions is constantly circulating the earth, deposited with every fall of rain or snow on these once pristine landscapes. On the bodies of ice that hold the key not only to our sea levels but possibly even our climate balance.

By the time Moth had gone to great pains to explain the formation of cryoconite, we had passed over a wide plateau with open peaks and undulations on every side and multicolored mountains stretching through 270 degrees of the horizon. The final ninety degrees was filled with ice slopes rising to the side and ahead and bringing a cold wind that blew in frozen blasts from glaciers just out of sight. A monument of mounded rocks and a small metal plaque drew us off the path. A memorial to a man of only twenty-five who had got lost in a blizzard on the hillside, not half a mile away from the safety of the mountain hut. These hills are no sanctuary for any living thing. Rock, ice and sulfur are all that belong here, in a land where summer can disappear in a breath, replaced by the remorseless grip of winter before a man has time to check his map.

I'm not a fan of walking poles. I've always found them cumbersome, unnecessary, more of a hindrance than a walking aid and just another few grams of weight that I don't want to carry. Moth had carried one for a year or two, something for those unstable moments when he needed to stop himself stumbling. I'd held out, resisting them as a symbol of giving in to the inevitability of decaying joints. But persuaded by YouTube videos that I would need them for river crossings, I'd bought one. Just one, and it was staying firmly strapped to my pack, despite having seen many under-thirties striding out with two, using them like cross-country skiing poles. Now we stood on the edge of a sloping ice sheet that stretched down the mountainside from high above to a few hundred feet below. I watched Dave and Julie set off, Dave holding his one pole on the downward slope and crossing without issue, Julie following with her two, not even a slip. Moth set off, the pole protecting him from slipping with his lopsided gait. He stopped and turned back, waving his stick in the air.

"Just do it. Give in to the pole and just get it out."

I looked around and self-consciously took the pole off my pack. Unsure of the feel of it in my hand, I stepped cautiously out on to the ice. I hated putting my trust in something other than my own legs, yet I walked across the ice slope without slipping.

"Oh, she's done it. Welcome to the world of the old ones."

"Thanks for that, Julie, it was just a precaution. I'm sure I'd have been fine without it."

"Oh yeah, you wouldn't have slipped once, like."

A beacon light at the edge of the ice marked the approach to Hrafntinnusker mountain hut. These huts sit like day markers on the path. Available for people to stay in, sleeping on small mattresses in their own sleeping bags, some provide food but all of them provide warmth and shelter from the harshest of environments. All of the huts along the way were fully pre-booked, and really expensive if they hadn't been, so we planned to camp near the huts each day if we could walk far enough, so we could enjoy the communal cooking tents that were erected outside and the wonders of their toilet facilities. As we reached the edge where the land fell away, green and red huts appeared on the hillside below. Clustered around the high viewpoint of the huts and scattered down the rocky hillside were stone circles. They had the look of a ruined ancient settlement, but each stone circle stood only one to two feet high and encased a tent. Elaborate wind protection for vulnerable nylon shelters on an exposed mountainside.

Just the sight of a tiny metal hut among the stone circles made me realize I hadn't peed for ten hours. I took a deep breath and went into the stinking shed. It still seemed infinitely preferable to dropping many layers of clothing and squatting in the ice. Strangely, dehydration wasn't something I'd considered in a subarctic climate, but in the cold, dry air I hadn't even thought of drinking. I closed the door behind me and exhaled.

We erected the tent on shale and black ash within the last remaining stone circle, set fifty meters down the mountain from the others. The girl in the red trousers was here and I watched her march up the hill near the huts, passing others on the path in a rapid ascent, as Moth blew some air into the self-inflating mattress that didn't inflate, then collapsed onto it.

"I'm done. Don't know if I've got the energy to get back up to the cooking tent for food. Can't we eat here?"

"We could, but I think Dave and Julie are already there; they'll be waiting for us. Shall I go up and tell them we're eating here?" I didn't know if I could even make it up there myself; my calves had seized into a spasm that felt as if they were in a vise and I needed sleep more than food.

"No, you go up. I can't let them see how tough I'm finding this. Get the water boiling and I'll be there—I just need a minute."

The cooking tent was dark, with a long camping table running down the middle of the damp ash floor. Inside Dave and Julie were already eating. Farther into the tent in the gloom at the back the couple with the huge rucksacks were laying out a huge array of food and frying pans alongside the girl in the red trousers.

"Wow, did you really carry all that?" Tins of baked beans, fresh peppers, a dozen eggs, a bag of flour, containers of herbs, salt, pepper, knives, forks.

"Yes, it was so hard." The girl with dark hair cracked eggs into the pan, while the boy, who close up clearly wasn't Ed Sheeran, watched the girl in red trousers as she stirred noodles in a pan.

"Why are you doing it? I hate dried food, but even I wouldn't carry all of that across the mountains."

"This is the first trek I've done. Eric asked me to come and said that we needed to bring all the food. It's okay, we're going to eat our way through it."

"Eric, is that your boyfriend with the ginger hair? I hope he's carrying his share of all this."

"Oh, he's not my boyfriend, just a friend. I came from Germany to study geothermal engineering in Iceland; I met him on the campus. He hasn't got room for much food, his sleeping bag is too big to fit anything else in."

"You must really like him."

She whisked her eggs; clearly more than just liked. I doubted she would carry enough weight to make a donkey's knees buckle if she only liked him.

"I keep my weight to less than ten kilos, even less when I hiked the Pacific Crest Trail. You're a fool to carry it. I was going to hike with you two guys tomorrow, but if you can't keep up I'll go on ahead." The girl in the red trousers ate her noodles while plaiting her hair, catching Eric's unwavering gaze. I looked at the dark-haired girl, who continued whisking. We all knew she'd be walking alone tomorrow.

"Saw you run up the hill earlier. Is there a good view up there, like?" Dave, oblivious to the dynamics between the group, had been focused on food.

"Yes, went up before I ate, superb views, took some great sunset shots."

"What do you reckon? Shall we go up and have a look before we turn in, like?"

Walk up to the top of a mountain for the view? I wasn't sure if I could even stand up. The first day of a trail, having done no physical preparation, and my legs had seized into painful unbendable stilts.

"Yeah, sure, why not."

We all dragged our end-of-the-day legs up an ash slope and on to the rocky hillside. The light began to fade as cloud flowed over the hill top: running wet air following the contours from the top of the hill and down into the valley as the summit disappeared under pink and orange water vapor. Lights came on in the stone-encased tents before they disappeared too.

"No point going up now then." Julie felt in her pocket and produced a bag. "Jelly baby, anyone?"

We sat in the murk and ate sweets as the mist caressed the land, lifting and falling as if moved by some force within the earth.

An ethereal communication between sky and land. The crackling, magnetized wet air lowered, momentarily becoming denser in the valley to display a faintly lit thermal inversion, before expanding again to obscure everything.

Shivering in the rapidly dropping temperatures we wandered in the direction of the campsite, our head torches illuminating nothing but fog and rock. We walked beyond the sound of Dave and Julie opening their flysheet zip to a rocky unfamiliar slope where there was no sign of our tent. The mist began to blow past on a rising breeze. I couldn't shake the thought of the young man who had died on the hillside, only a few hundred meters from the hut. So easy in this exposed land of ice, stone and electric air to slip through the cracks between life and death. My hand in Moth's, we retraced our steps uphill, eventually stumbling over the stone circle that hid the tent.

"I never thought I'd see something like this, thought the days of adventures were over." Moth was sitting up in his sleeping bag putting his hat and gloves on.

"But now we're on the side of a mountain in the wild heart of Iceland and, according to the tourist information office, winter's coming on Sunday."

"They can't know that."

"Of course not, but the buses stop running on Saturday night so I suppose they're moving on to the winter timetable. How are you feeling?"

"Like when I lie down I might never get up."

"You'll have to: the huts close in just over a week. We'd be under two meters of snow by the end of next month."

Huddled together in the middle of the tent, wearing most of our clothes inside our sleeping bags, we lay awake as a wild roaring wind shook the flysheet and blew through the vent holes.

"I'm so sorry we're here. I just had the memory of you on the Coast Path, how you almost walked yourself back to health, and

I just hoped . . . I keep pushing and pushing—you must be beginning to hate me. I'm not like your wife anymore, more like a parent who wants you to play football for England."

"Ray, you do talk crap. It was my idea anyway. I wouldn't be here if I didn't want to be, just go to sleep."

The wind shook the tent violently, the joints of the poles creaking with the threat of collapse.

"You do realize that today we actually did something we've never achieved before."

"Listen to that wind! I know, I'm on a mountain in Iceland."

"No, something much bigger than that. We did one of Paddy Dillon's day sections in one day not three."

"Oh wow, yes we did."

Álftavatn

I fell out of the tent, catching my foot on the pile of boots. No time to put them on: I rushed behind the stone enclosure and peed in the wind. The cloud was still low, enclosing wet air that rushed and swirled eerily in eddies of green-tinged vapor. Cold steam from a hot, boiling earth. I crawled back into the tent, picking lava and black ash from my socks and curled into the sleeping bag, pulling it closed over my head. Wrapped in a down cocoon, drifting in and out of sleep, I could feel a sense of air, earth and sky moving as one interwoven current of molecules.

I'd read a magazine article in the airport that discussed the role of the sea as a sink for CO_2 emissions. Apparently one-third of atmospheric CO_2 is taken up by the sea. In the surface ocean that volume is rising in line with rising atmospheric levels. But in the deeper, colder oceans it's rising at twice that rate: vast quantities of CO_2 held trapped in the deep oceans. It seems this whole system is only held stable by the salinity of the water. I put my duvet coat on inside the sleeping bag and tried to block the vision of the ice melting into rivers beneath the ice fields the day before. Fresh water running toward the sea. What will happen when the glacial melt increases? Could that CO_2 sink system be affected? If glaciers are melting then so too is the permafrost of the northern hemisphere, where unquantifiable volumes of CO_2 and methane are held. Greenhouse gases poised to be set free into the atmosphere. I could almost feel the coming heat, but not enough to stop me shivering into the morning light. One of the lucky ones, still able to feel the cold of the high north in late August.

I made tea and porridge while still sitting in the sleeping bag having hardly slept—my own fault for half-reading articles about science. But even as the water boiled, I couldn't shake the sense of the utter irrelevance of mankind to the terrifying, powerful forces that form the earth. The sense that despite our destruction of its equilibrium, the earth and the atmosphere would continue to move as one. In that wild place, close to the birth of the land, there was an overwhelming awareness of the earth gathering itself, preparing. Rising toward the moment when it would shake like a wet muddy dog and then go about its business. Rid for good of the annoyance of humanity.

"Porridge?"

"Oh, is it morning already? Can I have tea first?"

"No, it'll go cold."

"Why so grumpy? Did you sleep okay?"

"No, not exactly."

The other cold campers, and the warm ones who'd stayed in the huts overnight, set off into the mist, out of view before they'd even left the stone circles. We were alone again, shaking fog from the tents and drinking more tea as the cloud began to lift and the landscape reappeared. Below our viewpoint on the rocky, ash-covered mountainside, the trail markers fell into a flat valley bottom that appeared to stretch uninterrupted to a ridgeline in the far distance.

"Looks like a nice easy walk. What does Paddy say, Moth, you've got your glasses?" I knew mine were buried somewhere in my rucksack, probably wrapped in the sleeping bag.

Moth thumbed through the guidebook; then he looked again at the pages, slightly puzzled.

"Yeah, just seven and a half miles, no problem, nice and easy."

No, from your expression he doesn't say that at all.

"Read it out."

He raised his eyebrows above his glasses. There was no hiding from Paddy's words; we both knew what they meant.

"He says, 'As summer advances and the snow melts, crumbling gullies emerge, with rounded ridges between them, proving slow and tiring to negotiate.'"

We stood in a line looking out across what appeared to be a flat valley. There was no snow, not a flake between us and the high glaciers in the far distance.

"Oh shit."

We examined the open landscape. Black lines scored the surface, but it still appeared flat. Until a group of orange and blue coats appeared from a black line, then walked in a straggling group across a flat section of stone and ash before disappearing again into another line.

"What time did that last group leave from the hut?" Julie was scanning the valley with the monocular.

"About nine o'clock, like." Even Dave was shuffling uncomfortably.

"Two hours ago."

"Oh shit." Moth's hand squeezed my arm. So much in that squeeze. I don't know if I can do this, I'm going to find it really tough, don't let the others know. I didn't need the hand on my arm to tell me that. I lifted his rucksack onto his shoulder, unsure how I'd manage myself with legs that felt like lead and a pounding headache from lack of sleep.

Standing at the edge of the first gully, we knew Paddy hadn't been wrong. If this had been tiring for the superman of long-distance walking, we were going to find it really hard going. The black gullies were formed of slippery ash that moved like mud underfoot and sharp, jagged outcrops of glass-smooth obsidian rock. We slid down twenty meters and then scrambled back up a down escalator of moving earth. Exhausting. Looking ahead the plain of gullies seemed to stretch into the distance, only finally ending at an escarpment on the far horizon. It could be a few hundred meters or a lot more, hard to say, as the scale on the map in the guidebook didn't seem to relate to the gullies. I took a deep breath and carried on. Two hours later the ridge began to rise ahead, but still more gullies remained. Black gashes that became strewn with colored rock and sulfurous outpourings of vapor. At the bottom of the final gully a hole in the ground exposed an underground river of boiling water that raced past the hole at tremendous speed, spitting horizontal jets of hissing water at ankle level as it went. I watched the jet stream of violent, explosive heat in awe, unable to turn my eyes away. This isn't a quiet, stable planet that we live on, but a living, breathing entity powered by the boiling forces of heat and movement that melt rocks and move mountains. The core of its strength was visible here at this surface vent in this empty place where the earth begins and ends. That same strength lies under our feet in tarmacked cities where we live so far removed from the natural environment we could almost believe it has no relevance to us. But this is one earth and this wild, unstoppable power moves beneath all our lives.

Scrambling to the top of the ridge we turned to look back across the valley. Not a few hundred meters, but miles of gullies crossed. The huts of Hrafntinnusker were just green and red dots in the far distance. Ice-cold winds blowing from distant glaciers froze our sweaty clothes, yet the sun burned our faces from clear skies. We walked on for a while, away from the wind of the edge, but Moth dropped his pack, finally sitting down in exhaustion.

"Mars bar anyone?" Julie, far more in tune to Moth's body language than I realized, seemed to have the deepest pockets and the very best snacks.

"Thanks, Julie, can't think of anything better. Although I could actually kill a plate of beans on toast right now."

Was he hungry? I'd barely felt hungry at all; maybe the cold had reduced my appetite as well as my thirst. It was easy to see how people quickly perish in this environment. I fished around in my food bag for anything that he could eat cold.

"Oh, what the fuck? I don't believe it." Moth was holding his Mars bar up for us to look at. "Look." Two shards of white stuck out of the chocolate bar.

"What, how?"

He picked the white things out and held them in his palm. Two white shards of broken teeth.

"Where have they come from? Smile for me."

Moth smiled. Where once there had been a smile that made old ladies feel at ease, now he had a broken flash of spiky teeth that wouldn't have looked out of place on a boxer.

"Wow, not from the back then. I know your teeth are quite thin, but how could that have happened?"

"So where are they from? Oh jeez, the front, I can feel it."

"Does it hurt?" I began to panic about how to help him if he was in severe pain in an Icelandic wilderness. I didn't think a few ibuprofen would solve that one.

"No, I can't feel a thing."

I looked again at his teeth. One had sheared in half horizontally, the other had split vertically to the gum. How could that not be hurting?

"Moth, how is that not hurting? I broke my tooth and it was absolute agony, I had to get it fixed straightaway." Julie was looking at his teeth in astonishment.

"I don't know, but I really can't feel anything." For months he'd been saying he felt some numbness in his face and mouth. At times he'd bitten his tongue without realizing, but other than being amazed that he could be bleeding without knowing I hadn't given it too much thought. But this was surreal.

"So, no more cold Mars bars for you then."

Moth rolled the teeth in his hand, and then continued to eat the chocolate bar through the side of his mouth.

"I'll just have to warm them from now on. What shall I do with these though? Do you think if I keep them they could be stuck back in?"

"What, with a bit of superglue, like? Don't be daft. We should bury them. Let's put them here in the rocks around the marker post."

Moth dropped the broken teeth where Dave was pointing, in the rock pile that held the post upright.

"Good-bye, teeth, part of me forever in the Subarctic."

I scattered some ash over his brittle teeth; there was something almost funeral-like about the act. Something final. He would possibly never stand on a high Icelandic mountain again. But more than that, it was an unspoken acknowledgment of the frailness of his body and the almost imperceptible changes CBD was bringing.

The black ash of the valley behind us, we re-entered the multicolored hills, the sun still bright in the late afternoon, highlighting their colors with even greater brilliance. The path leveled at last and we walked parallel to an ice-capped mountain, the frozen wind keeping us in waterproofs despite the sunshine. And all around, the earth continued to breathe out plumes of sulfur which rose from the blues and greens that surrounded the vent holes. Two sheep walked slowly past a steam cloud. There are very few sheep in the southern highlands, despite there being more than twice as many sheep on Iceland as there are humans. There's nothing to attract them up here, just an occasional ribbon of green on a distant hillside, yet intermittently they appeared in twos and threes, small family groups. A harsh and difficult life trekking miles between sources of food and water, but here in the highlands they are free to be the unfettered, wild animals they really are. We carried on, touched by the sight of the only animals we'd encountered for two days. No animals or birds, no insects, no life other than humans. This vast, barren landscape wasn't a place for life. But as we walked through it, silent, each in our own state of wonder, I felt closer to my real self than I had since leaving the tent for the last time on the South West Coast Path. Only the land breathed here and I breathed with it.

Over a small crest, the path wound faintly away along the top of a rounded hillside of shale and boulders, the land spreading out around us in multitoned bare rock. A mounding landscape of muted gold and ochre, beneath a blue sky broken by white, scudding clouds. A landscape so new, so alien, my eyes could barely process the sight. The vivid colors of Dave's and Julie's clothing, already on the other side of a small valley, stood out in sharp relief. It was a photographer's dream view, and I took photos that I knew couldn't possibly capture the scene through the broken lens of an old mobile phone. But I stared until the brightness of their clothing passed out of sight, trying to imprint the wonder of the moment on my memory. A raw, open landscape. A land untouched by bacteria, microbes or ash, nothing here that could turn to soil or growth. Just an empty canvas, covered only by the wild, uninterrupted colors of a new earth. A place so thin both sides of infinity meet in a cycle without end.

At the edge of the ridge the world changed. The colored mountains ended abruptly, falling steeply down a rubble-strewn scree run of path to a black valley floor that spread for miles, scattered with lakes and vast waves of rock rising out of the land into peaking crests about to break in angry foam against some wild black shoreline. In the distance, spiked mountains streaked with green surrounded the black valley. Vegetation. Life. And beyond this strange landscape, rising huge and cold in the background, a distant glacier formed a white slice between earth and sky.

The four of us stood in a line at the edge of our known world as two men, tough, hardened mountaineers wearing the most up-to-date hiking gear and professionally packed rucksacks, took our photo before disappearing confidently over the edge and down the mountain.

Far away, at the edge of a lake, the sun caught the corrugated zinc of the Álftavatn huts. A shimmering oasis, for us still hours away. We inched our way down on unstable ground that slipped and ran beneath our feet, legs clenched in the hope of protecting knees from the pain of jarring. The slope went on unendingly. I sat on a boulder for a moment and looked across the scene, still only a third of the way down. Four people past the point when joints spring back from hard use, sixty getting closer for some and receding into the distance for others. But just for a moment I was twenty-two, standing on the side of Great Gable mountain in the Lake District, Moth at my side in a faded pair of blue tennis shorts that he'd worn through every day of every summer for years. We'd climbed the mountain in the early morning of a bright summer day; then we'd lain on the top, staring at the sky and passing clouds for hours. We were about to go down and it was still only midafternoon. We desperately wanted to head straight back up the other side of the valley and on to Scafell, the highest mountain in England, but we didn't have time, we needed to get back on to the motorway and head south for work the next day. A steep gray slope of broken rock fell down the mountainside in one continuous sheet to the bottom. The path we would follow passed through the middle of it on awkward, moving ground. Moth pushed his long hair off his face, the wind catching it and blowing the mousy blond strands upward, giving him a manic, half-crazed look.

"Scree run?"

"What?"

"Scree run, then there's time for a late lunch in the pub before we leave." He bent his knees, turned his feet sideways and began to run downhill on rocks that slipped like an avalanche beneath his feet. "Or you can crawl down like a granny while I'm eating pie and chips." And he was gone, daypack bouncing on his back, surfing the stones toward his lunch.

I always followed. There was no question; if he went I would be behind him. I took the pose he had, spread my arms like a surfer and let the rocks take me. Hips loose, knees bent, flying on an escalator of stones, to Moth waiting at the bottom, wild-haired, dust-covered, arms open to catch me.

When do we lose confidence in our bodies, forget how to trust them without thought or preparation? What was the difference between then and now? I watched the others making their way down. Dave, younger than the rest of us, already near the bottom. Moth, carefully picking his way down with the pole, not trusting his legs and feet to support him. Julie, older than all of us, placing each foot with the same care as Moth, fearful of knees that caused regular problems. It was the way we moved. We clenched our muscles, holding our legs stiffly like the walking poles, trying to protect our joints from jolting pain. When we were young our muscles were relaxed, they bounced, cushioning the compression, acting more like hydraulic suspension. I stood up and flexed my knees, releasing the tight angry tension in my thighs and hips. I could try; I could just let myself go. I turned sideways and thought about beginning a scree run, but a steeply curving path with boulders sticking out at dangerous angles was probably no place to risk it. So I put my pole away in my pack, flexed my knees and bounced slightly with each step, letting the mountainside take me. I was in another place, another time, another body as I reached the bottom without pain or stiffness. Maybe aging really is all in the mind.

Possibly the best way to defy it isn't through expensive serums, endless hours in the gym and overly sharp scalpels, but simply by trusting our bodies to be as strong and capable as they ever were, being in the wild outdoors whenever we can and not spending too long looking in the mirror.

At the bottom we faced our first river crossing. Too deep to keep our boots on and hop across the boulders, we would need to wade through the ice-cold, crystal-clear rushing water. Rolling up trouser legs and replacing boots with neoprene shoes we'd carried for this moment, we walked tentatively through the river. Halfway across, the force of the water pushed at my knees and I hesitated too long, allowing a cold pain to grasp my feet, but steadied by the pole they found gaps between the boulders despite their growing numbness. On the other side, drying my legs with a neck scarf that I'd just taken off, I looked over at Moth sitting on his upturned rucksack by the side of a river of water that had flowed from the ice-capped subarctic mountains, drying his feet on a red spotty bandanna, a glacier high in the distance. All I could think of was the doctor sitting on the edge of his table in his surgery in Wales after he'd told Moth he possibly had only two years left: "Don't tire yourself, or walk too far, and be careful on the stairs." But here he was, exhausted, bruised, hungry, but laughing as he put his boots back on to fresh cold feet. Already four years into borrowed time.

"When I googled the Álftavatn huts it said there was a café there."

I could see him smirking, knowing he'd saved this nugget of information until the moment when it would have the greatest effect.

"What, a café with real food, like?" Dave was tying his laces just a little faster.

"Well, it said food, and probably some sort of heating."

"About two miles away? Better get there then, before this food's all gone."

After only a few days, the novelty of a return to dried noodles had already worn off. The valley opened ahead, miles of flat ash and shale between the waves of mountains. We walked on, in an endless space where time and possibility seemed infinite.

Eric with the ginger hair and huge pack was standing outside the toilet block, shuffling his feet, his hands deep in his pockets, clearly waiting for someone to emerge.

"Hi, how was it coming down that mountainside with your heavy pack? It was so loose underfoot, wasn't it?"

"Hmm." He didn't even look up, but turned his back and stepped away. Maybe he'd forgotten we'd spoken the night before.

We pitched the tents at the edge of a shallow river and walked over to the lake. Piles of clothes lay at the edge, abandoned by a group who had hoped to dive in for a swim, but had waded naked into the water only to find that after fifty meters they were still only up to their knees. They had to run a third of the way into the lake before it was deep enough for them to hide, splashing and shrieking through the shallows. The water must have receded in recent centuries, as a man was supposed to have drowned in this lake. Falling off his horse while hunting swans with his daughter, he disappeared and although she searched the lake, his daughter couldn't find his body. She went back to her village to get help for the search, but in the night her mother had a dream in which her father asked the search team to look for his body under an overhanging cliff. The next day the villagers found him in the exact spot. Apparently not just folklore, but a true story, or so it said in a leaflet in the toilet block. Icelanders believe that their dead speak to them through their dreams, so the girl cleaning the toilets said, and obviously this story is proof. It's a shame the mother couldn't have asked the father how he drowned in water that only came up to his knees.

Moth hadn't been wrong. There really was a café. After the iced wind of the mountains, the heat that sucked through the door as it opened felt Saharan, and we happily left our boots at the door and went inside. Huge bowls of vegetable soup and toasted sandwiches were a luxury that we had only dreamed of: supplies brought to this remote spot by four-by-four trucks with immense wheels.

"Just a few more days, then the trucks will be in to take away the huts that are on wheels. Two weeks and we'll shut up the remaining huts for the winter and get out before the snows come. Just staying open for the last few stragglers on the trail, like you, then after that anyone who comes up here is on their own . . . well, if they're mad enough to set off out of season we just hope they're prepared." The German boy behind the counter poured steaming tea from a pot, happily telling us that his bags were already packed, ready for a return to civilization. "Four months up here—believe me, you've had enough."

I sat by the window, watching the last of the light fade across the water, highlighting the mountains in shades of gray and silver. Outside, Eric seemed to be holding court at a picnic bench, the girl in the red trousers with the wild eyes sitting next to him and others that we'd spotted along the route listening intently to what he was saying. The engineer who carried his food was nowhere to be seen. Battery lights came on in the café hut and I realized the tough mountaineers who'd taken our photograph were sitting on the table next to us. They ignored me, heads buried in guidebooks, tanned skin and week-old beards glowing in the faint light. The German from behind the counter began lighting candles, placing them in the dark corners and put one down on the mountaineers' table.

"A romantic light, so you can talk of love." One of the men raised his head and merely nodded at the German. As I looked away I noticed their feet, heavily padded in thick woolen socks, intertwined beneath the table. I was as guilty as the people whom we'd met on the South West Coast Path. Like them I'd jumped to conclusions about these men. I'd just seen two weather-worn, hardened mountaineers on an efficient expedition; I hadn't seen the rest of their story, or even considered that there was one. No different from the people who had immediately assumed we had issues with substance abuse or mental health the moment we said we were homeless, I had assumed these were straight men with patient girlfriends waiting at home. Not two people in a loving relationship having the trip of a lifetime. And they had really great socks.

"Excuse me, where did you get those amazing socks?"

"In the Mountain Mall bus at Landmannalaugar, so nice, made from Icelandic wool."

"Damn, wish I'd bought some, my feet have been freezing at night."

We reluctantly left the café hut, the wind feeling even colder after the extreme warmth inside. Despite that, at this much lower level the cold was almost tolerable, but I still longed for woolen socks.

Emstrur

The morning broke in a faint light as I tripped over the guy rope getting out of the tent and rolled toward the river, but stopped myself before my only dry socks got wet. The engineer was walking slowly along the path from the lake, her head down, hands in pockets.

"Hi! You're out early. Ready for another day with that big pack?"

"I still have to carry that pack for two more days, then there's talk of going farther."

"Aren't you enjoying it?"

"Nothing is what I thought it would be." She walked slowly away, hunched and quietly crying. On the picnic bench Eric and the girl in red trousers sat side by side, heads close together, as others came to join them and he handed out the biscuits the engineer had carried.

The other backpackers had long gone by the time we'd eaten porridge and packed the tents. A cold wind blew off the lake from wild gray skies framed by black mountains, giving the morning a threatening edge, the damp air heralding turbulence to come. The path snaked away from the safety and warmth of the huts and café, climbing over a ridge and falling to a river crossing: fast iced water at knee height gripping my legs in tight bands of pain as rain began to fall. Black ash slowly replaced shale and lava as we reached a small hut that was rarely used so late in the season. The wind lifted over the ridges to fall on to the lower ground with force, driving rain against waterproofs until they flapped like wet, ash-covered sails. We made tea on a bench sheltered behind the hut and took it through an open doorway to drink it sitting on the floor of the drying room, dripping waterproofs hanging from racks overhead.

Moth leaned against the wall, soaking up the heat. He'd been quiet all morning, barely speaking as we'd walked away from the lake. He'd been so hard on himself, suggesting we come to this place of subarctic weather systems in a desert of volcanic soot, where there was no choice but to keep walking, no other way out. In the hope of what? That we could re-create an effect that he'd experienced on the South West Coast Path, when we knew that was probably impossible? Then we had walked for months; there was no way we could get that same result in just a few days. I couldn't shake the thought that maybe it was time to just let it be, to stop pushing and let him rest. Were the farm and the orchards enough to slow the decline and allow us time to acknowledge his illness fully and prepare to let go, as I'd thought I'd been able to once before? I watched the tremor in his hand as Julie passed him a cereal bar and started to move my aching body off the floor to cross the room. Opening wrappers takes far more dexterity than is available to hands that move unbidden and uncontrolled. But then I sat back down. Slowly, but firmly, he grasped the wrapper and opened it, the same dexterity that had put the spring back into the strimmer head. He ate the bar, carefully avoiding his broken teeth, and pushed the wrapper into his pocket, seemingly unaware of what he had just done.

The rain passed, leaving a gray air drying in the cold wind. Over a small lip away from the hut, a wide-open soot field stretched ahead for miles, all the way to the horizon. Either side of this apartment, matte-black valley, near-vertical mountains rose to jagged crenellations. But before we could reach the soot field there was another river to cross. Wider, deeper, faster. Muddy brown icy water straight from a glacier.

Dave and Julie were looking for something in a rucksack and

Moth had his boots off before anyone, hanging them around his neck and standing at the side of the water.

"I'll go over and see how deep it is."

"But wait for . . ."

He had gone, feeling his way across, finding gaps between the boulders of the riverbed to wedge his pole in and following confidently with his feet, the water above his knees.

"Bugger, I didn't realize he'd gone. Is he all right? I'll catch him up then come back for you, Ju." Dave was on his feet, hurrying to get into the river, but I caught his arm.

"No, let him go; he'll be okay."

We watched as he climbed out on the far bank, waving for us to cross. Dave and Julie waded in and were gone, but I stood on the bank. On the opposite shore Moth was drying his feet on the red bandanna. I shoved my trousers in the pack and waded thigh deep to a meter-wide island of land in the middle of the river. Fiercely cold water rushed by on all sides, driven into the sky in jets of wind as it pounded against the boulders. I closed my eyes and felt my body swaying with the force of the elements. Here in a place where the land was reborn, where it stripped away its surface and found a new earth beneath, where mountains ended and began. Devoid of all but a fleeting microbial chance, in this raw upheaval was the start of life, the start of hope.

I watched Moth on the opposite bank, boots on, laces tied, beckoning me to him. For a moment, the rush of water seemed to slow and I thought I saw a young man push the long hair from his face and wait to catch me as he called me on into his world. A fleeting moment of connection. The earth, our lives, entwined, dependent. Stripped back to an earlier, raw state. Unfettered, reformed, renewed. And I could hear the voice for the first time in this alien land. Roaring in deep-throated tones from mountainsides streaked with green growth painted across the black. New life growing from the destruction. Fresh, clean; the same, but new. Here in the icy tumult of a world beginning was our connection to it all. A chance, a hope, a breath. I stepped into the raging water and picked my way across to a man who was surviving the upheaval in his body, a man returning to a raw state of being. Neurons refiring, new connections forming, a primeval simplicity being refound.

On, through soot so heavy the wind couldn't move it. A feather-soft, yet solid, unmoving black blanket. Across a plain of dust that appeared flat and featureless, but hid deep gorges, blasted by ferocious meltwater, crossed by a bridge of flimsy wooden poles. Yet all around I could see it: more new life. Thrift, bladderwort and sharp silver grasses, species that would be at home on a British sea cliff, hung on in pockets of eroded, composted black mush. Soot evolving miraculously into the starting block of vegetative life. Roots somehow finding a purchase in the loose, inhospitable earth. A future meadow in the making, before the next eruption presses the reset button on evolution and the land returns to the beginning of its endless cycle. A cold wind came in blasts and eddies, skating over the half-pipe of the valley in an endless battering, plucking motion. We fell into a metronome of movement: four bodies moving slowly, steadily through the black landscape. As the land finally rose to an escarpment I looked back to Moth, but he wasn't at my shoulder. Two hundred meters behind, a figure stood on a boulder; he wouldn't have been visible if it hadn't been for the blue cover on his rucksack. Green waterproof arms outstretched, wrapped by the wild air, in a moment of acceptance of the raw blankness of the landscape. I closed my eyes, feeling the same wind he did, imprinting the sight of him as he would always be to me: free in the wide embrace of the natural world.

Dropping down from the small ridge and the Emstrur huts appeared at last. Tucked in a narrow ravine where scrubby bushes clung to the side of a fast-flowing stream, overhung with thick growths of angelica and Himalayan balsam. Unwilling to head down into the ravine, I stayed on the higher levels where the wind blew unfettered, sitting on a bench in the cooking tent, looking down into the deep, damp camping area below.

"Don't sit here and sulk, Ray. Just look at the way this tent's moving—and it's tied down with winch straps. We've got to move down out of the wind or we'll just get battered. People are piling rocks round their tents for a reason; it's not decoration." Moth refused to take his rucksack off, but stood in the cook-tent doorway. "Let's just do it. I need to get this pack off and make some food."

Familiar tents scattered across the flat areas along the stream. The girl with red trousers and a now familiar group of young people gathered around Eric's tent, but the engineer was nowhere to be seen. We pitched the tent on a slope of shale and grit and headed back up to the communal space offered by the cook-tent, through rain that had come without warning. Exhausted and cold, we longed to cook food while sitting in our sleeping bags in the tent, but the slope made that impossible—the noodles would have poured out of the pan. The tunnel tent shook and leaked waterfalls of rain through rips in the plastic. Eric and his growing band of followers gathered around two tables pushed together. Bedraggled wet people gazed at him in awe as two American girls made him coffee. Moth lay on a bench among dripping waterproofs and steaming hikers while the water boiled on the stove, adding to the fog in the shelter.

"So where are you all heading then?" Moth sat up on the bench and moved closer to the young backpackers. Bored by the them-and-us barrier that seemed to have developed between the twenty-somethings and ourselves, he tried to break into the circle.

"Þórsmörk," someone replied. The others barely acknowledged him.

"Oh, right, yeah, us too. Any of you heading over the Fimmvörðuháls?"

They looked up at him then, slightly sneering, slightly amused.

"Ha, no, weather's looking too rough. We're getting the bus out of here. If you're heading over there you might need some more sticks." They closed ranks, sniggering among themselves, and Moth returned to the bench.

"Don't worry about it, mate, they're probably scared of you with those teeth like, you look like a right bruiser."

"But I was just trying to have a chat."

"Forget it, mate, eat your food."

We'd been walking long enough for a packet of dried pasta and a piece of chorizo that had survived in the rucksack since Reykjavík to taste like a plate of wonder from a Michelin-starred Italian restaurant. Water boiled for a third cup of tea and we shared some chocolate raisins in the hope that they would be soft enough to allow Moth to hold on to the last of his teeth.

The huddle on the other tables tightened around Eric, who was taking another food bag out of his rucksack. I put my water-proofs on as he handed out small sachets of herbs, obviously oregano, and the group slowly dispersed, heading away to their tents, leaving just Eric leaning against the scaffold pole that held the tent up and the girl with the red trousers lying on the bench next to him with her head on his lap. Why hadn't I thought of that before? They were all following him for the quality of his seasonings. We completely understood how dull dried food can be after a while; it would definitely be improved by a pinch of oregano.

There was still no sign of the engineer.

Langidalur

I lay in a curled ball of pain near the tent doorway. When would I ever learn that camping on a slope always resulted in my sleeping bag sliding relentlessly toward the lower end of the tent? It was pitch black, not a scrap of light filtering through the flysheet, but Moth's knees under my head and the pain in my hips said I'd done it again. Why didn't Moth ever slide downhill? Was it his weight that held him down, or because he seemed to lie perfectly still all night, not constantly wriggling like I did? He was in a deep sleep, groaning lightly with each breath. Was he in pain and his brain registering it even as he slept, or was it the forerunner to a full-throated snore? I shuffled in a snake-like motion back uphill, joints pinging in agony as I uncurled. In the absolute blackness I imagined designs for sticky self-inflating mats that didn't move on the nylon groundsheet and Velcro attachments that fixed the sleeping bag in place no matter how extreme the slope. The groan didn't develop into a snore but continued as a low moan of pain. However hard he tried to convince me in the daytime that he was coping, in his sleep he couldn't hide. Had I really seen a change in his movements yesterday, or was it no more than wishful thinking, hoping for the same miracle we'd had on the South West Coast Path, yet knowing it was impossible in such a short space of time? Rain began to beat on the flysheet, thunderous rain that fell from the tent with the sound of torrents from a gutter. I fumbled around in the darkness and pulled the waterproofs over him.

★

Leaving the Emstrur huts in warm sunshine, the pounding rain of just a few hours earlier already drying, we climbed away from the ravine into a fresh cool wind blowing from the higher mountains covered in heavy snow.

"What the hell, what day is it?"

"I'm not sure. Is it Sunday?" Moth glanced at his watch to check the day of the week.

"Winter came early then?"

"What?"

"It was supposed to come today, on Sunday—obviously came last night like, with all that snow."

How could the Icelanders predict the season so accurately in a land where the weather systems seem to emanate from the very earth itself? Accurately enough to set the bus timetables by it? Maybe the 350,000 permanent inhabitants of the island still have an unacknowledged connection to the elements. Maybe even the inhabitants of Reykjavík can look across the ice-gray water and sense a cold front on the horizon. Possibly the ancestry which reaches back to Viking longboats that crossed those same seas still holds in its genes the ability to sense movement in the skies, or a change in the wind. Or perhaps the high level of volcanic activity here means it's the most geologically and meteorologically scrutinized bit of rock on the planet and great weather forecasting comes from that.

I stopped, panting for breath on a path of loose stones, looking back across the black ash of a valley bottom and another river just crossed. Moth and Dave walked past, chatting easily about life in the boy scouts and the merits of Firestarter badges. Julie strode by in her relentless metronome of perseverance. All disappearing over the edge of the jagged lip of the flat-topped escarpment above. Alone on the windswept mountainside, I was as close to the others unpacking lunch on the flat top as I was to the glacier that moved through this valley millennia ago, carving it into a classic U shape. Or to the deer we'd heard sing on the hillside at Lochan Tuath a lifetime ago, or the green stones we'd picked from the beach at the Bay at the Back of the Ocean. All those moments felt huge and present in the air as it moved along the valley, pushed by the river. A background roar of the rushing elements of air and water, a sense of the earth moving without time. I've read arguments that say time doesn't exist, that it's only a human construct to measure change. If that's true, then on that rocky slope I was in a place outside of time, where all things existed and nothing was lost, only re-formed.

What is it about boys and badges that fifty years after they pinned them on their green jumpers and straightened their scarves, they can still hold such relevance in their lives? As I left the timeless valley behind and stepped over the edge of the escarpment I could hear the conversation still going on, as if the badges had been handed out yesterday and the years between hadn't happened. Moth sat on a flat rock, already holding a cup of soup. Chatting as if he'd just taken a stroll in the park, as if life had barely touched him and his hold on it was as permanent as the mountains. A world without time, or just a moment in life: is there a difference?

The flat top of the escarpment was disconnected from the neighboring mountain. A high cliff face of red chevrons of rock forced up by huge tectonic uplifts was separated from where we stood by a cavernous ravine where a river rolled and boiled far below. It was as if we stood on a column that had just risen from the earth. A white sea bird spread its wings and glided on the air currents above the river. As I watched it rise high on the wind across the cliff face, stark against the black and red rock, I realized it was the first bird I'd seen since passing a group of whimbrels near the coast while on the bus to the lava head in Landmannalaugar. I watched the fulmar glide into the distance, following the ravine and the river away to the south. All that was left was the roaring, wild silence of an empty land without vegetation or animal life. A heaving, crashing chasm of noise and movement, overlaid by a veneer of stillness.

The earth beneath our feet has no need of humanity. It exists in a state of fixed impermanence, a volcanic equilibrium of rock and ash in constant realignment. The only transition is in the changing state of molecules on its surface. The archaeological eras of Nordic, Neolithic, Roman and Plastic erupt and fold in chevrons of change, across an earth that will undoubtedly eject any presence of life that threatens it, as surely as a splinter from a human thumb. We packed the cups away and followed the fulmar south through a landscape of shrinking glaciers and warming skies.

The molecules on the surface were visibly changing. As the path progressed gradually south, so more and more patches of ash had evolved into soil that held low grasses and thrift. Dave and Julie walked on ahead, casually pointing walking poles at some distant peak. Moth meandered behind them, stopping repeatedly to take photographs or move the weight of his rucksack across his shoulders, but then disappeared from view. The ash thinned, replaced by stony shale, then dropped into a huge bowl in the land. The others were already over the rim on the opposite side, but in the bottom was a bush, just one bush, alone in a hollow, shining yellow. A yellow so bright that it reflected its color onto the surrounding earth. Not a recognizable shrub to my eye, but something totally unknown, dazzling the dark earth with its brilliance. I walked around it, held by the wonder of it being able to grow in such a hostile landscape, as Moth walked back toward me and dropped his rucksack down.

"I just went over the top to see if there were any other bushes like this on the other side."

"Are there?"

"No. This is so unreal, like something totally new has been created and just put here."

"Thought you didn't believe in stuff like that? That sounds almost creationist."

"No I don't, but it's as if the earth has made something that can only grow in this one spot where nothing else can thrive. As if the molecules have moved to allow life to exist in another form."

A pale yellow light bathed him in the shrub's reflected glory as he picked up his rucksack and swung it on to his shoulder, then lifted mine for me to put my arms through. A changing landscape, where molecules, life and time shifted and transformed.

As the land fell into a wide river valley the vegetation increased. Scrubby growth of bilberries, birch and tough grasses scattered the riverbank. An occasional insect lifted from the path. Sparse but forceful life was emerging. The final river crossing of the Laugavegur Trail lay ahead. Not one river to be crossed, but a valley of water that separated and diverged and rejoined. Veins of water across a body of rock and shale.

"How the fuck are we going to cross that? It's like ten rivers in one." Moth's rucksack was down and his boots were already off by the time I reached the edge of the river.

"Well, we'll just pick our way over with the poles, like. I think we should go this way." Dave was pointing upstream through a maze of water.

"Not sure about that. I think here, where it's wider but shallower." Moth was already wading in the opposite direction.

"What, are you telling me there's no boy-scout badge for river crossings?" Julie strapped her sandals on to her feet and headed into the river, delicately testing each step with her walking pole. I watched the three of them, nervous, excited, but sure enough of themselves to step out into the fast-flowing iced water, and then, checking that each step was secure, find their way to the opposite shore. Moth sat on his rucksack drying his feet as I stepped into the water, the noise of the river almost deafening as it pushed at my knees, sharp pain gripping my ankles. But I barely acknowledged either. *Don't tire yourself . . . and be careful on the stairs.*

Refreshed feet warm in boots, we climbed away from the noise of the river into a thicket of birch and undergrowth. Iceland faded away and as we followed the narrow path through the branches we could have been in the foothills of Snowdonia, walking on peaty ground past tiny streams of clear water. But when we climbed a ridge Iceland was back in full view, the edge of a glacier filling the skyline. Then down, down among birch and sky to a tiny campsite by the Langidalur hut at Þórsmörk, the edge of a wide, stony, tree-lined river valley, surrounded by high-peaked mountains. The end of the Laugavegur, but the start of something bigger. Rising beyond, the Fimmvörðuháls loomed, barring the way to something hidden and foreboding.

Clusters of people sat on benches around the hut. We found a space at a picnic table where two men were sitting. Shorter than me with very similar, unusual gnome-like expressions. They stared at us, smiling and nodding. Moth caught their look.

"Hi."

"Well, hello, are you staying in the hut?"

"No, we're camping."

"Of course, maybe that's because you like camping?" They were nudging each other and laughing. Possibly German.

"It's okay, getting a bit chilly though."

"Yes, but you're used to it being cold, no?"

"Well, we're from the UK, so . . ."

" 'Ere, come and look down at the bottom, some good pitches down by the river." Dave had already explored the site.

We wandered down to the edge of a riverbed that in full spate would be a vast and terrifying expanse of angry muddy water nearly a quarter of a mile wide, but was now a scattering of streams, with just a narrow central river.

A small cooking tent looked out to the mountains. Eric, the girl in red trousers and a collection of others who had come and gone from their group sat inside, filling the tent with steam and food. But—again—no sign of the engineer. They shouted out from the tent.

"Didn't think you'd make it!"

"Well, here we are. Are you all finishing here, or going over the Fimmvörðuháls?"

"They're all finishing here, but we're going over. Just straight over in the day tomorrow. I don't feel as if I've had a proper walk yet, so it will make a good stretch to finish on." The girl in the red trousers looked confident but Eric stirred his soup, looking down at the table. He'd probably need to add some more oregano to that, if he was to have any chance of walking the twenty-five kilometers over the mountains to Skógar near the main road to Reykjavík, in one day.

On the opposite side of the riverbed an off-road bus wound its way slowly through the boulders, lifting, jerking and twitching as it came toward a small group of people sitting on the riverbank. Among them was the engineer with her rucksack, straps tightened and looking half its original size.

"Aren't you going over with Eric?"

"No. This hasn't been a good holiday for me. I thought Eric was my friend, or something more. But I'm just his donkey, his packhorse carrying his frying pan. And I had a dream."

"A dream?"

"Last night, I dreamed about my grandmother who died years ago. I never dream of her."

"Was it a bad dream?"

"No, it was a beautiful dream. She was making *kuchen* in our family kitchen. She said, 'Come home, the strudel is ready.' So I'm going home. Iceland is not for me."

I waved as the huge wheels of the bus bounced back across the riverbed. Sad for her, but a sadness tinged with envy. No comforting arm reached through my dreams with plates of strudel.

We sat in the cooking tent with freeze-dried rice and the last six Jelly Babies.

Shivering in the darkness, there was no choice but get out of the tent. The cold had woken me, biting through the down sleeping bag and all my clothes. That and too many cups of tea the night before. Desperate for a pee, I shoved boots on and scrambled to get the zip open before it was too late, but the zip wouldn't open. The flysheet was solid with ice and the dampness of the night before had frozen the zip closed. I ran my fingers up and down it until it thawed enough to unzip, folding the tent door back like the cover of a hardback book. Beyond the tent the night spread in an ice-still vastness of mountains and sky. The huts and campsite were unlit, as if they had melted back into the birch woods, leaving only a deep dark world of ridgelines, sky and stars. The bonfire of the evening before smoked with only the faintest glow at the edge of the riverbed. Silence. Switching off the head torch as I left the toilet block, a faint light spread and wavered around the eastern horizon. Maybe the first movement of dawn? No, too early. Or starlight refracted from the white glow of the glacier? But the light moved, lifting in brightness, a hesitant spreading mist of light, a fluctuating ripple of energy. Then without warning it broke into fingers of whiteness, then falling, hanging curtains of color that blew in some wild polar wind from horizon to horizon. Pink, blue and the faintest green painted the sky in moving brushstrokes of charged particles.

"Moth, Moth, get up, the aurora, it's here."

People were emerging from tents and huts, awestruck by the

vast magnificent spectacle of the earth displaying its aura. A chance encounter with the atmosphere that's always there, but so rarely seen. Fingers of the universe reaching down to include the earth in its constant motion. I thought of the engineer in her bed in Reykjavík, sleeping after packing her bags ready to fly away tomorrow, held safe by the call of home and family. There were no dreams of home or comforting arms holding me in some subconscious half-remembered childhood warmth, nothing calling me back through time to a table set and waiting for my return. But Moth's hand was still in mine and as the light wrapped us in curtains of infinity I held it just a little less tightly. Whatever was lost or found in life he would always be a part of this. A part of the charged movement of molecules from the earth to the universe. He would never leave.

Baldvinsskáli

Eric and the girl in the red trousers had already left the campsite by the time we got out of the tent. But even we made a much earlier start than normal, knowing that if we were to reach even halfway over the Fimmvörðuháls, we would have to set off before eleven thirty. The first half of this short trail was thirteen kilometers of uphill slog along a path that is renowned for weather changes and mist rising without warning. Paddy Dillon, the master of underestimation, describes this path as "steep and rugged climbing with narrow, exposed ridges. Snow and ice on the highest parts." But we weren't ready to end the trail and catch the bus. The path had already started to strengthen its hold. Just one more hill; just one more valley. Moth adjusted the pack on his back and spied on the hills ahead with his monocular. *Be careful on the stairs.*

Above the birch line the path returned to the landscape we had come to recognize. Rough stony tracks followed narrow ridgelines and broad plateaus to a mountainside that we'd spotted from the tent. Even from there we were able to see the brown line of a path crossing the flank. What we hadn't been able to make out was that the gently inclining thirty-degree track actually crossed a seventy-degree hillside of gravel, grit and mud. The Þórsmörk valley stretched away as snow-clad mountain tops began to reappear and finally another broad plateau. All sight of the vegetation in the valley bottom disappeared and we were back in the savage, rock-strewn landscape of ash, boulders and obsidian. And above us, the summit of one of the most disruptive volcanic explosions of recent years.

In 2010 Eyjafjallajökull erupted, spewing out an ash plume that rose five and a half miles into the air, shutting down most of the air traffic across Europe. But it wasn't just the ash that caused the problems. The eruption was beneath a glacier and as the glacier melted, the water poured back into the crater causing the lava to cool really quickly, forming glass crystals in the ash cloud. Bad for jet engines and horrid to walk on. In the tourist shops of the capital, walls are lined with photographs of the eruption. Dramatic pictures capturing red-hot lava as it was ejected from the mountainside. Photographs of heat, ash and disruption. But the one picture that held me transfixed was of the ponies. The farmers had evacuated the area as the volcano began to erupt, escaping from the danger zones. But as they left, they remembered the horses trapped on the hillside, so turned back to find them. The picture is of a herd of ponies running down the road and behind them a dark and furious ash cloud chasing them at high speed.

What the picture doesn't show are the farmers behind the ponies, guiding them down the road to safety as they ran to safety themselves. The dramatic crisis of a volcanic eruption, a blast of raw, instant power, bringing the human and animal worlds together to face the same threat, the same possibility of extinction. Seismic activity had begun in 2009, allowing the inhabitants of the area nearly a year to prepare, and yet it wasn't until the lava was running down the hillside that people finally reacted. Mainly for economic reasons, they refused to acknowledge what they knew was coming. The much bigger volcano, Katla, is heating up. History says it usually erupts in the years following an Eyjafjallajökull eruption and information boards about it litter the hillsides. Plastic-coated signs that normally describe local birdlife now instruct people to get to high ground when they hear a warning siren, away from the predicted lava-flow channels. And yet undoubtedly people will still be walking on these hills as the ground is shaking and the water heating up, unable to admit that danger is imminent until it's visible.

I watched my feet finding their way through the ash and rock and my thoughts drifted back to the farm in Cornwall, to the dust-dry fields and bare hedges of our first visit. No insect life other than the flies that hatched in the window frames, or bird-life other than the crows waiting for the sparse growth of apples to fall. A crisis unfolding, but invisible to most as they drove to the supermarket. The immense form of Katla looms unseen to the east. The horses will be running, the birds will have flown and the insects will lie dead on the ground, but the volcano will have erupted before humans look up and say, "Maybe the signs were there, but we walked on the hills anyway."

A via ferrata awaited us. A precipitous path traversing a near-vertical hillside of loose, shifting rock: a scree run, in fact, at a few thousand feet, crossed by this narrow track with a chain attached to steel pegs hammered into the rock for the walker to hold on to. Moth's head for heights disappeared one day in his forties when he fell through the barn roof. Especially exposed heights where he can see directly to the bottom of the valley. Dave and Julie inched their way across, keeping their eyes fixed on the chain. But Moth was looking the other way.

"Just give me a minute."

"There's no other way around, it's too steep. We have to cross here."

"I know, I know, just give me a minute."

We stood on a narrow ridge between the plateau and the scree run while he tried to breathe. Views of mountains stretched out to either side, but ahead only the sheer mountainside and a path that had to be crossed.

"All right, mate, your turn, but don't trust the chain, we're just fixing it." Three men in high-vis jackets were looking in a bucket of long steel bolts. Talking to each other in broad north of England accents.

"What are you doing up here? You're clearly not Icelandic!"

"No, obviously. I'm from Doncaster. I normally work in Scotland, the Lake District, Northumberland, you know, round the north. But this job came up and I thought, why not, can't be that different to home. Didn't think I'd be on the side of a volcano for a week though. Bloody cold up here. Right, get across then, but like I say, don't rely on the chain; we've just taken some pegs out. Off you go."

Moth took a deep breath; his pale waxy complexion had fear written across it in capital letters, but he knew he was going to cross anyway. He kept his back to the northerner, so the man didn't see his hands shaking, and stepped out on to the loose ground. The same man who had stood at the bottom of the scree run in the Lake District, arms wide, laughing as I hurled myself down, began to reappear. His shoulders loosened and his back straightened as he stopped momentarily, one hand on the chain and, looking back, beckoned me over, the color returning to his face. Don't "be careful on the stairs," run up them. Run up them two at a time if you can, while you can. I followed him, eyes fixed on his back and away from the valley bottom a thousand feet below.

Ash and rock crowned the volcano. An alien landscape of desolation. Sleety hail-filled rain began to fall, loud on waterproof clothing. In a confusing landscape of mounds, dips and soot, Dave and Julie's red and blue jackets stood out in stark relief. Even the reliable Paddy seemed a little confusing here.

"I think it's left of the hill, following the yellow marker posts." Moth sat on a rock to examine the map more closely, but quickly got up again, surprised by how warm it was.

"But we've been following the blue markers all the way, it wouldn't suddenly change." The landscape made no sense to me.

Maybe something about the magnetism was shifting the compass in my head. How could I possibly doubt Paddy?

"And I saw some people go the other way round that hill. Maybe Paddy's wrong, like," Dave was gathering his things, preparing to follow them.

Moth looked at us all in exasperation as Julie stayed out of the argument and sat quietly eating a cereal bar; but then she looked up slowly.

"I thought that was a lake over there and it was just mist rising from it. But there's no water. It must be the hot top of the volcano. It has to be if these are the two new cones that were formed in the eruption. Check in the book, Moth, these must be Móði and Magni." She casually finished eating the cereal bar.

We all looked in the direction she was pointing—to the two cones and the waterless lake of steaming rock beyond.

"They are."

"Well, that's solved it. I'm not walking across that; it'll melt my boots, like. Let's go left."

We set off, Moth smiling smugly, heading to the left of the Miðsker hill ahead.

The wind picked up, blowing in strong cold gusts from the snowfields all around. Crossing a valley of packed ice, past metal cases housing instruments for measuring seismic activity and more warning signs to head away from the lava flows. I wondered where exactly we would head to. Where can you go when you're standing on the top of a volcano and all the activity you've been warned of finally comes together into one catastrophic moment? Too late then to consider a change of route.

The ice took us into a precarious ravine of melting rivulets and the black bacterial growth. I peed behind a boulder; it froze instantly, leaving a trail of yellow ice. Dehydration. I needed to drink, but although I knew I needed to drink, something about the cold air, or the cold water, meant that again I hadn't. Ahead was an A-shaped zinc hut, the tiny Baldvinsskáli hut that only sleeps twenty and is recommended for emergency stops only.

"Paddy says there's often no water at this hut."

"Well, I've carried this water filter all the way and haven't used it, so let's get it out and fill all our bottles now, then if I have to I'll come back for more later." Dave unwrapped his new filter and slowly filled the four bottles. There wouldn't be room at the hut for us to stay, but as the light was falling, reflecting pink rays across the ice, we were hoping to camp nearby. I thought about Eric and the girl in the red trousers. Would they be at the hut or, fueled by oregano, already on the bus to Reykjavík?

Out of the ravine, on the flat area where the hut sat, the wind ripped in, pushing us hard toward the path that led away and down the mountainside. But darkness was coming and we needed to stop: this wasn't a landscape for a night-hike with a feeble head torch. The leeward side of the hut offered some shelter from the wind, so might be a spot where we could camp.

We opened the door and walked in, instantly hit by a wall of hot, clammy, noodle-flavored air. A woman with unwashed hair and layers of fleeces emerged from the heat. She was in her late thirties with an open welcoming face.

"Get in, get in, shut the door." Lauri had a commanding presence that anyone would obey without question.

"Hi, we just wondered if it would be okay to camp outside? There's no other shelter from the wind."

"No."

"Oh."

"No, you can't camp, the forecast's too bad. Your tents will blow away. We're full in the hut. Completely to the rafters."

"Well, thanks anyway." We opened the door and picked our rucksacks up to head out into the darkness and the iced rain blowing in gusts from the glacier.

"Where are you going?"

"If we can't camp here we'll have to head down to find some shelter."

"No, no. I'm not turning anyone away tonight; it's a death trap out there. Certainly not you four."

"Us four?"

"Well, you're not exactly a group of tough twenty-year-olds, are you?" What *exactly* was she saying? "All the bunks and the spare mattresses are taken, but if you can find some floor you can use it. But close the door."

Lauri, it transpired, wasn't a hermit, or a recluse living wild on the hillside, but a mother with a family of young children at school in Reykjavík. For four months every summer she left them with their father and moved on to the volcano to take care of her other children: the people stranded on the mountainside at night, who often only survived because of her diligent care and ethos of "no one left outside."

Beyond the porch in the main part of the hut the heat and noise was an intense assault on senses attuned to the wild landscape outside. Rows of tables, all crowded with people in trekking clothes. Heaps of rucksacks on every available meter of floor space. And a queue of people cooking, waiting to cook or fighting over pans by a small two-ring fixed gas hob.

"Cook your food if you want to, but no camping gas stoves, on the cooker only—we don't want to catch fire, we don't have enough water to put it out."

"Where do we sleep? Is there another room?" I'd never spent a night in a trekking hut and was already feeling myself withdraw. Too many people in such a small space and the familiar sense of panic was rising. I hung back by the door. I couldn't do this; I'd rather risk the wind on the volcano summit than this. "Moth, please don't make me do this. You sleep in here if you want, but help me put the tent up first. I can't be in here."

"We can't. The tent will just rip away out there."

"I can't be in here." But there was no escape, his hand was on my arm, forcing me toward a chair by a table Dave had cleared. "You can, it'll be fun. You're not going out there."

What the fuck was I doing here? My head was pounding, breath catching in my chest as the noise and the room began to pulsate. How could these people think this was okay? It was not okay. I was in the street in Polruan, running to hide behind the chapel, while trapped in a chair unable to escape.

These were a new set of people; we'd encountered very few of them before, most of them had started the trail at Skógar and were heading north to Þórsmörk where they would catch the bus back to Reykjavík. No sign of Eric; the girl in the red trousers must have forced him over the mountain to Skógar as she'd planned. But opposite us were two familiar faces, the obviously related Germans from the Langidalur campsite.

"So why are you in the hut, why aren't you camping?" They were nudging each other again and staring. Why were they so keen that we should camp, were they concerned that there wasn't enough floor space for four more bodies?

"It's blowing a gale out there, like."

As the water boiled for noodles Julie chatted easily with them in her fluent German, but all the time they were nudging and looking from Moth to myself with broad gnome smiles. I ate noodles that wouldn't rehydrate because the water wasn't hot enough and drank lukewarm tea, eyes fixed on the bowl, struggling in an attempt to exclude the wider room. I had to get outside and slipped Moth's grip with the excuse of going to the toilet hut. Beyond the sleeping hut was a smaller replica A-shaped hut that housed a chemical toilet and a wooden seat. I went inside and bolted the door. The wind rattled the zinc and pushed through in icy drafts, but I was alone. The air was cold, not a voice to be heard, and I sat there until my head stopped spinning and someone was hammering on the door to come in.

Outside the wind blew in strengthening gusts, parting the clouds that had engulfed the volcano. For a moment a deep, dark sky appeared through a tunnel of cloud, a black hole strewn with bright points of starlight. A stillness finally came with the wind blowing at my back and the cold as it puckered my face. I inhaled long slow breaths. This was outside the door; all I had to do was to walk out of the door whenever I needed to and I'd be able to make it through the night.

"Where have you been? Your tea's nearly cold." Julie handed me a mug. "You'll have to drink it quickly, we're supposed to move the tables and put the mattresses out before lights out."

"Oh wow, like school camp."

"Seems so."

A mad delirium followed of bodies, tables, chairs and rucksacks. A scene that could have been accompanied by the theme tune to a Benny Hill sketch show. I didn't wait for my mat to inflate but threw it down in the corner and claimed my space at the edge. Moth squeezed in next to me with the last of the foam hut mattresses.

"You'll be okay; I'm between you and everyone else. Face the wall and it'll be as if it's just us."

But that was always going to be impossible in a room full of people, few of which spoke the other's language, when one of them, a young man with dark hair, was frantically rushing round the room, throwing the rucksacks about and looking among the pans.

"It's lost, it's lost."

"What's lost?"

"A black zip bag. It has my important night things in it."

More madness, as the whole room got out of their sleeping bags and began to search for the important bag, obviously containing his valuables and medication. I stayed in the corner, afraid of losing my spot. But the bag couldn't be found. The two

Germans didn't get involved, but sat on their beds, occasionally looking to my corner and smiling their knowing smiles. I looked the other way.

"What exactly is in it? Will you need a doctor?" Lauri was in the doorway, hands on hips, and the room fell silent.

"My important night things."

"Medicine?"

"No, my things." The young man's voice was rising to a quaver of panic, but Lauri was swelling with exasperation.

"Just tell me what things."

The whole room turned to him in expectation of a life-threatening revelation.

"My toothbrush."

The exasperated room got back into their sleeping bags as Lauri turned the lights out.

"Goodnight, children, and no one gets up until six."

I got up. In the darkness of the early hours I crept over the bodies, picked up a coat and went outside. The wind had dropped to a whisper and on the far eastern horizon a slither of pink wove between the dark gray gaps in the clouds, lighting the glacier tops in hints of faintest blue. The silence was total. The complete silence of an earth at its beginning. Or its end. Even in the warmth of a stranger's parka, I felt this was no place for human or animal and yet the world went on without either. The pink light spread through the gray, not time passing, just light changing.

Skógar

The Germans left the hut at first light, tiptoeing out before the chaos of breakfast and furniture-moving began. They waved as they passed my mattress, whispering, "Enjoy more camping."

An hour later Lauri stood on the raised wooden decking outside the hut, hugging each of us as we passed her.

"Be careful today, it looks nice now but it's going to rain later. Just follow the river downhill, you can't go wrong."

We descended the mountain over a blank, featureless, rock-strewn land, falling into silence as the hillside folded ahead and the glacier retreated behind. We'd found our rhythm, an easy pace on the last day. Or was it because we were going downhill? We finally found the river as Lauri said we would. A frantic rush of muddy meltwater, racing downhill beneath a small wooden bridge, erected in memory of a man who had tried to cross the river here but didn't make it and was washed away toward the valley, miles below. I hesitated on the wooden platform above the water as it burst into brown spume over the boulders. Nothing could have made me step into that wild river.

Dave squatted behind a boulder and boiled water for tea as a fine drizzle began to fall. Before the stove was packed away the beat of rain on waterproofs began to drown out the sound of the river. Muffling the volume of millions of gallons of water as it fell through a cascade of waterfalls, increasing in drama, height and width as it went. Water from the sky, underfoot and in deep echoing ravines. Everything was water. Beyond the desolate fields of rock and ash crowning the volcano's summit, pockets of bacterial mush became patches of peat, then a blanket of soil.

Below the icy reach of the glaciers, protected by sheltering cliff walls, tentative fingers of green growth stretched away from the water. The earth underfoot transformed into the landscape of foothills, a familiar world where the green threads massed and spread into blankets of coarse grass and thrift.

Moth walked on ahead through the cold, driving rain. Walking alone in his own world, on his own path. As the waterfalls grew in size the noise increased in volume until all we could hear was water. Water in a furious, pounding roar against rocks, clothes and earth. A maelstrom of noise and moisture, turning the peat soil into a moving conveyor of treacherous mud. But still Moth walked on, the distance between us growing.

People began to file past in ones and twos, then in groups and columns of school trips. We were getting closer to Skógar, to the cafés and buses where day trips to the waterfalls start and end. Nearly running on the slimy pathway, I caught up with Moth.

"What's the rush? I can't keep up with you!"

"What? I can't hear you—it's so loud."

"What's . . . the . . . rush?"

"What do you mean? I'm not rushing. I was just walking, remembering bits of the path from the last few days."

"Maybe that's how you should always walk then, without thinking about it. Maybe you need headphones, so your movements become more automatic; perhaps the problems are in the connections between thought and action."

"I can't wear headphones in the wild, I'd rather listen to the silence."

"No chance of that here."

Two women walked uphill toward us, wiry women with bright-colored clothing. Mustard-colored waxed waterproofs jackets and red trousers, with wide brimmed hats tied on with beaded cord, which hadn't come from the hangers in any outdoor shop I'd seen. They stopped on the path ahead, watching us walk toward them.

"Hi, lovely day."

"*Guten morgen*." Germans. "It is not lovely, it is raining."

"You're right, it is."

"What did you say?"

"It's raining."

"So you've noticed. My friend and I, we think we know you."

"No, I don't think so."

"Yes, this man, we've met, but we can't remember . . . we know your face."

"No, I really don't think so."

They continued to stare with puzzled expressions as we walked away.

"So, Moth, secret life in Germany then?"

"Don't know what they're talking about. Great coats though."

We looked back and they were still standing on the brow of the hill watching us.

The waves of land shallowed and the river broadened as I followed Moth, disappearing rapidly ahead of me down the hillside. Maybe there was something in what the women had said: a secret trip to Germany in the past, possibly. Or was he walking alone because he was bored with my trivial conversation, or lack of it? Tired of talking about boy-scout badges and food, he just wanted to be alone. I waited for Dave and Julie, who were walking carefully on the slippery grass.

"What's up with him, like, what's the rush?"

"I don't know, I can't keep up with him. I think he's bothered by the German women."

"What?"

Moth was waiting for us on a viewing platform at the top of the final waterfall. The vast Skógafoss waterfall thundered down to a riverbed sixty meters below, where busloads of tourists stood, photographing themselves in the cloud of spray that formed as the water landed. Two Icelandic trails behind us, we had walked through ice, rain and sulfur to the end of a strange and unknown land. To a cliff edge that used to be the end of the land, before sea levels fell and took the coastline three miles farther out to sea. Folktales say this is the place where the Viking Prasi Porolfsson dragged his boat ashore for the first time and buried a chest of gold, obviously just traveling money, in a cave behind the roaring power of Skógafoss. A buss trip of Chinese girls clearly thought it was still there, but appeared from the spray empty-handed and dripping in their plastic ponchos.

"Don't you want to walk with us today, like, or do you fancy catching the bus back to Reykjavík this afternoon?"

We all stood by the railings, squeezing together for a selfie at the falls.

"Course not. It's my legs, I had to just go with them."

I'd been too focused on the thought of the strange German women—I hadn't considered that he might be having a problem going downhill. Struggling to put the brakes on.

"Could hardly have left them behind, like."

"They felt real today, like my old legs, as if I was completely in control. I had to go with it, seize that sense of normality and go with it. Sorry, didn't mean to ignore anyone."

"No, Moth, if you have a moment when life is in balance you seize it and forget us." Julie handed out the last of the chocolate raisins.

At the bottom of the fall, feeling tiny against the backdrop of wild power, we asked one of the girls in ponchos to take our photo. We leaped into the air, all the wrong side of middle age, seizing a moment of life in defiance of infinity, or because of it. A moment of the wild, loud cacophony of life caught in flight. Two fulmars circled in the currents of the air above the waterfall as we breathed in the empty volcanic possibility. There, where the earth begins and ends and life goes on in another form.

The daily bus had long gone as we pitched the tents by the river, sat in the warm dry café and ordered food. Logging in to wi-fi for the first time in Iceland, I scanned through an enormous list of unanswered emails. Among them was one from the literary agent. *The Salt Path* had reached the top ten in the German book charts and had been featured in a widely read magazine. A selfie that we had taken, homeless but laughing near Godrevy Lighthouse on the South West Coast Path, was all over the magazine racks of Germany.

Only Change

To pass through the cracked and splintered oak-wood doors of the cider barn was to pass through time. To another world, where dark stone walls, barely visible in the low light, still held the sweet smell of centuries of crushed fruit and fermentation. Through lofts where apples fresh from the orchards would stand in hessian sacks, past cobwebs hung low, cloaking every beam and corner, forming curtains across doorways, where generations of farmers had stacked the press with crushed apples and watched as the juice ran. Oak barrels lined the walls, racked in rows of deep, musky anticipation. Waiting for the moment when the cloudy sharpness of fresh pressed juice refilled them and the cycle of production would begin again.

But the sense of the past had been hidden in more farm waste and plastic bags, until Moth worked his way through the barn, slowly brushing, sweeping and bagging rubbish. Washing the walls with water until the smell of cider returned and with it a breath of the barn's history. As he closed the door, the shadows in the darkest corners could almost have been of monks, tapping the barrels, tasting the pink fermenting liquid. It was nearly time.

In the farmhouse, the rucksacks stood in the bedroom propped against the wall, exuding a faint smell of sulfur. It had been three weeks since we'd returned but neither of us were ready to unpack. We still carried something of the vast, wild turmoil of the volcanoes in our thoughts, a sense of uncontained horizons that we weren't ready to put back in the cupboard. Outside, apples hung full and ripe on overladen branches, the warmth of the low autumn sun tracing patterns of light across their damp red skins. I cupped one in my hand to see if it would easily leave the branch and it came off with only the slightest twist. It was time; they were ready to pick. Soon they would be in the barn and the cider season would begin.

I gathered the first few into a basket as the yellow leaves began to move on the tree, the wind slipped into the north and, almost without warning, the soft tones of autumn picked up a harder, sharper edge. Before darkness had fallen angry gales were ripping over the hill, battering rain and hail powering through in relentless waves.

When it finally stopped, tons of apples lay on the ground, bruised and broken, the trees were stripped of leaves and the weak sunlight held the wateriness of early winter.

"What a waste. These need to be off the ground and into the cider barn before they rot." Moth squatted under a tree picking a few undamaged apples from the ground and putting them in a bucket.

"We'll have to just pick up what we can. What else can we do?"

"Just me and you? We'll never do it; there's too many. We can pick up a few but the bulk of these will be lost. What a mess." We looked across the orchard at the devastation; we couldn't possibly pick them all up before they began to rot, but who could possibly help us? There was no one to ask.

Cars parked in front of the house, packed full with people from Polruan. Sarah, armed with bags of sandwiches, bottles of wine, gloves and buckets. Other people that we'd briefly met, or hadn't met at all, people loaded down with boots, hats and enthusiasm. Then, from the last car, Gill and Simon, happy, laughing. Together for anyone to see.

"Gill, I thought you'd gone back to London."

"No, I've stayed. I'll be here until after Christmas this time, unless Simon kicks me out before then."

"I won't be doing that; you've always known you can stay. It's always been your choice." Trust, such an elusive thing, but given the slightest chance it can grow and flourish. They walked into the orchards, as inexplicable but inevitable as thrift growing in the Icelandic ash. Within days the loft of the cider barn was stacked with hessian sacks full of salvaged apples, and freshly pressed juice began to fill the barrels.

The half-light of a November morning lit the horizon, the faintest slice of pink catching the underside of the clouds in a wash of color beneath the towering blue mass. Through the smallest breaks in the cloud a pale sky held the suggestion of a clear day and unknowable infinities just out of reach. Mist cleared from the field nearest the house, dissipating in the weak sunlight, to reveal brown shapes moving across the grass. We watched the scattered forms as they came together, then dispersed again.

"I can't believe they're here."

"I didn't think they would ever come, but just over a year and here they are." I squinted into the binoculars to get a clearer look. The curlews had come. Tall brown birds with unmistakable curved bills pushed into the grass in search of bugs and insects. Birds who know where the food sources are simply by the feel of the land. An endangered bird, a rare and fragile life, feeding in a field that so recently had been devoid of all but the loneliest of worms. We watched, transfixed, until the sun burned the colors from the sky and the curlews headed back to the creek.

Moth folded the binoculars back into their case, his hands moving as he directed them. We walked down into the orchard to find our usual seat on the goat-moth tree. The fresh wet sap that had oozed from the holes in the summer had dried into hard resin drips. Maybe whatever was in the tree had transformed and flown, or maybe they were still there, hiding and growing for years yet to come. Maybe time would tell, but then only if we were there at the right moment, on the right day.

"Shall we go to the coast? I feel as if I want to be on the path today, to hear the sea."

We would always need to find our way back to the path, however far away from it we traveled, to smell the salt and spread our arms into the wind on the cliff top. We walked across a familiar headland to a spot in the gorse where we had pitched our tent only a few brief years earlier, homeless, with no money or food, but, here at the edge of the land, miraculously unafraid. We sat in a clearing among the scrub on a bare patch of rocky earth, the sea disappearing into a gray horizon, still the same people who had shivered in the cold of the tent as we walked this coast—only the landscape had changed around us. In the cold wind, blowing salt-laden winter air from the sea, no doubt remained. No drugs or doctors could help Moth, but he didn't need them. Simply by living as he was built to, his body had found a way to sidestep the failures and go on. As surely as removing heavy human interference from the land was allowing the wildlife to return to the farm, so Moth was surviving by returning to a more natural state of existence. Life re-forming and reshaping, not with man's intervention but without it. A winter squall blew curtains of rain toward the land, a storm we'd seen coming from the far horizon. Don't "be careful on the stairs," run up them, run as fast as you can, with no fear of clocks ticking or time passing. Nothing can be measured in time, only change, and change is always within our grasp, always simply a matter of choice.

I closed my eyes and let the sounds come, let the voice come. Calm and hushed on a rising wind hissing through rocks, in clear water falling through sunlight. Carried on a gull's cry over sea against cliff, somewhere beyond the blurred line between water and air. The sound in the leaves as I'd hung in the branches of the willow tree, and crouched in the dark woods. It had always been there, whispering with the water voles in the ditch, the deer on the mountainside, the seals calling beneath foggy headlands. The voice behind it all . . .

. . . a sound beyond connection, or belonging.

The hum of particles
vibrating to the energy of life.
The voice of the
beating
pulsing
wild silence
of the earth.
The voice
of . . . . .
home.

It was a fortunate wind
That blew me here. I leave
Half-ready to believe
That a crippled trust might walk
And the half-true rhyme is love.

The Cure at Troy, Seamus Heaney

Acknowledgments

Lying on the forest floor, my fingers pushed into the leaf litter, I reflected a lot on what led me there. But my thoughts rarely moved beyond Moth and our life. I certainly didn't consider what might be happening beneath the soil's surface. Since then, thanks to Rob MacFarlane's fascinating book *Underland*, I'm aware there's another world down there, a world of fungus. A magical, magnificent network of mycorrhizal fungi beneath the forest floor, connecting tree to tree and one species to another, transferring nutrients, water and minerals in a maze of correlation, allowing seedlings to grow in the shadow of the adult plant and unrelated species to share resources. An invisible world of natural connections that helps each plant thrive as a part of the beautiful connected whole. Maybe, with my fingers in the earth I found a connection to that network; a connection that helped me get through the harshest times. It could also be the reason why my toenails are rotting!

But writing a book has connected me to a network I am aware of, enabling me to thrive as part of a system where everyone matters, and no one person succeeds without the help and support of the whole. Without every person involved in *The Wild Silence*'s development it would still be just a seedling that had yet to grow.

Huge thanks to Jen Christie of Graham Maw Christie, who holds all the details together. To Fenella Bates, the irreplaceable Olivia Thomas, Jen Porter, Aggie Russell, Richenda Todd, Louise Moore, Dan Bunyard, Catherine Wood and everyone else at Michael Joseph who make working with them such a pleasure.

Thanks to Dave and Julie for their friendship and for sharing wet tents on cold hillsides. To my Polruan friends who have opened their hearts and their doors in ways I thought I wouldn't experience again, and to Sam and Rachel for having a dream and the overwhelming generosity of spirit to choose to share it.

But most of all thank you to the Team. All three of you. For the time, space and love it has taken to create this book. Time without end, space without borders and love without restraint—the most important network any of us can have.

The Salt Path

A Memoir

Just days after Raynor Winn learns that Moth, her husband of thirty-two years, is terminally ill, their house and farm are taken away, along with their livelihood. With nothing left and little time, they make the brave and impulsive decision to walk the 630 miles of the sea-swept South West Coast Path. From Somerset to Dorset, through Devon and Cornwall, they live wild in the ancient, weathered landscape of cliffs, sea, and sky. Yet through every step and every test along the way, their walk becomes a remarkable and life-affirming journey.

"Polished, poignant . . . an inspiring story of true love."
—*Entertainment Weekly*